Homicide:
The
Hidden
Victims

Interpersonal Violence:
The Practice Series

Jon R. Conte, Series Editor

Interpersonal Violence: The Practice Series is devoted to mental health, social service, and allied professionals who confront daily the problem of interpersonal violence. It is hoped that the knowledge, professional experience, and high standards of practice offered by the authors of these volumes may lead to the end of interpersonal violence.

In this series...

LEGAL ISSUES IN CHILD ABUSE AND NEGLECT
by John E. B. Myers

CHILD ABUSE TRAUMA: Theory and Treatment of the Lasting Effects
by John N. Briere

INTERVENTION FOR MEN WHO BATTER: An Ecological Approach
by Jeffrey L. Edleson and Richard M. Tolman

COGNITIVE PROCESSING THERAPY FOR RAPE VICTIMS: A Treatment Manual
by Patricia A. Resick and Monica K. Schnicke

GROUP TREATMENT OF ADULT INCEST SURVIVORS
by Mary Ann Donaldson and Susan Cordes-Green

TEAM INVESTIGATION OF CHILD SEXUAL ABUSE: The Uneasy Alliance
by Donna Pence and Charles Wilson

HOW TO INTERVIEW SEXUAL ABUSE VICTIMS: Including the Use of Anatomical Dolls
by Marcia Morgan, with contributions from Virginia Edwards

ASSESSING DANGEROUSNESS: Violence by Sexual Offenders, Batterers, and Child Abusers
Edited by Jacquelyn C. Campbell

PATTERN CHANGING FOR ABUSED WOMEN: An Educational Program
by Marilyn Shear Goodman and Beth Creager Fallon

GROUPWORK WITH CHILDREN OF BATTERED WOMEN: A Practitioner's Manual
by Einat Peled and Diane Davis

PSYCHOTHERAPY WITH SEXUALLY ABUSED BOYS: An Integrated Approach
by William N. Friedrich

CONFRONTING ABUSIVE BELIEFS: Group Treatment for Abusive Men
by Mary Nõmme Russell

TREATMENT STRATEGIES FOR ABUSED CHILDREN: From Victim to Survivor
by Cheryl L. Karp and Traci L. Butler

GROUP TREATMENT FOR ADULT SURVIVORS OF ABUSE: A Manual for Practitioners
by Laura Pistone Webb and James Leehan

WORKING WITH CHILD ABUSE AND NEGLECT: A Primer
by Vernon R. Wiehe

TREATING SEXUALLY ABUSED CHILDREN AND THEIR NONOFFENDING PARENTS:
A Cognitive Behavioral Approach
by Esther Deblinger and Anne Hope Heflin

HEARING THE INTERNAL TRAUMA: Working With Children and Adolescents Who
Have Been Sexually Abused
by Sandra Wieland

PREPARING AND PRESENTING EXPERT TESTIMONY IN CHILD ABUSE LITIGATION:
A Guide for Expert Witnesses and Attorneys
by Paul Stern

TREATMENT STRATEGIES FOR ABUSED ADOLESCENTS: From Victim to Survivor
by Cheryl L. Karp, Traci L. Butler, and Sage C. Bergstrom

HOMICIDE: THE HIDDEN VICTIMS—A Guide for Professionals
by Deborah Spungen

Homicide: The Hidden Victims

A Guide for Professionals

Deborah Spungen

Foreword by Marlene Young

Interpersonal Violence:
The Practice Series

SAGE Publications
International Educational and Professional Publisher
Thousand Oaks   London   New Delhi

For information:

SAGE Publications, Inc.
2455 Teller Road
Thousand Oaks, California 91320
E-mail: order@sagepub.com

SAGE Publications Ltd.
6 Bonhill Street
London EC2A 4PU
United Kingdom

SAGE Publications India Pvt. Ltd.
M-32 Market
Greater Kailash I
New Delhi 110 048 India

Printed in the United States of America

Library of Congress Cataloging-in-Publication Data

Spungen, Deborah.
    Homicide: The hidden victims—a guide for professionals
/ by Deborah Spungen.
        p.   cm. — (Interpersonal violence; v. 20)
    Includes bibliographical references and index.
    ISBN 0-8039-5776-9 (cloth: acid-free paper). — ISBN
0-8039-5777-7 (pbk. acid-free paper)
        1. Murder victims' families. 2. Murder victims' families—
Services for. 3. Homicide—Psychological aspects. 4. Bereavement.
I. Title. II. Series.
HV6515.S65 1997
362.88—dc21   97-4895

99 00 01 02 03 10 9 8 7 6 5 4 3

Acquiring Editor:	C. Terry Hendrix
Editorial Assistant:	Dale Mary Grenfell
Production Editor:	Diana E. Axelsen
Production Assistant:	Karen Wiley
Typesetter/Designer:	Danielle Dillahunt
Indexer:	Mary Mortensen
Print Buyer:	Anna Chin

Contents

Foreword   xi

Acknowledgments   xiii

Introduction: Making Known the Hidden   xix
     Recognizing Co-Victims   xix
     Preview of the Chapters   xxii

1. The Dynamics of Murder   1
     The Interaction of Violence and Murder   2
     The Impact of Homicide   7
     Summary   16

2. Traumatic Grief: A New Model   17
     Understanding Trauma   18
     Understanding Grief   23
     The Synergism of Trauma and Grief   40
     The Emotional Experience of Traumatic Grief   44
     Cultural and Gender Influences   51

Mental Health Implications 56
Summary 61

3. Murder and the Family System 63
   The Uniqueness of Family Loss 64
   Intrafamily Homicide 83
   Summary 91

4. Circumstantial Influences 93
   Co-Victims of Police 93
   Alcohol-Related Vehicular Homicides 99
   No-Arrest Cases 101
   Bystander and Random Killings 107
   Community Disasters and Multiple
      and Serial Murders 110
   Murder-Suicide 112
   Summary 117

5. Death Notification: The Long-Term Impact 119
   Role of Caregivers and Service Providers 120
   Consequences of the Death Notification 133
   Summary 137

6. Interventions and Advocacy 138
   Who Are the Intervenors? 139
   What Are the Interventions? 155
   Summary 176

7. Justice for All: Do Co-Victims Have Legal Rights? 178
   The Criminal Justice System 180
   Additional Legal Issues 200
   Summary 215

8. Facing the Media 216
   Media Perspectives 217
   Impact of the Media on Co-Victims:
      The Second Wound 224
   Positive Effects of Media Coverage 230

Strategies for Working With the Media   232
Summary   237

9. Reconstructing a New Life:
    Endings and Beginnings   238
        Healing   239
        Summary   246

    Resources   249
        Organizations   249
        Books and Journals   250
        Audiovisual Materials   250
        Clinical Instruments   250

    References   251

    Index   259

    About the Author   271

Foreword

I remember the first time I met a parent whose child had been murdered. By chance, I sat down beside her outside of a courtroom. She held herself stiffly and wadded a handkerchief in her hands. I was there on other business and paid little attention to her. After a few minutes of silence, she asked me why I was in the courthouse. I told her. She replied, "I'm here because my daughter was murdered." I was stunned and, truthfully, uncomfortable. I didn't know what to say or do.

This was over 23 years ago. I think I said something like, "How terrible. I'm sorry." But I don't really know. I do know that I listened to her story for about 20 minutes and then had to leave on an errand.

I've thought about those moments a great deal over the last two decades, as I've journeyed through the evolution of the victims' movement in the United States. I've thought how inadequate I was, and how far I have been carried toward understanding by the thoughtful survivors of crime I have come to know.

Inevitably, I often reflect on how much progress we have made through the establishment of some 10,000 victim service programs throughout the country to provide services to victims from the time of the crime through the court process and after case disposition. I marvel over the thousands of laws that have been passed to protect the rights of victims in the criminal and juvenile justice systems. I have witnessed the birth and maturation of a great force, as state after state has passed constitutional amendments on victim rights; and even now I am witness to a great debate over a federal constitutional amendment to ensure that victims' rights are protected, informed, present, and heard at critical phases in the justice system—criminal, administrative, juvenile, and military.

I've watched as society and the criminal justice system have better responded to all kinds of criticisms.

But the memory of 23 years ago still haunts me. It haunts me because, despite the tremendous growth in trauma research and the revolutionary changes in victim rights and services, the distress I experienced over that encounter with a homicide's victim's mother is recurring today with thousands of others who find themselves in the same situation—even among people who meet such victims not by chance, as I did, but on purpose. For even well-meaning caregivers often lack the skills and understanding to provide the support that homicide co-victims deserve and need to survive.

I believe this gap in services is due to a number of factors. First, there is little training for professionals on how to work with co-victims. This is illustrated simply by the vast numbers of law enforcement officers, emergency workers, coroners, doctors, and crisis interveners who have never received death notification training. As Deborah Spungen aptly points out, "All caregivers who serve co-victims of homicide, even if they do not actually deliver death notifications, need to be familiar and comfortable with the death notification model."

Second, the interconnected issues of trauma and grief have only recently begun to be examined. It is in a sense ironic that the fields of traumatology and thanatology have emerged as independent disciplines complete with different professional associations representing them. While some professionals are members of both fields, many have yet to see the essential union of research and thought that is needed when addressing sudden, violent death. Even in the studies that have emerged on traumatic grief, there has been little thought given to the uniqueness of grief occasioned by homicide and its varieties.

Third, most public interest in homicide and murder has focused on the offender. At times, this is due to the sensationalism of an individual case or mass murder. But at times, it seems to be because the victim is dead and the offender is alive. The co-victims are subjected not simply to a conspiracy of silence but to a state of invisibility.

Fourth, and perhaps most distressing, is the fact that homicide co-victims are stigmatized by their fate. Homicide victims may be blamed and even slandered for the way they died, and sometimes for the way they lived. They, of course, have no voice to tell their own stories. Co-victims endure the aspersions cast upon their loved ones.

But co-victims often endure more. They may be isolated because others are distressed by their distress. They may be disparaged because they "will not let go," or "fantasize about revenge," or "talk about the evil done." They may be ignored because no one wants to hear about the murder anymore. And, at times, they are even shunned because others fear the contagion of death and murder in their lives.

Finally, what complicates the preparations of caregivers and professionals who deal with co-victims is the remarkable breadth of knowledge they need. They need to comprehend the issues of traumatic grief, but they also need to understand the criminal justice system, the civil legal system, the juvenile justice system, the media, compensation and insurance systems, family systems, and the emerging law of victim rights. This multidisciplinary basis for intervention is not new to professional victims advocates, but other professionals have not been exposed to this maze of structures and functions.

And many victims advocates have focused on victims of crimes other than homicide. This is true despite the fact that homicides are committed in burglaries, robberies, rapes, domestic violence, and child abuse—so many of the subspecialities in victim assistance lead their practitioners to confront murder.

Deborah Spungen's book fills a major gap by examining more closely the intricate nature of the effects of homicide on its co-victims and by addressing the complexities of the interactions of multiple systems on their lives. It is particularly helpful because it draws upon the experience of the author as a co-victim herself, as well as the experiences of many other co-victims with whom she has worked. There is growing recognition that those who are traumatized are often able to better deal with traumatic events when they are able to put words to their reactions and a story to their experience. Storytelling may be a helpful coping strategy for co-victims, but it is also a compelling education for those who listen to the stories. Nothing can tell of the anguish and agony of homicide and its aftermath like the words of those who continue to live after murder has occurred. The fact that those words can still startle or amaze is a testament to how much there is to learn.

Chapters 2 and 9 should be of particular interest to anyone working in the field of grief or trauma. Spungen's discussion of why there is a need for a new model for understanding grief in the aftermath of homicide is insightful and raises many issues that bear further study and thought. I hope her suggestion that it may be useful to develop a new schema to address normal homicide bereavement and to differentiate it from complicated homicide bereavement is taken seriously by researchers and practitioners. Chapter 9 provides an excellent summary of critical tools that can be used for co-victims, and I hope every caregiver will use it as a guide in presenting options as co-victims continue to live their lives.

As I read this book, I thought of the grieving mother I met in 1975. I hadn't even asked her name. Through the many years since, I have sat, talked, walked, wept, and laughed with many other co-victims—Charlotte and Bob Hullinger, Betty Jane Spencer, Roberta and Vince Roper, Bob and Pat Preston, Dick Kramer, Greg Novak, Bob and Dee Dee Kouns, Jack Russell, Odile Stern, and so many, many more.

I hope that I have learned their lessons well, and that my response today to co-victims is more skillfully compassionate than it was 23 years ago. But this book offers me additional perspectives and has shown me ways to do my work better.

And for professionals who have not had the gifts given to me over two decades by co-victims, Deborah Spungen's *Homicide: The Hidden Victims* is an essential guide to better comprehension of the challenges faced by them.

Marlene Young, Executive Director
National Organization for Victim Assistance
Washington, DC

Acknowledgments

The completion of *Homicide: The Hidden Victims—A Guide for Professionals* has been one more step for me on my journey since the murder of my daughter Nancy on October 12, 1978. Her death started me on a road that I never could have envisaged for myself. Nancy's murder was the catalyst for my work with crime victims. At some point, however, my work began to stand on its own. I truly believe that the universe is unfolding as it should and that I am exactly where I need to be in life.

When I sat down to write the acknowledgments for this book, I found myself not knowing where to begin. So many colleagues, friends, professionals, teachers, institutions, organizations, agencies, research assistants, computer consultants, members of the criminal justice system, and co-victims of homicide all played a role in the creation of this book. I hesitate trying to list them individually because I fear that I will inadvertently neglect to mention someone. I apologize to those whom I do not name personally, and I thank them for their time, effort, information, and support. Some names I never knew or cannot remember, but the assistance and encouragement of these individuals was always appreciated.

This book has a long history, and I want to acknowledge Dr. Lenard Kaye, my professor at Bryn Mawr College Graduate School of Social Work and Social Research, for providing me with the focus and title for *Homicide: The Hidden Victims* and the impetus to write it. I would also like to mention some of the people who made special contributions during the 8 years that it took for the book to go from the germ of an idea to reality. Jennifer Cousar Costa, my first research assistant, helped me organize my thoughts for this book and taught me where to put commas and quotation marks. Suzanne Lanza and Sarah Matthews also ably assisted me in my endeavors. A special thanks goes to Sharron Russell, my number one research assistant, who worked with me on this project for the last 2 years. I truly could not have completed the book without her loyalty, commitment, skills, and patience. She also provided the focus and motivation that I needed when I began to despair of ever finishing and created the wonderful tables throughout the text. I also want to thank Krista Ely, who came late to the team and was there for the final word. She played an integral role in applying the finishing touches to the book. Ann West, my developmental copy editor, was the sculptor's assistant who came in to polish the rough edges and give me the confidence to complete the book. I commend C. Terry Hendrix, Senior Editor at Sage Publications, for his remarkable patience, understanding, and tolerance in the 3 years it took me to write the book. A large vote of appreciation goes to Dale Grenfell at Sage. She was always responsive to my questions and concerns, and it was a pleasure to work with her. Thanks to Dr. Jon Conte, the editor of the **Interpersonal Violence: The Practice Series for Sage Publications**, who believed in my book from the beginning.

Many colleagues in victims' rights organizations and agencies inspired me with their commitment to the field and were always available to provide me with the answers and information that I needed while writing the book. I thank all those individuals at the National Organization for Victim Assistance (NOVA), National Victim Center (NVC), Mothers Against Drunk Driving (MADD), Pennsylvania Commission on Crime and Delinquency (PCCD), Office for Victims of Crime (OVC), Philadelphia Coalition for Victim Advocacy (PCVA), National Association of Crime Victim Compensation

Boards, and the Association of Traumatic Stress Specialists (ATSS) for their time, support, and effort on my behalf.

The Board of Directors of the Anti-Violence Partnership of Philadelphia (AVP) supported me by ensuring that AVP would continue to flourish and grow even when their "charismatic leader" resigned as executive director to find more hours to work on the book. Special words of appreciation go to Julie Good, my colleague and friend, who replaced me as the executive director of AVP. Her professionalism and commitment to the agency and its mission allowed me the peace of mind to continue writing. Under Julie's leadership, AVP has grown beyond its early grassroots days as we address the entire cycle of violence. I especially appreciate her understanding of my emotional ties to AVP and allowing me to continue that relationship.

I thank the Philadelphia District Attorney's Office, especially the homicide unit, for allowing the Families of Murder Victims (FMV) program to exist within the office and for the opportunity to serve the co-victims of homicide in Philadelphia. Thanks also to all my friends in the Philadelphia Police Department, especially the homicide detectives (present and retired), for their hard work and dedication.

I appreciate my family and friends for their faith in me and for never asking, "Aren't you finished with that book yet?" To my children, Susan, David, and Liz, who found their own way in the world, I thank them for their love and for being there for me.

The most special thank-you goes to my best friend, my husband, Frank, who offered me all his love and support and never questioned my commitment to writing this book. Only he knew how arduous a task I had chosen for myself and understood that it was a necessary part of my journey.

*   *   *

Grateful acknowledgment is made to the following for permission to reprint excerpts from previously published articles.

Associated Press:
"Simpson Case Backlash Keeps Camera Out of Other Courtrooms." (1995, September 17). *New York Times*, p. 35.

Skorneck, C. (1990, December 22). "Shootings No Longer Faze D.C. Children." *Philadelphia Inquirer*, p. A3.

The New York Times:

Baker, R. (1993, September 10). "A Slight Plague of Murder," p. 21.

Blumenthal, R. (1990, November 6). "With Detective Hard Pressed, Family Joins Hunt for Killer," pp. B1, B5.

Bragg, R. (1996, December 26). "Prisoner's Pittance Is Meant as a Reminder of a Great Loss," pp. A1, A16.

Fried, J. (1990, December 14). "Confession Forces a Family to Relive Decade-Old Killing," pp. B1, B4.

"The Girls Who Had Everything." (1986, October 22), p. A30.

Goldberg, C. (1996, February 22). "Boys' Families Hope for Release as Freeway Killer's Execution Nears," p. A14.

Gross, J. (1990, August 12). "Bystander Deaths Reshape City Lives," p. 18.

James, G. (1992, December 24). "The Endless Quest for a Daughter's Killer," pp. B1, B5.

Jones, C. (1995, October 13). "Nicole Simpson, in Death, Lifting Domestic Violence to the Forefront as a National Issue," p. A28.

Kolbert, E. (1994, December 14). "Television Gets Closer Look as a Factor in Real Violence," pp. A1, D20.

Leary, W. E. (1994, October 23). "Gun Violence Leading to Better Care for Injuries," p. 32.

"Man Tells of Learning About Wife's Slaying." (1995, January 25), p. B4.

Richardson, L. (1993, July 1). "For a Grieving Mother, Freshened Tears," p. B6.

The Philadelphia Daily News:

Daughen, J. R., Costantinou, M., and Sheehan, K. (1994, January 12). "Woman Slain on Highway," pp. 5, 22.

Laker, B., and O'Dowd, J. (1993, December 22). "Medical Student Killed: Newlyweds' Plans End in Tragedy," pp. 4, 5.

The Philadelphia Inquirer:

Barnard, A., and Henson, R. (1996, June 26). "Father Slays Son, 2½, Then Kills Himself," pp. B1, B4. Reprinted by permission of A. Barnard.

Cipriano, R. (1996, June 13). "Business Scrubs Away Death," p. A3.

Colimore, E., Raphael, M., and Sanginiti, T. (1994, November 3). "Wife of a Cherry Hill Rabbi Found Beaten to Death at Home," pp. A7, A17.

Gammage, J. (1993, June 18). "Shooting Took a Life, Shattered a Second, and Shook Many More," p. A1.

Gibbons, T. J., and Gelles, J. (1996, November 21). "Arrest in Killing of Penn Chemist," p. A1.

Goodman, H. (1995, December 3). "2d Jury Convicts Ex-Guard in '84 Drexel Slaying," pp. A1, A13.

Jamieson, K. H., and Romer, D. (1995, August 27). "If It's (Black and White) Crime, Television Will Give It Time," p. E5.

Lewis, C. (1995, November 29). "Our Fear of Crime Is Exaggerated, and Lurid News Stories Are to Blame," p. A19.

Lopez, S. (1997, January 1). "Enduring the Loss of a Child to Violence," pp. A1, A9.

Loyd, L. (1994, December 7). "Man Sentenced to Die for Shooting Teen During Deli Dispute," p. B5.

Loyd, L. (1995, November 1). "Life Sentence for Man Who Killed Officer," p. B1.

Loyd, L. (1996, February 28). "Polecs Get Chance to Tell Killer Their Pain," pp. A1, A13.

Matza, M. (1991, July 28). "The Innocent Bystander as Victim," pp. A1, A10.

Paik, A. (1995, March 11). "Kin's Anger Erupts in a Murder Trial," p. B7.

Phillips, N. (1991, July 21). "Memorial for a Child Slain at Five," p. B2.

Sabatini, R. V. (1996, June 26). "Murder-Suicide Ruled in Bristol Fire Deaths," p. R3.

Samuel, T. (1996, July 16). "Victims' Kin Running for Office to Change Nation's Gun Laws," p. A3.

Seplow, S. (1996, November 27). "Without Camera, Trial Isn't As Riveting," p. A2.

Terry, R. J., Colimore, E., and Gibbons, T. J., Jr. (1996, July 11). "Wait for Answers in Dellapenna Case Grows One Day Longer," p. R3.

Valbrun, M. (1996, January 12). "A Philadelphia Officer Is Mourned as Colleague, Mother, Friend," pp. A1, B7.

Vigoda, R. (1996, December 10). "Judges Rules du Pont Ready to Stand Trial," pp. A1, A14.

Weiner, J. (1995, June 8). "A Shooting Victim Now Crusades Against Violence Aimed at Gays," p. G4.

Woodall, M. (1995, August 20). "When Mom's Boyfriend Gets Violent, Children Die," pp. A1, A16, A17.

Knight-Ridder/Tribune Information Services:

Cannon, A. (1996, December 25). "Father of Slain Man Joins Kin of Teen Killer to Fight Violence," p. A25.

Introduction:
Making Known the Hidden

❏ **Recognizing Co-Victims**

What is homicide? "The willful (non-negligent) killing of one human being by another" (Bastian, 1995, p. 3). The family of a murder victim has a different definition: the blackest hell accompanied by a pain so intense that even breathing becomes an unendurable labor.

I became personally acquainted with the above definitions when my own daughter Nancy was murdered in 1978. In 1980, my husband and I founded a peer support group for families of murder victims in Philadelphia. In its original format, it was a chapter of the national group of Parents of Murdered Children (POMC). Edward Rendell, then district attorney of Philadelphia, attended the third meeting and encouraged the families present to get more involved in the criminal justice system by attending trials and other court proceedings. This would, he said, help provide information and a support system for the families involved.

It became clear to the original families of POMC that it was not possible to deal with grief and bereavement issues without also dealing with the impact of the legal system on the families and friends of a homicide victim, the co-victims of homicide. The sociolegal model of service delivery to co-victims evolved in response to the personal insights and experiences gained from my interactions with the various systems and individuals who deal with homicide.

The support group was helpful and important, but it was not enough. As our group prepared to widen our scope of clients and services, we changed our name to Families of Murder Victims (FMV). In 1986, FMV established a freestanding victim advocate office within the homicide unit of the district attorney's office to help guide the families of homicide victims through the criminal justice system and the grieving process. FMV was the first victim advocate agency in the United States developed solely to provide services for the co-victims of homicide. Initially, our other priorities were twofold: (a) sensitizing the criminal justice system, the media, the lawmakers, and the community at large to families' feelings and requirements and (b) providing case and system advocacy for individual co-victims as well as for the entire class of co-victims.

The murder of my 20-year-old daughter in 1978 allowed me to say "I understand" to families that I met in my work, but that was not enough. I could generalize from my own experience, but that still was not enough. As I worked each day with the co-victims of homicide, I began to see how much more information was needed to respond effectively to their many needs. Our group modified and expanded its original list of priorities in response to the knowledge we were acquiring from working with co-victims and the systems that affected them.

The subsequent growth of FMV paralleled the growth of the victims' rights movement in the United States. One of the few grassroots endeavors of the 20th century, this field was launched in the early 1970s and emerged in the 1990s as a formalized profession with its own technology and knowledge base. FMV advanced from the part-time, volunteer-based organization of 1980 into the full-service victim advocate agency that it is today. A critical participant in the national victims' rights agenda, FMV is serving as an agent of change. Each year brings new victories, albeit small ones, and co-victims of homicide are receiving greater recognition as victims of violence with additional legal rights.

During the developing years of FMV, there were no resources or experts to turn to. The organization itself became the place to learn about the experience of homicide and how to translate that knowledge into appropriate services for co-victims. In gathering information for my own use as director of FMV, and to assist in training other victim advocates, I discovered that the primary interest in murder was aimed at the perpetrator. Consequently, the majority of research and academic writing on murder followed suit. The resulting gap in literature has consistently hindered service delivery to co-victims because there have been few references or resources about this perspective for caregivers. How to best notify a family of the murder of a loved one, the effects of murder on the family and friends of the victim, media influences, traumatic grief, and "second wounds" have not been examined, collectively, until *Homicide: The Hidden Victims*.

This text is a direct product of my personal experience as a co-victim of homicide coupled with 16 years of work with families of homicide victims. In May 1989, I completed two graduate degrees in areas related to my expertise (Master of Social Service and Master of Law and Social Policy). In 1995, during National Victims' Rights Week, I was a recipient of the Presidential Crime Victims' Service Award, giving national recognition to co-victims as crime victims. The establishment of FMV and the creation of the term *co-victim* have resulted in positive modifications in the way that victims are viewed by the American criminal justice system and by society. FMV is considered a model program and standard for the establishment of similar programs in jurisdictions around the country. It is my hope that caregivers, and the agencies for whom they work, can learn from my experiences at FMV, build on them, and contribute to the much needed research in this field.

Homicide: The Hidden Victims is a crossover text that makes multidisciplinary connections and is intended for advanced undergraduate courses as well as for training at the M.S.W., M.A., or Ph.D. levels (e.g., social workers, clinical psychologists and counselors, pastoral counselors, and other mental health practitioners). It is also a training manual for recent graduates and new service providers, a reference for experienced caregivers, and a definitive resource for those who come in contact with or formulate policy for co-victims of homicide (e.g., journalists and police officers). *Caregiver, service provider, intervenor,* and *victim advocate* will be used interchangeably here to describe professionals who work with this victim population including, but not limited to, trauma workers, mental health professionals and clinicians, criminal justice workers, clergy, emergency or medical professionals, volunteers, and students.

This book focuses on the invisible victims of crime, the co-victims or survivors of homicide—their ordeal, their grief, their pain, and their reconstruction of new lives. The purpose of such research, however, is not merely to chronicle the co-victim experience but also to use this perspective to acquaint intervenors with an understanding of the ordeal that homicide co-victims face. I am interested not only in the promotion of empathy for the co-victims but further in encouraging caregivers to use relevant information for creating better helping models. Case studies, anecdotes, and quotes garnered from interviews are used to illustrate the challenges confronting co-victims. The suggested reference material represents only a small segment of the information available. Some of these supplemental resources are quite current and suggest pioneering paradigms, theories, and interventions. It is imperative for caregivers, whether individual practitioners or those based in public or private agencies, to be familiar with such information, making every effort to be aware of new modalities.

❏ Preview of the Chapters

The first chapter provides an overview of murder in the United States and defines the concept of the victim-survivor. This essential foundation is presented as a basis for providing helping professionals with the knowledge to develop, frame, and deliver appropriate services to co-victims.

The idea of traumatic grief represents a new paradigm arising from the need to merge issues related to both trauma and grief, the commonality of which binds co-victims. Chapter 2 provides the lens through which the co-victim's experience is examined throughout the text.

The next two chapters provide a thorough discussion of the situational influences or special circumstances of co-victims, looking at the relationship of family and friends to the victim and then at the circumstances under which a murder occurred. From this assessment, professionals will gain greater understanding of the nuances and extent of the co-victim experience and mourning process.

The most defining event of a homicide, other than the murder itself, is how a family is notified of the victim's death. Empathic and informed death notification is an essential part of the co-victim's recovery process. Chapter 5 includes a field-tested training model and death notification protocol so that caregivers, if not notifiers themselves, can train others in effective death notification.

Interventions and tools specifically designed for use with co-victims are offered in Chapter 6 to guide the service provider. These interventions include techniques to use in individual and case advocacy; individual, family, and group counseling; and peer support groups.

Because most co-victims will need to confront legal matters—criminal, civil, or both—caregivers need a full understanding of these systems and knowledge of the legal rights of co-victims, discussed in Chapter 7. As the likely liaisons between co-victims and the system, victim advocates must know the rights of co-victims and legal terminology to provide effective services.

The media are a powerful, and often overwhelming, force in contemporary society. To best advise clients, service providers must understand the media rights of co-victims and the responsibilities of media professionals. Chapter 8 provides an in-depth look at the right to know versus the right to privacy.

Is it possible for co-victims to recover from the murder of a loved one? Will they ever "get over it"? The last chapter about reconstructing a new life explores these questions, provides caregivers with realistic expectations for co-victims, and differentiates between recovery and reconstruction.

Homicide: The Hidden Victims—A Guide for Professionals
is dedicated to all the co-victims of homicide. Thank you
for your strength and courage and for sharing
your love, laughter, and tears with me.

1

The Dynamics of Murder

Violence and crime in America are not new phenomena, but the recent increased awareness of these issues has caused a change in perspective for many people. Besides becoming more interested in understanding the roots of violence, we are beginning to study and comprehend the effects of violence and crime on those most affected—the victims. For caregivers to better serve individuals and communities affected by murder, they have had to gain more knowledge of both the roots and consequences of violence.

This chapter's overview of the dynamics of violence and murder includes the following: the causes of murder, the effects of witnessing violence and of viewing violence on television and in movies, current homicide statistics, and the public perception of violence. The impact of violence and murder is addressed by defining the victims of murder and their subsequent "second wound" and by examining theories regarding the role of stigmatization and blame.

❏ The Interaction of Violence and Murder

It seems that America cannot get enough violence. But for an increasing number of people, violence is no longer confined to the 6 o'clock news, to the front page of the newspaper, or between the covers of a book. Not only do people want to understand the perpetrator, but there is a growing communal need to believe that justice will be done and to be witness to the recovery of the victim or survivor—for the restoration of hope. This new focus helps assuage the uneasiness besieging U.S. society. The average citizen is challenged and concerned by the angst of the victim. The direction of this shift of attitude is still in a transitional state, resulting in some noticeable tensions in society's reaction to murder.

The steady diet of violence that intrudes on many aspects of everyday life has caused many people to internalize the victim's humiliation, pain, and suffering. Although the heightened awareness of the victim's experience can be viewed in a positive light, it also serves to increase the public's feelings of vulnerability. It makes the unthinkable a reality—that bad things can happen to good people. It is easier to deal with the violence that surrounds us if a person considers it as something that happens to someone else—that "the victims must have done something to cause their own deaths, and if I or my loved ones don't behave in the same manner, then we will be safe."

CAUSES OF MURDER

Crime and homicide in the United States are linked to complex issues, and it is not the purpose of this discussion to analyze or project the causes of murder. Caregivers and other service providers, however, need to be cognizant of the extent of the problem of violence and its contributing factors to gain an understanding of who gets murdered in our country and the significance of those murders on their clients—the families and friends of the victims.

Violence is a part of American culture, an accepted form of conflict resolution. Homicide is often the result of escalating violence (Mitchell, 1992). The idea of an American frontier mentality is sometimes blamed for this country's passion for violence. This mind-set, however, cannot be considered the definitive rationale. Other countries with similar traditions do not even come close to demonstrating America's level of violence (Lore & Schultz, 1993).

The Centers for Disease Control and Prevention (CDC; 1990) have identified a number of factors as important contributors to homicide: "immediate access to firearms, alcohol and substance abuse, drug trafficking, poverty, racial discrimination, and cultural acceptance of violent behavior" (p. 872). The questioning of governmental authority that came into being with the Vietnam War and the movement of America into a postindustrial economy are also implicated among the influences that seem to be related to the rise of the homicide rate in the United States as well as in other Western nations. This is noted as "the breakdown of the urban social fabric, the splitting up of family structures and the growth of drug addiction and unemployment, particularly amongst the most disadvantaged minorities" (Chesnais, 1992, pp. 218-219).

Witnessing Violence

Witnessing or experiencing violence, or both, "generates expectations about others' intentions that promote the use of aggression in interpersonal relationships" (Newberger & Newberger, 1992, p. 87). Young people in the United States, especially in urban areas, continue to be exposed firsthand to increasing amounts of violence in their homes, neighborhoods, and schools. A growing number of research studies are connecting the extreme increases in juvenile commission of violence to the huge numbers of children who are direct or indirect victims of violence. In "Preventing Black Homicide," Bell and Jenkins (1990) associate an increase in

> *Young people are exposed firsthand to increasing amounts of violence.*

aggression and behavioral problems with the witnessing of and exposure to violence, citing unresolved grief from the murder of loved ones as a major reason why some boys act out aggressively. According to the American Psychological Commission on Violence and Youth,

"The experience of being victimized by crime has been found to increase certain individuals' propensity for perpetrating violence, juvenile crime, adult criminality, and adult violence toward family members" (Eron, 1993, p. 43).

In her book *Deadly Consequences*, Prothrow-Stith (1991) notes,

> Many, perhaps most, homicides and assaults do not readily fit into the model that assigns total blame to one party and total innocence to the other. . . . The study of homicide and violence has pinpointed dozens of traits the victim and aggressor in a homicide may share with one another. Both are likely to be young and male, both are likely to be of the same race, both are likely to be poor, both are likely to have been exposed to violence in the past—to have been the victim of violence themselves, both may be depressed, both may use or abuse alcohol, both may use drugs, both are likely to see themselves as persons under attack, threatened, needing protection. (pp. 5, 22)

Viewing Violence on Television and in Movies

In any discussion of the causes of violence, the effects of violence as portrayed on television and in the movies are often cited as a major negative influence on children. Children are bombarded daily with violent images from a myriad of sources that fall under the guise of entertainment—television shows, cable programs, movies, cartoons, and even news programs. The problem is not limited to the amount of violence viewed as entertainment but extends to the manner in which it is shown. Much of the violence that is portrayed within media and entertainment venues is intense, gratuitous, and glamorous and is displayed without regard for the resulting consequences.

Whether viewing violence on television leads directly to more violence is still unclear. Both views have their proponents and accompanying studies. Researchers who have conducted lab, field, and correlational studies strongly agree that "taken together the results point to a statistically significant connection between watching violence and participating in it" (Kolbert, 1994, p. D20).

Regardless of the skepticism that remains about these findings, many people are concerned about the indirect effects of viewing media violence. The important question is not whether television violence causes violent behavior but rather what are the consequences of the attitudes and perceptions that result from watching television. For example, a disturbing influence of violent entertainment is the dehumanizing and desensitizing effect that repetitive viewing of violent acts has on the emotions of young children. As a result, children may lose the ability to empathize with others. Teenagers as well as young children are adversely affected. Teenagers are impressionable and will model their behavior on others. These are the same children who are increasingly showing up in the violent crime statistics as today's victims and perpetrators.

Cartoon violence can have as strong an impact on children as does other television violence. Most cartoons portray multiple violent acts in an unrealistic way. For example, what could be identified as the Wile E. Coyote Syndrome on the *Road Runner* cartoon is demonstrated as the Road Runner character assaults Wile E. Coyote by engaging him in almost every violent scenario imaginable—hitting him, running over him, pushing him off cliffs. Yet in the next frame of the cartoon, Wile E. Coyote is always restored to his former state; there is no evident remains of any wounds or pain. This representation of violence, presented via a cartoon that purports to be amusing, gives children a distorted picture of reality. In the *Road Runner* cartoons, death is depicted as a transitory state, and violent acts have no consequences.

HOMICIDE STATISTICS

Many experts in the field of criminology attribute recent changes in the murder rate, in both the increasing number of homicides and in the younger ages of the victims and perpetrators, to the increase in youth violence. Youth violence is more random; teens kill strangers more frequently than do adults. The following statistics offer a picture of who gets murdered in the United States and how that picture has changed during the last few decades:

- The federal CDC in Atlanta reported that between 1985 and 1991, the rate of homicide among males ages 15 to 19 increased 154% from the rate in the previous two decades (Leary, 1994, p. 32).
- From 1960 to 1980, the population of the United States increased by 26%; the homicide rate due to guns increased 160% (Koop & Lundberg, 1992, p. 3075).

- The rate of 10.5 murders per 100,000 people made 1991 the bloodiest year in American history (MacKellar & Yanagishita, 1995, p. 1).
- Since 1979, firearm homicides have been the leading cause of death for black males ages 15 to 19. Homicide is now the leading cause of death for African Americans, both male and female, between 15 and 24 years of age, and the second leading cause of death for all people in that age category (MacKellar & Yanagishita, 1995, p. 5).
- In 1993, 47% of murder victims were known to be either related to (12%) or acquainted with (35%) their assailant. Fourteen percent of victims were murdered by strangers, whereas 39% of victims had an unknown relationship to their murderer (Bastian, 1995, p. 3).
- In most industrialized countries, except the United States, murder is a rare occurrence. The homicide rate of approximately 10 deaths per 100,000 people, per year, is 17 times higher than the rate in Ireland or Japan and 10 times higher than the rate in Germany, France, or Greece (MacKellar & Yanagishita, 1995, p. 4).

THE PUBLIC PERCEPTION OF
CRIME AND VIOLENCE

The perceptions that individuals have about crime and violence have a myriad of roots that go beyond statistics. These yield a different picture from what experts and researchers are typically promulgating. People react to their impressions of crime and violence and not necessarily to the realities of the issues.

Some of the public's conceptions of crime and violence are a result of watching television. Dr. George Gerbner of the Annenberg School of Communications at the University of Pennsylvania has analyzed the contribution of television to these fears. He has investigated the relationship between television viewing and people's general attitudes regarding crime and has concluded "that heavy viewers tend to suffer from . . . 'the mean world syndrome' " (Kolbert, 1994, p. D20). They tend to "overestimate their chances of encountering violence, to believe that their neighborhoods are unsafe and to assume that crime is rising whether or not it actually is. They are also more likely to buy guns for protection" (p. D20).

The public's fears of crime may also be exaggerated by the extensive media coverage of violence. Fed a steady diet of crime meant to both frighten and titillate, individuals not surprisingly experience anger, fear, and frustration. "Lurid stories contribute to the public's feelings of vulnerability and powerlessness, and create a law and order climate exploited by politicians" (Lewis, 1995, p. A19).

In studies conducted by the *National Law Journal* (NLJ) in 1989 and repeated again in 1994, changes in the American view of crime's causes and solutions have come to light. In its first crime poll, 66% of Americans thought that drugs were the greatest cause of crime. The second NLJ poll found that only 28% believe that drugs are the leading cause of crime today. "The NLJ's second crime poll also finds more Americans now say crime is a societal problem that won't be curbed until conditions for the poor are improved" (Sherman, 1994, p. 19).

In the past 20 years, the face of murder has changed: Prior to this time, most people assumed that murder happened to others and was not an issue that would affect them. Not so today. Most researchers conclude that Americans are not any more violent than they were a generation ago; more guns, however, are available today. They are more powerful; they hold more bullets; they leave more dead and wounded. The result is a perception among the general population that violence has increased, but the reality is that today's violence is just more deadly.

❑ The Impact of Homicide

Who is a victim? "One who suffers some injury, hardship, or loss, is badly treated or taken advantage of" (*Oxford English Dictionary,* 1989, p. 607). Quinney (1972) notes that a "victim is a conception of reality as well as an object of events" (p. 314). Within a social framework, we all construct a definition of *the crime, the criminal,* and *the victim.* Therefore, we think we understand who the victim is in each circumstance. But we may also eliminate certain candidates from our concept of the victim. Under the law, the concept of the victim recognized in any legal definition of crime. Many of our legal statutes indicate who the victim is and that identifying the victim is the purpose of the criminal code.

The conceptions of the victim become more complicated when re-
moved from the criminal law. But it is this realm of common sense
conceptions that gives meaning to the question, "Who is the victim?"
It is these conceptions that affect the administration of the law and our
everyday reactions to crime. They also influence the formulation of
new laws and the way we regard and treat the victims among us.
(Quinney, 1972, p. 316)

THE HOMICIDE VICTIM

An examination of current information regarding homicide indicates that the majority of the victims of homicide are (a) young black
males who were most likely known to their assailants, (b) victims of
random felony murder, or (c) female partners of male abusers. Before
the last two decades, demographics and statistics alone defined the
homicide victim. Neither reliance on this information nor an understanding of the issues, however, takes into account *all* the victims of
a homicide. As the family and friends of homicide victims became
more vocal and visible, there seemed to be a need for an appellation
that included them.

The definition of the term *homicide victim* was expanded to include
the family and friends of the victim as a result of the victims' rights
movement that surfaced in the early 1970s. In its early days, the
movement turned its attention to the victims of sexual assault and
then to battered women. From this point on, sufficient interest was
raised for service providers and the federal government to begin to
look at the entire spectrum of victims of violence, with the co-victims
of homicide being the last group of victims of violent crime to be
recognized and identified.

Although the criminal laws defining murder have as their object
the victim whose life has been taken, murder creates an additional
class of victims. The surviving family and friends have no status
under the law, unless they were actual witnesses to the crime. In a
sociolegal context, however, they do exist. A framework that acknowl-
edges them should serve as the foundation for the sociolegal model
of service delivery. In 1986, Families of Murder Victims (FMV) pio-
neered such a model for co-victims of homicide. For services to be
beneficial to victims of violent crime, they must be designed to

respond equally to the human service component and to the construct of the criminal justice system.

Family members—mothers, fathers, spouses, siblings, children, and friends—become victims at the time that their loved ones are murdered. The designation *co-victim* responds to the need for a term to specify this category of victims. Some may feel that the term *co-victim* is pejorative, but as Burgess (1975) states, "to be acknowledged as a victim involves people validating the crime as a crime" (p. 397).

The term *homicide survivor* or *survivor-victim* is preferred by some victim advocates, mental health providers, and other caregivers. This label, however, often prematurely moves victims to survivors before they have had the opportunity to advance to that level of healing.

Conceptually, it is essential to understand that the family and friends of the murder victim have also been victimized by the crime and have had to assume new and permanent identities. This societal recognition via the term *co-victims* confirms that a crime has taken place and that the people affected are indeed victims. When referring to a homicide, too many people still operate under the concept that the "victim is dead," without acknowledging all the victims of a homicide.

In the aftermath of the murder, it is the co-victim who represents the murder victim; it is the co-victim who deals with the medical examiner, the criminal justice system, and the media. These interactions may go on for several years, some for a lifetime. It is not unusual for the trial phase (assuming there is an arrest in the case) to take several years to unfold. Sentencing, appeals, and parole may become a continual journey. The immediate and shocking reaction to the murder of a loved one is only a small part of the victim experience; it cannot be thought of as a single moment. The effects on the co-victims will last forever.

Family members and friends become co-victims when their loved ones are murdered.

The term *co-victim* may be expanded to any group or community that is touched by the murder—a classroom, a dormitory, a school, an office, a neighborhood. Most of the individuals who make up these communities are wounded emotionally, spiritually, and psychologically by a murder, some more deeply than others. To deny the ripple effect of a murder is to deny the human capacity for empathy. Frankl (1985) states that "suffering completely fills the human soul and conscious mind, no matter whether the suffering is great or little. Therefore, the 'size' of human suffering is absolutely relative" (p. 64).

It is estimated that each homicide victim is survived by an average of three loved ones for whom the violent death produces a painful and traumatic grief. If approximately 24,000 people are murdered each year, then the number of those who are personally victimized by homicide is an astonishing 72,000 victims a year. This means that in the last decade, almost *three quarters of a million* individuals carry with them the deep psychic wounds caused by the murder of a loved one (National Organization for Victim Assistance [NOVA], 1985).

THE SECOND WOUND

Co-victims are often victimized repeatedly by (a) the action of the defendant, (b) intrusions of the media, (c) insensitivity of prosecutors, (d) the process of the criminal justice system, (e) police, (f) would-be helpers, and (g) family and friends. Collectively, they all serve to produce what has been termed a *second wound*. The co-victim's experience is thus complicated by this second injury or secondary victimization.

The literature on victims tends to organize crime victims according to particular types of crime, but there are reactions that are common to all crime victims. These include shock, confusion, isolation, help-lessness, blame, fear, and anxiety. These reactions often serve as the basis for the second violation as they further illustrate the loss of the victim's assumptive world. Symonds (1980) states, "The second injury is the victim's *perceived* rejection by—and lack of expected support from—the community, agencies, and society in general, as well as family and friends. This second injury often follows any sudden, unexpected helplessness" (p. 37).

The term *secondary victimization* is not an appropriate term to describe this phenomenon because in some ways, the second injury is even worse than the murder itself. The second wound is inflicted on the co-victims by those from whom the co-victims had expected help in dealing with the loss and in remedying the injustices caused by the murder. Co-victims are especially vulnerable to this second injury because of the circumstance surrounding the murder of a loved one and the multiple contacts that they have with so-called helping systems.

THEORIES OF BLAME AND STIGMATIZATION

Individuals have a tendency to blame victims for the misfortunes that befall them. This attributional bias toward victims is well documented in literature. The stigma extended to victims and co-victims of homicide, however, has not received the same attention, but the material can be adapted to apply to co-victims as well.

Caregivers, service providers, criminal justice personnel, and other officials may not be as cognizant of these issues as they should be and may even aggravate the problem. In some cases, the stigmatization is inadvertent, but at times, it is a blatant act. Being more informed about the issues of blame and stigmatization will give service providers the opportunity to provide significant interventions and, one hopes, avoid inflicting a second wound on the co-victim. Several theories may assist caregivers in understanding the roots of this phenomenon.

The "Just World"

In general, people adhere to the belief that this is a just world and that bad things do not happen to good people. As a result of empirical studies in the 1960s, Lerner and Miller (1978) formulated the "just world" hypothesis:

> Individuals have a need to believe that they live in a world where people generally get what they deserve. The belief that the world is just enables the individual to confront his physical and social environment as though they were stable and orderly. Without such a belief it would be difficult for the individual to commit himself to the pursuit of long-range goals or even to the socially regulated behavior of day-to-day life. Since the belief that the world is just serves such an

important adaptive function for the individual, people are very reluctant to give up this belief, and they can be greatly troubled if they
encounter evidence that suggests that the
world is not really just or orderly after all.
(pp. 1030-1031)

> Blaming a homicide victim is less disturbing than facing the uncertainty of life.

When a loved one is murdered, the world
is no longer safe or secure. It is no longer
correct to think that such an event cannot
happen; the world is now viewed as ma-
levolent. This is true for any type of victimization, but the definition of murder brings
the intentions of a third party into the equation. This deliberate,
conscious violation by another opens the wound even more deeply.

When people learn that many homicides are random happenings
or that the murder victim is similar to themselves or their loved ones,
their faith in the world as an orderly and secure place is threatened.
This raises the possibility that such violence can happen to anyone;
people generally see themselves as less likely than others to have
such bad things happen. People have a problem considering that the
unspeakable can happen to them. Blaming the victim in a homicide
is a less disturbing alternative than facing the uncertainty of life.

Blaming the Victim

Mourners typically do not meet negative reactions when experiencing the loss of a loved one. Unfortunately, negative reactions are
often the case with respect to a homicide. Co-victims encounter many
unexpected feelings and reactions at every turn. Co-victims are as-
tounded to discover that the violent death of a loved one carries with
it an explicit social stigma. Not only are victims diminished, but they
are often vilified as well. This phenomenon has been experienced by
many families who have lost a loved one to murder. Much to their
shock, people often imply that the victims must have done something
to cause their own deaths. There is a strong analogy to the rape
victim's experience, although for the family of a homicide victim, the
blame and the resulting implications extend beyond the victim to
include them as well.

I have experienced this blaming and stigmatization. About 6 months after my daughter's murder, I was standing outside at my college reunion talking to some of my classmates. Out of the corner of my eye, I saw someone whom I barely knew point at me, and I heard her say in a loud voice, "That's the one whose daughter was murdered." She was standing directly in front of my husband. It was as if our daughter's murder had made us at fault and deaf and dumb at the same time. I doubt that the same reactions would have occurred if she had died of cancer or in a car accident.

Social Regulation of Grief

In her theory of the "social regulation of grief," Fowlkes (1990) cites a number of examples of "stigmatized, morally illegitimate" losses, such as the "death of someone who is a convicted criminal, a suicide, an alcoholic or a drug addict, a mental patient, a retardate. . . . The person who does not possess a 'virtual social identity' in life does not possess it in death either" (p. 645). Homicide falls under that same umbrella. In many homicide cases, the loss not only is socially and morally undervalued but even is devalued. In many situations, the murder victim is stigmatized, as is the family, so the loss may be considered as illegitimate. In my first book, *And I Don't Want to Live This Life* (1983), I tell the story of my daughter's "spoiled identity" and how that affected the family's ability to grieve her death. The usual sympathy and respect that are accorded to mourners were replaced with derision and ostracism (Fowlkes, 1990).

She died the subject of ridicule and scorn. The press called her Nause-ating Nancy. Their stories made it seem like she had "asked for it," just like a rape victim in a provocative dress "asks for it." They made it seem like she got what she deserved. In life, the media had made my daughter into a distasteful celebrity; in death, they made her a freak. There was a derisive skit about her on *Saturday Night Live*, jokes about her in Johnny Carson's monologue. Some people were selling Sid and Nancy T-shirts. Others were buying them.

Nobody wanted to hear of her pain, her sadness, her sensitivity. Nobody wanted to understand Nancy. Nobody cared. (Spungen, 1983, p. 7)

Goffman's (1963) work on stigma further illustrates the relationship of Fowlkes's "spoiled identity" to the lack of understanding of
the loss to the co-victim:

> While the stranger is present before us, evidence can arise of his
> possessing an attribute that makes him different from others in the
> same category of persons available for him to be, and of a less desirable
> kind—in the extreme, a person who is quite thoroughly bad, danger-
> ous, or weak. He is thus reduced in our minds from a whole and usual
> person to a tainted, discounted one. Such an attribute is a stigma,
> especially when its discrediting effect is very extensive. . . . It consti-
> tutes a special discrepancy between virtual and actual social identity.
> . . . Not all undesirable attributes are at issue, but only those which are
> incongruous with our stereotype of what a given type of individual
> should be. (p. 3)

By assigning certain attributes to individual murder victims, society, with some assistance from the media, tends to categorize the
victims into "good" and "bad" classifications with almost no middle
ground. The greater preponderance of homicide victims are placed
into the "bad" category. This societal belief promotes the stereotypical thinking that the murder victim is somehow different and, therefore, less valued than *we* are.

Minority Homicide Victims

The stigmatization of blame occurs more frequently in the murders
of women and minorities than in murders of nonminorities. Certain
circumstances of the murder may further stigmatize the female victim by implying contribution, such as (a) a woman who was murdered in a domestic violence incident, especially if the murder occurred as the result of a reconciliation with the abuser; (b) a victim of
both rape and murder; (c) a victim who was engaged in prostitution
at the time of her death; and (d) a victim who exhibited less than
"respectable" behavior. Murders of African Americans are often
linked to illegal activities prior to any evidence being put forth by
authorities or the connection being proved. Besides society's need to
prove that the world is just, many of the attributions directed toward
women and minorities are a result of stereotypical thinking.

In examining the tendency of society to place a weak response to the victimization of women, many imply that women's rights are not really worth "recognizing, protecting, and enforcing" (Schur, 1984, p. 134). The female murder victim may be treated as if she, not the male perpetrator, were the deviant. This contributes to the gestalt of female victim blaming. The attribution that the female victim has somehow violated a gender norm, particularly if her behavior can be considered as having a causal relationship to the crime, may be used to justify treating her as if she were guilty.

The labeling of female murder victims as deviant is reinforced by the social science concept of victim precipitation, which highlights the interaction between the victim and offender that may have preceded the murder. The concept of victim precipitation does not describe the victim's behavior but rather someone else's interpretation of it. This explanation of the contributing circumstances is often misconstrued and unfounded. It is important to call into question the sources of the description of the precipitating circumstance. They are most likely to be offered by a man—the perpetrator or the homicide detective. Police reports are also culpable in furthering these misconceptions. These reports are written in the immediate aftermath of the murder and may not be a correct and complete representation of the facts. Initial police reports are rarely updated to reflect additional information. Focusing on the conditions that precede the murder serves to deflect the responsibility away from the perpetrator and adds to victim blaming.

Rape-Murder

"Many states have . . . enacted shield laws to protect rape victims against harassment through questions about past sexual behavior" (Gifis, 1984, p. 443). These statutes do not apply if the rape victim was also murdered during the commission of the rape. During the criminal justice process, the victim of a rape and murder, who cannot speak in her own defense, may be demeaned and blamed. Her background is often brought into question, and this may include inferences about her sexual relationships, her possible use of drugs and alcohol, and her lifestyle. Frequently, this information, elicited out of context, allows the defense attorney to cast serious aspersions on the character of the victim, often leading to the assumption that the victim "asked for it." Generally, this sort of questioning is no longer legally allowed to be put forth during a rape trial, but it is still frequently presented during a homicide trial. Not only is the victim blamed, but also the co-victim may feel shamed and humiliated and is usually without recourse to respond within the criminal justice system or in any other venue.

❏ Summary

An understanding of the dynamics of murder in the United States is essential to defining the victims and co-victims of murder. Caregivers need to be cognizant of the repercussions of violence on individual co-victims and on the community to apply this information in developing new approaches to service delivery. The current lack of relevant literature, research, documentation, and information about the co-victim has hindered this process, and immediate efforts should be undertaken to remedy this problem. Only by effecting change in how we deal with violence and its ramifications can we hope to begin addressing the problem of homicide in America.

American society seems to want to bury the results of homicide along with the victim. By advocating for the use of the term *co-victim*, caregivers ensure that the loved ones of the murder victim are not forgotten. At the same time, one needs to remember that there is a next step: becoming a survivor. Eventually, co-victims need to lay aside any "victim" mentality that exists and begin living their lives again. Chapter 9, "Reconstructing a New Life," discusses this healing process, particularly, how to move from victim to survivor, and beyond.

2

Traumatic Grief: A New Model

Any approach to an investigation of the aftermath of a violent death must include a discussion of the models for trauma, grief, and bereavement. Historically, the focus of caregivers has been on the co-victim's grief issues, often without considering the impact of trauma issues that may also be present. Without recognition of the traumatic components of the experience, co-victims have been provided with services and treatment that primarily emanate from the grief model. This often causes co-victims to feel uncomfortable and anxious because their type of grief is not addressed by current models of treatment.

This chapter explores pertinent theories and issues from the fields of both trauma and grief as they relate to co-victims' experience. This information serves as background for introducing the rationality of merging the two fields to construct a new paradigm of service delivery that specifically relates to co-victims. Discussions of the emotional experience, cultural and gender influences, and mental health implications of traumatic grief then follow.

17

❑ **Understanding Trauma**

Since 1980, the expansion of the definition of posttraumatic stress disorder (PTSD) through the development and publication of the *Diagnostic and Statistical Manual of Mental Disorders* (American Psychiatric Association, 1994) has given rise to a greater acceptance and increased interest in the trauma experienced by victims of violent crime (see Table 2.1). The diagnosis of PTSD was initially applied to victims of crime on the basis of their witness status. This effectively dismissed most co-victims of homicide from consideration because they rarely witnessed the event. As more research became available, it was evident that the same concepts of trauma that apply to victims of violent crime apply to co-victims of homicide as well. The field of trauma is still in its infancy, compared with the field of grief and bereavement; therefore, less information is currently available. This situation is quickly changing, however, with the advent of more research. Professionals should stay informed about current theories of trauma and interventions with trauma victims.

Concepts of trauma apply to co-victims of homicide as well as to victims of violent crime.

TRAITS OF CO-VICTIM TRAUMA

For most co-victims, trauma begins with the death notification, unless they have been actual witnesses to the homicide. Typical responses to a stressful life event include a wide array of both physical and emotional responses that stimulate the sympathetic nervous system (see Chapter 5, "Death Notification"). The physical reactions include (a) shock; (b) confusion; and (c) increased adrenaline, which may cause heart palpitations, sweating, hyperventilation, nausea, and vomiting. Emotional responses can include (a) anger, (b) fear, (c) frustration, (d) guilt or self-blame, (e) shame or humiliation, and (f) grief and sorrow (Young, 1994, pp. 2:6-2:7). If the body has been put in a high state of alert to rapidly cope with a stressor, it may react. When the amount of information that must be processed is too great, the body and the mind are overwhelmed and become disorganized. No action can take place. The result of this sequence is a traumatic reaction.

For many crime victims, the threat that arouses a flight-or-fight reaction often involves imminent personal danger or threat of danger. The human system processes any stressful life event in the same manner. Although they do not witness the homicide of a loved one, co-victims are similarly overwhelmed.

> I lost all control. I began screaming and crying. Physically, I felt all my muscles go limp, my head felt like it was going to explode, I couldn't breathe, my heart felt like it was being squeezed, I was nauseous. (Significant other of a murder victim)

RETURN TO EQUILIBRIUM

People's lives are usually conducted in a state of balance as they encounter the positive and negative stresses of everyday life. For the most part, people remain in a comfortable range of equilibrium, and if not, they can usually reestablish their balance. The emotional trauma of having a loved one murdered is so profound that co-victims cannot restore this sense of equilibrium to their lives (Young, 1994). Co-victims feel out of control, weak, frightened, powerless, and helpless in the wake of events beyond their control.

The equilibrium of the co-victim's life is so radically changed that the prognosis is poor for a complete return to the state that existed prior to the homicide. The process of reconstructing a new life is a realistic goal, but it should be understood by both caregiver and co-victim that this is a continuing process. Intervenors should be sensitive to the use of the terms *healing* or *recovery*, which can be considered pejorative because these labels may convey the idea that the co-victim is ill.

Reconstructing the Assumptive World

Much of the psychological trauma of being a co-victim of homicide is derived "from the shattering of very basic assumptions that victims have held about the operation of the world" (Janoff-Bulman,

TABLE 2.1 Diagnostic Criteria for Posttraumatic Stress Disorder

---

A. The person has been exposed to a traumatic event in which both of the following were present:

 1. The person experienced, witnessed, or was confronted with an event or events that involved actual or threatened death or serious injury, or a threat to the physical integrity of self or others.

 2. The person's response involved intense fear, helplessness, or horror. Note: In children, this may be expressed instead by disorganized or agitated behavior.

B. The traumatic event is persistently reexperienced in one (or more) of the following ways:

 1. Recurrent and intrusive distressing recollections of the event, including images, thoughts, or perceptions. Note: In young children, repetitive play may occur in which themes or aspects of the trauma are expressed.

 2. Recurrent distressing dreams of the event. Note: In children, there may be frightening dreams without a recognizable content.

 3. Acting or feeling as if the traumatic event were recurring (includes a sense of reliving the experience, illusions, hallucinations, and dissociative flashback episodes, including those that occur on awakening or when intoxicated). Note: In young children, trauma-specific reenactment may occur.

 4. Intense psychological distress at exposure to internal or external cues that symbolize or resemble an aspect of the traumatic event.

 5. Physiological reactivity on exposure to internal or external cues that symbolize or resemble an aspect of the traumatic event.

C. Persistent avoidance of stimuli associated with the trauma and numbing of general responsiveness (not present before the trauma), as indicated by three (or more) of the following:

 1. Efforts to avoid thoughts, feelings, or conversations associated with the trauma

 2. Efforts to avoid activities, places, or people that arouse recollections of the trauma

 3. Inability to recall an important aspect of the trauma

 4. Markedly diminished interest or participation in significant activities

 5. Feeling of detachment or estrangement from others

 6. Restricted range of affect (e.g., unable to have loving feelings)

 7. Sense of a foreshortened future (e.g., does not expect to have a career, marriage, children, or a normal life span)

TABLE 2.1 *Continued*

D. Persistent symptoms of increased arousal (not present before the trauma), as indicated by two (or more) of the following:
1. Difficulty falling or staying asleep
2. Irritability or outbursts of anger
3. Difficulty concentrating
4. Hypervigilance
5. Exaggerated startle response

E. Duration of the disturbance (symptoms in Criteria B, C, & D) is more than one month.

F. The disturbance causes clinically significant distress or impairment in social, occupational, or other important areas of functioning.

SOURCE: From *Diagnostic and Statistical Manual of Mental Disorders* (4th ed., sec. 309.81, pp. 424-429), by American Psychiatric Association, 1994, Washington, DC: Author. Copyright © 1994 by American Psychiatric Association. Reprinted with permission.

1985, p. 17). The stress syndrome described by PTSD is largely attributable to the shattering of victims' basic assumptions about themselves and their world. Janoff-Bulman suggests at least three highly related types of assumptions, shared by most people, that are especially affected by victimization: (a) the belief in personal invulnerability, (b) the perception of the world as significant and comprehensible, and (c) the view of ourselves in a positive light. The experience of having a loved one murdered leads to an intense questioning of the co-victim's self-perceptions and activates feelings of negative self-images in the co-victim that may involve a feeling of deviance.

Loss of equilibrium and subsequent loss of meaning shatters the presumption of invulnerability; an individual can no longer say, "It can't happen to me." It behooves the victim of violent crime to reconstruct the event to find meaning to the trauma. Herman (1992) states, "The traumatic event challenges an ordinary person to become a theologian, a philosopher, and a jurist" (p. 178). This leads the co-victim to formulate a series of questions beyond the realm of human understanding, questions for which there are no acceptable answers. The first question—"Why?"—is "spoken more in bewilderment than in outrage" (p. 178). A newspaper reported the words of a rabbi presiding at a memorial service for a murder victim:

"We come here because we have nowhere else to go. We don't know what to do," he said, his voice choking. "We come here with many questions, the main one being, 'Why, why?' " (Colimore, Raphael, & Sanginiti, 1994, p. A17)

This question is uttered, indeed screamed out loud, by the co-victim—often to no one in particular. The next question often posed by a co-victim of homicide is "Why me?" or "Why did this happen to me?" rather than focusing on the question "Why did this event happen?" Sometimes, the co-victim includes the murder victim within the scope of this question. Even in cases in which the actual victim of the murder has led a lifestyle that may have resulted in greater vulnerability to violence, the searching for the answer to the "why" question remains applicable. And there is still no satisfactory answer.

Recognizing Long-Term Symptoms

Horowitz (1986) explains that "stress-response syndromes are composites of signs and symptoms that occur after serious life events or threatening life circumstances" (p. 241). Although working through a traumatic experience is considered a normal process, some individuals suffer symptoms ranging from temporary to severe, and many continue to reexperience crisis reactions for long periods as certain events act as a trigger to reactivate the trauma. The rebuilding of an individual's "shattered assumptions" (Janoff-Bulman, 1992, p. 1) about the world and self is an integral part of the stress response.

Common response patterns to trauma have been identified in co-victims, but long-term stress reactions are unique to each person. Many co-victims suffer from long-term stress or crisis reactions, although not every co-victim will develop PTSD. Brom and Kleber (1989) indicate that 15% to 25% of co-victims will suffer from PTSD (p. 341).

Caregivers should be cognizant of these reactions to assist co-victims in processing their trauma. Working through a traumatic experience serves a necessary and important function; PTSD may occur if the victim has not had the opportunity to perform this task. On the other hand, it is incorrect to think that the co-victim should automatically be traumatized because something bad has happened.

Time has lessened the feelings of being vulnerable, helpless, and completely out of control; however, I will never feel the way that I did before he was murdered. The ever present fear that some other horrible thing will happen to me no longer controls my life. (Significant other of a murder victim)

The long-term impact that the murder of a loved one has on a co-victim cannot be underestimated. "Traumatic events have primary effects not only on the psychological structures of the self but also on the systems of attachment and meaning that link individual and community" (Herman, 1992, p. 51). On the basis of firsthand observation, anecdotal reports from co-victims, and contemporary research, strong evidence indicates that the initial trauma causes a permanent alteration to the co-victim's nervous system. The responses evoked by the event continue long after the trauma is over—in many cases, forever.

❑ Understanding Grief

An overview of the grief process is presented here as a component of the structure of traumatic grief. Grief is the second stage of a two-part process that co-victims face, and it is necessary for the caregiver to have some insight into the issues and problems that the grieving process presents. Knowledge of "normal mourning," compared with "complicated mourning," is also a significant component of this process because almost every co-victim will present complicated mourning issues. Again, as in the area of trauma, the material tends to be generic in content and will need to be adapted to the specific issues relating to co-victims. Whatever definitions and time frames are employed to describe the theories of mourning will need to be revised to fit the co-victim's individual experience.

One of the hardest parts is people telling me that I have to let go. What does that mean? A year hasn't even passed since my mother's murder, and people are trying to pressure me to be okay. No one can tell you how long to grieve. You have to allow yourself time and space to feel and to take care of yourself while doing so. (Daughter of murder victim)

PERSPECTIVES ON "GRIEF WORK"

The distinction between the terms *grief* and *mourning* as explained by Rando (1993) suggest that "grief refers to the process of experiencing the psychological, behavioral, social, and physical reactions to the perception of loss" (p. 22). Grief is a natural reaction and takes place at the beginning phases of mourning, but "mourning requires more than the passive reactions of grief: it demands *working actively* [italics added] to adapt to the loss" (p. 23). It is exceedingly important for caregivers to provide support during the early acute stages of grief and throughout the entire mourning process.

> *Caregivers must provide support throughout the entire mourning process.*

Co-victims, as a group, report that caregivers generally do not inform them about the concept and realities of grief work. Grief work needs to be clearly defined for co-victims and presented as a flexible process. Just as attention is paid to normalizing the effects of trauma, the same should be done with respect to grief. Even homicide support groups seem to pay insufficient attention to this process. Co-victims state that if they had had more education regarding what grief work entails, they would have felt better prepared to carry it out. Much of the frustration and fear that co-victims experience might be lessened if they had more knowledge regarding the possible tasks and expectations of their painful journey.

Grief work is even more complicated and intense because of additional tasks that co-victims must undertake as they interact with other individuals and systems. In the aftermath of a homicide, the co-victims are often involved in various activities imposed on them by the medical examiner, the criminal justice system, and possibly the media. This is true whether or not an arrest is made. Such involvement is not by choice, and these endeavors are time-consuming, physically and emotionally exhausting, and sometimes quite public. Co-victims are left with little energy to traverse the rest of the grief process, which is distinct from that experienced by those whose loved ones did not die violently. As a result, co-victims may be incapable of moving on to other phases until there is some finality to the legal aspects of the case, such as the completion of the trial. Several key theories and concepts regarding issues of grief, grief work, and mourning are highlighted below as a background for caregivers.

Freud

From a historical perspective, Freud's research on mourning has provided insights into the process necessary to accomplish the work of grieving. It has also spurred others to build on his theories. His classic *Mourning and Melancholia* (1917/1953), although not his first writing on the topic of mourning, is regarded by many as a benchmark. One of Freud's most important influences in this area came from his assertion that mourning the loss of a loved one is normal and necessary:

> It is also well worth notice that, although mourning involves grave departures from the normal attitude to life, it never occurs to us to regard it as a pathological condition and to refer it to medical treatment. We rely on its being overcome after a certain lapse of time, and we look upon any interference with it as useless or even harmful. (pp. 243-244)

Prior to the publication of *Mourning and Melancholia*, this concept was neither accepted nor understood.

Another major contribution made by Freud was his recognition that the "work of grief" is difficult and arduous. In *Mourning and Melancholia* (1917/1953), he wrote, "Normally, respect for reality gains the day. Nevertheless its orders cannot be obeyed at once. They are carried out bit by bit, at great expense of time and cathectic energy" (pp. 244-245).

Although some of Freud's writings and theories of mourning have met with controversy, his contributions to the field cannot be negated. For serious students of thanatology and others who wish to investigate the field from a historical perspective, a more thorough reading of Freud's writings is strongly suggested.

Lindemann

In his classic work on loss, "Symptomatology and Management of Acute Grief," Lindemann (1944/1994) also refers to the issue of the work that is involved in the processing of grief. He delineates three tasks: (a) emancipation from bondage to the deceased, (b) readjustment to the environment in which the deceased is missing, and (c) the formation of new relationships (p. 156). Caregivers can assist grievers with the initial grief work. This assistance usually involves teaching new skills to survivors for which they were dependent on the deceased and helping in the establishment of new confidants or primary group relations, which researchers have found essential to well-being (Lohmann, 1977). Lindemann is also concerned with the duration of grief; it depends on the manner in which the mourner takes on the grief work.

Bowlby

Bowlby's (1980) work in attachment theory, separation anxiety, and mourning provides a framework for looking at the typical bereavement responses, as well as the issues that might lead to pathological mourning. Bowlby's bereavement model has become the standard to follow for many caregivers who work with mourners. The four main phases of response are

1. numbness that, in adults, usually lasts from a few hours to a week and may be interrupted by outbursts of extremely intense distress and anger, or both;
2. yearning and searching for the lost figure, often lasting for months and sometimes for years;
3. disorganization and despair; and
4. greater or less degree of reorganization. (p. 304)

Bowlby's model was instrumental in establishing the linear structure of grief and mourning. This linear process often disintegrates as caregivers may attempt to impose a rigid and artificial progression on the mourner that is not necessarily applicable for all co-victims. As a result, caregivers, and even the co-victims, may labor under the mistaken idea that some complication or pathology exists when there is none. When co-victims are informed of the usual stages of mourning and feel they are not adhering to them, they may experience unnecessary fear and anxiety.

The use of a linear model does not imply a fixed sequence, although most co-victims will ultimately have to work through all the stages. In the long term, the mourner tends to move in a forward progression; in the short term, the mourner will move back and forth among the stages, sometimes even completely bypassing a stage. This is considered quite normal. Some thanatologists and bereavement specialists are beginning to investigate the use of a circular model to replace the linear paradigm of grief. This may be a more realistic way to view the process because it does not force the mourner into a subjective time frame.

Worden

Worden (1991) has formulated four tasks of mourning into his approach of assisting the mourner with the grieving process. In *Grief Counseling and Grief Therapy,* he uses "the term *mourning* to indicate the process which occurs after a loss, while *grief* refers to the personal experience of the loss" (p. 34). Worden finds the terms *stages* or *phases,* used by some experts in the field of grief, to be inadequate to describe the process of mourning.

> Tasks, on the other hand, are much more consonant with Freud's concept of grief work and imply that the mourner needs to take action and can do something. Also, this approach implies that the mourning can be influenced by intervention from the outside. (p. 35)

Worden relies on his four tasks to provide a deeper insight into the mourning process and offer the caregiver a more practical approach to assisting the client. He suggests some ordering of the tasks, but a specific sequence is not imperative as long as the griever completes all of them. The following are Worden's four tasks of mourning:

1. To accept the reality of the loss
2. To work through the pain of grief
3. To adjust to an environment in which the deceased is missing
4. To emotionally relocate the deceased and move on with life (pp. 10-18)

Worden, like Freud, Lindemann, and Bowlby, does not specifically identify co-victims within the category of mourners; therefore, their unique needs are not addressed. The caregiver will need to look at the various approaches to working through the mourning process and adapt the salient components to the co-victim's situation.

CHARACTERISTICS OF HOMICIDE BEREAVEMENT

Because homicide co-victims are continually interrupted by outside influences and circumstances, these disruptions cause them to feel even more out of control, as if taking "a ride on a roller coaster without anyone at the controls." Co-victims may feel that they are taking two steps forward and four steps back—probably a true interpretation of the reality of the situation. The avoidance and fear of grief can lead to problems. Doka and Rando are two researchers whose work specifically relates to homicide bereavement.

Doka

When a loss is not or cannot be openly acknowledged, publicly mourned, or socially supported, mourners cannot be supported in their bereavement. First, there needs to be an acceptance of the idea that support is needed. Such mourners find themselves in a state of *disenfranchised grief*, represented by a lack of social validation and recognition of the loss (Doka, 1988). Doka's theory, much like Fowlkes's social regulation of grief (see Chapter 1), has profound implications for the co-victim; they both speak to the issue that these are mourners who have been shut out of the grieving process. Doka explains that "this has created an underclass of grievers whom we describe as disenfranchised by society from the normal grieving process" (p. 14).

Doka (1988) states that "there is both an intersocial and an intra-psychic aspect of disenfranchised grief" (p. xv). Whenever there is evidence of disenfranchisement, there are parallel events taking place on the intrapsychic level. The psychological and sociological dimensions may blur, be undifferentiated, or influence each other. The core of self-disenfranchised grief is the mourner's own lack of acceptance and understanding. Shame, which will be discussed further in this chapter, is the underlying psychological basis controlling this phenomenon.

Typically, an AIDS death is presented in the literature as a prime example of stigmatized loss or disenfranchised grief. Other examples of disenfranchised grief include the grief that is experienced by lovers and significant others, friends, pet owners, and ex-spouses. References to homicide co-victims, in this context, are conspicuously absent from the literature. Yet the grief that homicide co-victims experience certainly falls within the same parameters.

Doka (1988) points out several reasons that a mourner may be positioned in disenfranchised grief: (a) The relationship is not recognized, (b) the loss is not recognized, and/or (c) the mourner is not recognized as a legitimate griever. Rando (1993) adds two additional categories: (a) The loss, even if it is recognized, is not supported by the mourner's social group; and (b) it is believed that the loss of a person whom one may have devalued should not elicit grief.

Victims of homicide are often devalued because of the perceived or real blame that is ascribed to them. For these reasons, the family often has difficulty in getting permission to legitimately mourn a loved one and to receive support in that process. Simply giving permission to grieve the loved one may be all the homicide co-victims need to be able to begin the process. Caregivers should be aware of this and be available and willing to open the door.

> With Paula's [the therapist] help, David made some progress. He was at least able to get in touch with what was upsetting him.
> I was really angry at Nancy for so much of what she did to us . . . I wouldn't let myself grieve for her. I fought it. I didn't think it was right to grieve for her. That really messed me up, because I also loved her. She was my sister. (Spungen, 1983, p. 399)

Rando

On a contemporary basis, Rando has done some of the most definitive research on grief and mourning. Her latest book, *Treatment of Complicated Mourning* (1993), is probably the most complete exploration of the subject presently available. Rando's schema of the *process* of grief and mourning work divides the responses into three periods or phases, each characterized by a major response set toward the loss:

1. *The Avoidance Phase* covers the time periods in which the news of the death is initially received and briefly thereafter. It is marred by the understandable desire to avoid the terrible knowledge that the loved one is lost.
2. *The Confrontation Phase* is a time when grief is experienced most intensely and reactions to the loss are most acute. . . . The Confrontation Phase has been described as a time of angry sadness. There are extremes of emotion.
3. In *the Accommodation Phase,* formerly called the *reestablishment phase,* there is a gradual decline of the symptoms of acute grief and the beginning of social and emotional reentry into the everyday world. . . . The goal of accommodation is to learn to live with the loss and readjust one's new life accordingly. (pp. 33-41)

Rando (1993) has developed six major processes of mourning, which coincide with her three phases of grief and mourning. She views mourning as processes rather than tasks. This schema allows the caregiver to be more focused on outcome and provides for more immediate feedback. Rando's schema, "The Six R Processes of Mourning," are as follows:

1. Recognize the loss.
2. React to the separation.
3. Recollect and reexperience the deceased and the relationship.
4. Relinquish the old attachments to the deceased and the old assumptive world.
5. Readjust to adaptive movement into the new world without forgetting the old.
6. Reinvest. (p. 45)

Without a formal model for bereavement, many caregivers, thanatologists, victim advocates, and mental health professionals do not recognize and integrate the unique perspective of the homicide co-victim into the theories of grief and bereavement. The stages of grief

that are delineated and recognized by caregivers are often uninten-
tionally delayed or postponed by co-victims who must divert their
time to other tasks involved with the murder—the criminal justice
system, the media, and so forth.

Complicated mourning has currently displaced the term *pathological
grief* as a more accurate description of grief in which "there is some
compromise, distortion, or failure" (Rando, 1993, p. 149). Acute grief
as defined by Lindemann (1944/1994) falls into the same classification: "Acute grief is a definite syndrome with psychological and
somatic symptomology" (p. 155). As used in Rando's book, complicated mourning means that the mourner attempts to deny, repress,
or avoid aspects of the loss, its pain, and the full realizations of its
implications for the mourner and hold on to and avoid relinquishing
the loved one. One of the criteria for ascertaining the above complications is the timing of the mourner's response, that is, the response
relative to the time that has elapsed since the death and the circumstances, sudden or anticipated, under which the death occurred.

In homicide, caregivers may misunderstand the loss reactions of
the co-victim and may make a premature diagnosis of complicated
mourning or other problems. The unique quality of the grief makes
homicide bereavement different, but does it necessarily make the
mourning complicated? To answer this question, more research needs
to be directed to this issue. The goal is to develop a new schema that
adequately explains normal homicide bereavement and, at the same
time, differentiates it from complicated homicide bereavement.

HOW PARENTS GRIEVE

One of the greatest problems experienced in parental bereavement
is that although parents are viewed as representing a dyad, they are
distinct individuals. Their disparities can be especially profound
when it comes to the grieving process. Not only do men and women
grieve differently because of social and gender role conditioning, but
they commonly grieve in different rhythms. In addition, each parent
has a unique relationship with his or her child, and, therefore, each
experiences the loss differently. It is often wrongly assumed that the
loss is the same for both parents.

Depending on the specific personal situation—unmarried, divorced, separated, or widowed—single parents will face a number of circumstances that can further complicate their grief and trauma. The burden may become heavier because one parent often assumes the role of both mother and father in interactions with the various systems. Others, however, will continue to judge the parent from a gender-oriented perspective. Single parents may experience emotional difficulties because they are not part of a parental dyad, but they can also operate in a more independent manner, without having to consider the impact on a partner.

Grieving Fathers

The father is expected to be strong and to cope with many of the details that arise after the death, as well as to continue to work, although these expectations may become less gender focused as more women enter the workforce. When parents are unable to cope and to carry on their traditional roles, society tends to be less forgiving of the father. This may help explain why men appear to return to their normal day-to-day activities more quickly than do women.

The expectation by society that fathers must be strong may deny to men the opportunity to be comforted by others and to express their grief. Fathers often serve as the caretaker of the family and as the connection between the family and the larger, more perilous world. Men are so strongly indoctrinated with this function that they often feel greater pressure from within themselves than from other people. It is not surprising that many fathers express some resentment for such a burden.

On the other hand, the father may feel that he is helping his wife by overseeing her grief. Many wives, however, express criticism of their husbands' seeming inability to communicate their feelings. It is easy to see how these competing tensions can lead to problems within the marital dyad. Spouses often need outside support to understand gender differences in the mourning process, but this may not be readily available or even solicited. A rapport can be achieved, with effort and a good deal of patience. This, too, can be considered as part of the grief work.

In the aftermath of a child's homicide, the father is routinely asked, "How's your wife doing?" Rarely does he receive a similar inquiry into his own needs and feelings. This may be perceived by the father as a denial of his pain and grief and cause him to shut the door on any effort to discuss his responses to the murder.

Grieving Mothers

Bereaved mothers are often the more verbal partner in articulating their anger, their reactions to the murder, and any second injuries. Mothers are more likely to show their emotions and to do so without attempting to contain their feelings; they may cry, scream, keen, and wail.

The mother of a murder victim is more likely than the father to be labeled as unfit, as somehow bearing some of the responsibility for the death of the child, regardless of the age of the child or the circumstances of the murder. "Conceptions of the 'unfit' mother may also reflect the dominant cultural tendency to put the female in the wrong" (Schur, 1984, p. 88). Minority women, who encounter additional stereotypes of a gender and cultural nature, are doubly victimized when a child is murdered.

Spouses, friends, and family often make attempts to comfort the mother and to calm her down in the mistaken idea that it is "for her own good." The often strong reaction to her emotional displays and the attempts of others to intervene may impart the impression to the bereaved mother that there is something wrong with her or that she is "going crazy." It is important to reassure the bereaved mother that she is not "sick" and that others have had similar reactions. Crying and other emotional displays often provide a great deal of relief and are part of the healing process. When individuals suppress their emotions, they will find few other outlets to express themselves and may even manifest their feelings in adverse physical symptoms. Well-meaning family and friends often encourage the bereaved mother to go to a doctor in the misguided idea that there must be a pill that can be prescribed to anesthetize the pain. This can lead to a plethora of secondary problems, including the inability of the co-victim to experience her grief and to actively participate in the funeral and other rituals, which can have their own healing effect.

The Parental Dyad

After a child has been murdered, each partner needs the other to serve as a strong support, sometimes even to function in therapeutic ways. Previously, the parents may have been able to work together in solving problems, but they may now find themselves in conflict. A breakdown in communication between partners often breeds anger and blame as issues accumulate. This can lead to the development of problems that place severe stress on the relationship and become the cause of deep and often irreparable divisions. It behooves parents—indeed, it is often imperative—to make every effort to continue an open dialogue. It may require the assistance of a professional counselor to keep open the lines of communication, but it is well worth the effort.

> It is a strong marriage, and we have been through a great deal. It is a different marriage, and the murders played a very big part. I wish I could say we are cohesive, sharing, aware, etc., etc. I think we have dealt with it each in our own way. (Mother of two murder victims)

Research has shown that the divorce rate after the death of a child is higher than average, especially if the child has died as the result of a prolonged illness. In all cases of child death, regardless of the manner of the death, the state of the parental relationship prior to the death plays an important role in determining what happens next to the relationship. Osterweis, Solomon, and Green (1984) reported that marital problems and divorces occur in 50% to 70% of families whose child has died from cancer (p. 81). The pain of being witness to a child's serious illness and impending death leaves many scars that do not heal easily and can disrupt a marriage.

In a violent death, the grief work occurs almost entirely after the death, rather than being anticipatory, as in the death of a child from an illness. This may explain why the divorce rate in the aftermath of a homicide does not seem as high as the occurrence after the death of a child from other causes. The difference may lie in the circumstances of the death.

Studies focused on the effects of homicide bereavement on marital relationships have been too few to reach statistically reliable conclusions. More research needs to be conducted regarding the issue of differences in the divorce rate. The unique tasks that are required of the parents of a murdered child can be intense and add another dimension to grief work.

Parents of a murdered child may find that grieving now draws them together rather than causing conflicts, as it might in other types of parental bereavement. They are often surprised to discover that they are functioning as a team, although they may be experiencing some division over certain aspects of the grieving process such as gender differences. This forging of a new and sometimes stronger bond may protect these bereaved parents from any friction they may encounter.

There is a great and immediate need for the development of a new model of parental bereavement that takes into account traumatic or violent death. Increasingly, the literature provides information about parental grief and bereavement. Empirical research, however, is lacking concerning variables that reflect the extent of grief experienced by co-victims of homicide and, more specifically, that focus on the grief of parents of murdered children. In addition, little clinical recognition and attention have been paid to the types of interventions that are employed with this victim group. Much of what is available is the result of anecdotal accounts and other subjective material.

THE GRIEF OF CHILDREN

Although a large body of current literature is available about children and grief and children and trauma, little of the material seeks to bridge the two issues. Currently, the subject of children who witness violence, particularly domestic abuse in the home, has received increasing attention by professionals. The issue of children who have had a loved one or friend murdered, whether or not they were witness to the event, has not been dealt with to the same extent.

In parts of the nation's capital, violence does not seem to rattle the kids anymore. Not even when five of their classmates are shot and wounded, as they were on Thursday when rivals opened fire from a passing car. In many communities, the day after a multiple shooting of children—the youngest 6 and the eldest 15—would have meant a rush of counselors into the local schools. . . . But not here. . . . Students generally did not mention the shooting. "And teachers made no special effort to

TABLE 2.2 Normal Grief Reactions in Children

1. Shock or numbness
2. Denial
3. Panic or alarm
4. Fears
5. Anger
6. Guilt or regrets
7. Idealization
8. Tears
9. Relief at death (could apply in domestic violence situations)
10. Physical reactions
11. Disorganization
12. Regression
13. Lowered self-esteem
14. Loneliness or yearning
15. Depression and apathy
16. Searching, hyperactivity, or restlessness
17. Changes in roles (child becomes caregiver)

SOURCE: Adapted from Beckmann, 1990, pp. 6-14.

draw them out," one teacher said as students chatted animatedly during lunch period. (Skorneck, 1990, p. A3)

As will be noted in the next section, an appearance of "being fine" often masks traumatic grief in children. Normal grief reactions in children are shown in Table 2.2.

Some children are upset and angry and exhibit regressive behaviors in the first few days after a homicide. This may be displayed by obvious symptoms such as crying, somatic manifestations such as stomachaches and headaches, acting out, aggressive behavior, and nightmares. Sometimes, their sadness is sporadic, as they "remember" and "forget" their grief at various times of the day. Adults become concerned and often ask a victim advocate or physician for a referral to a professional counselor. At the same time, children appear to return to a normal life more quickly than adults, and so it is not unusual for them to be back playing with their friends within

TABLE 2.3 Trouble Signs in Children's Grief

---

1. Problems in school
2. Delinquent behavior, acting out in school or home
3. Self-destructive behaviors, including excessive use of substances
4. Acting out sexually
5. Slamming doors, smashing items
6. No emotions, loss of feeling
7. Overactivity
8. Psychosomatic conditions
9. Personality changes
10. Isolating behaviors
11. Hinting about suicide
12. Giving away possessions
13. Remaining angry or depressed
14. Unusual vulnerability to new separations
15. Underachievement

SOURCE: Adapted from Beckmann, 1990, pp. 15-16.

a week or so of the murder. Adults, usually relieved to see the rapid dissipation of symptoms, take this to mean that their children "are doing just fine now." When parents see this change, they may postpone any plans for counseling, often indefinitely. Trouble signs in children's grief are shown in Table 2.3.

There is some disagreement about the ability of children to mourn significant losses. Nevertheless, adults should tell children the truth about death and give them as much factual information as they can developmentally handle. It is often difficult for parents to determine how much their children can handle, but research has shown the extent to which children at various developmental stages understand the concept of death. Younger children do not need to know all the gruesome details of murder, but they do need to understand the finality of death. Issues regarding death should be dealt with concretely. Several good children's books are available to use with young children; they focus on the death of a parent from illness or accident, however, and do not take into account the circumstances of homicide.

TABLE 2.4 Indicators of Resolved Grief

 1. Restoration of positive self-esteem
 2. Focus on present instead of past and ability to make plans for future
 3. Making new friends
 4. Improvement in school grades
 5. Ability to give encouragement to others
 6. Increased verbalization about death and feelings without fear of being different
 7. Decreased frequency of tears
 8. Ability to feel warm affection for others
 9. Return to normal activities
10. Return of humor
11. Ability to give human qualities to the deceased loved one
12. Ability to problem solve and make decisions

SOURCE: Adapted from Beckmann, 1990, p. 15.

A series of books by Debra Whiting Alexander (see Resources) deals specifically with homicide bereavement.

Small children may incorporate some aspects of the event into their play. This is not at all inappropriate; such play can provide an opportunity for further discussion with children about the murder. On the other hand, older children and teens may not want to initiate these conversations and may need to be drawn out. Techniques such as asking teen co-victims what they think *other* children are feeling or doing in reference to the murder, or inviting them to write or draw about what happened, can be helpful. Indicators that grief has been resolved are shown in Table 2.4.

Another factor that complicates grief for child co-victims is that the adults around them will usually be co-victims as well. Parents in this situation, overwhelmed by grief and trauma, want to avoid all reminders of the murder and, as a result, often avoid talking to their children (Eth & Pynoos, 1985b). Parents may also avoid discussing a murder with their children if the stigma often attached to murder has caused the topic to be taboo. In this case, children usually sense that they are not supposed to talk about the murder with their family. Parents in such situations are unable to pay attention to their children or to recognize their children's need for professional assistance in the immediate aftermath of a murder. Furthermore, many children, particularly in cases in which the homicide victim is from the same family, take on the role of protector and, regardless of their age and relationship to their parents, want to shield them from further pain (Applebaum & Burns, 1991). Children know which of their emotional displays upset their parents and learn to avoid such behaviors. This period is crucial for children, as it is for all co-victims, because it sets the tone for future coping and healing.

Children who have experienced the murder of a family member often do not grieve until years later, especially if normal mourning was delayed or inhibited because of insufficient therapeutic attention (Eth & Pynoos, 1985b). Therefore, it is not unusual for adults to join their first support group for co-victims of homicide 10 to 20 years after the murder.

THE ROLE OF RITUALS AND COMMEMORATIONS

Rituals and commemorations are both important and necessary aspects of the grief and mourning process. These tasks should not be overlooked; rather, they should be encouraged by family, friends, and caregivers. Everyone has a unique way of remembering the victim, but most co-victims have a need to commemorate their loved one's life and death. Poetry is a common of way of remembering a loved one.

Rituals and commemorations are important and necessary in the grief and mourning process.

The sun still shines, but it's not as
    bright.
The snow still falls, but it's not as soft.
The flowers still smell, but they're not so sweet.
The tears still fall, but they're not as bitter.
The night is still long, but it's not as dark.
The wound has healed, but the scar still hurts.
I see life through a #4 filter.
                    —Deborah Spungen, 1979

The first ritual that the mourner engages in usually revolves around the funeral. The actual funeral and the associated activities are often governed by the co-victims' religious, ethnic, and cultural beliefs and background. Co-victims will commonly engage in some form of religious or spiritual services and some other informal or formal rituals (e.g., wake and shivah). In addition to the funeral, a more public memorial service may be held at a later time. Co-victims may also want to arrange for a permanent memorial, such as a tombstone or memorial plaque. In addition, co-victims might choose to remember a loved one through the establishment of a charity, scholarship, or some type of activity (e.g., a baseball game or golf tournament). Each of these outlets will carry some symbolic meaning, provide an appropriate outlet for emotion, and give co-victims an increased sense of control.

When blame and stigma are attached to the event, as often occurs in murder, public rituals may be seen as inappropriate. Group memorials can allow the co-victims to participate fully in a meaningful ritual without feeling shame or embarrassment. During National Victims' Rights Week, many victim advocate agencies throughout the United States hold memorial services to remember victims of violence and homicide. The Families of Murder Victims Program of the Anti-Violence Partnership of Philadelphia has a yearly candle lighting and memorial service, one of the largest gatherings of co-victims in this country. A co-victim has the opportunity to light a candle and recite the name of the loved one who was murdered. Memorial services of this nature are healing because victims and co-victims are equal at this event; there is no consideration of the circumstances of the homicide.

❏ The Synergism of Trauma and Grief

The current paradigms used by caregivers serving co-victims of homicide have proved less than effective because they do not address the diverse psychological and emotional repercussions of homicide. As more caregivers became aware of the difficulties that this approach created for co-victims, some responded with a blending of the ories and interventions drawn from the fields of both trauma and grief. Although this was a step in the right direction, it did not go far enough. There is increasing recognition of the need for a new model, rather than to simply adapt or marry existing ones to fit the circumstances.

Much of the normal grief and bereavement process is generalizable to the grief experience of homicide co-victims. It should not be assumed, however, that information about dealing with grief and bereavement can easily be applied without being integrated into a new model that includes all the complexities of homicide bereavement. Presently, no model is in widespread use that encompasses the features of homicide bereavement as well as the traumatic aspects. A new model must take into account the suddenness and intensity of the experience, plus that the death has occurred at the hands of a third party. This model should be constructed as a two-level approach, that is, trauma based with the grief and bereavement integral to the second level. Such a model should not be constructed with two completely distinct and isolated interventions, each emerging from different specialties. The goal should be an amalgam developed from the fields of both trauma and grief and bereavement. The resulting multidisciplinary approach would address both issues in the context of a dynamic process. The trauma work would ultimately be incorporated into the grief work and serve as a stepping-stone to the next level. As counseling continues, it might be necessary to shift the focus back and forth from trauma counseling to grief and bereavement counseling as the need arises.

Researchers in the 1980s (Kilpatrick, Amick, & Resnick, 1990; NOVA, 1985; Rinear, 1985) began to recognize the link between trauma and the experience of the co-victim and to document it in literature. Redmond, whose discipline is thanatology, wrote in 1989:

> Homicide survivors may present symptomatic behaviors characteristic of PTSD up to five years following the murder of a loved one. This becomes a normal range of functioning for this distinct population. All homicide survivors with whom I have worked were assessed at intake with some characteristics of PTSD. (p. 52)

Even after conclusive research, clinicians continued to overlook the role of the trauma while primarily focusing on the individual symptoms presented by the co-victim. These symptoms, which may include depression, sleep disorders, somatic complaints, and anxiety, were treated without integrating them into a multidisciplinary approach that addressed both the trauma and the grief.

As Figley (1992) notes, "Although the fields of grief/bereavement/death studies and therapy/counseling and traumatology have different origins and, to this day, are remarkably distinct and insulated from each other, they have much in common, both conceptually and empirically" (p. 7). One of the key connections between the two fields revolves around the idea of *functionality*.

The same precipitant that leads to a reactivation of the trauma for the co-victim of homicide may simultaneously trigger a *subsequent temporary upsurge of grief* (STUG) reaction long after the murder. Little attention is paid to this area, one in which trauma and grief intersect and that highlights the validity of the duality of the experience as incorporated in the traumatic grief model. It would be helpful to have a schema that better illustrates the phenomenon and conceptualizes the precipitants of both trauma and grief.

STUG reactions are often misdiagnosed as pathological responses, although many of them are representative of uncomplicated mourning. Co-victims may become upset and fearful when they experience a STUG because they do not understand it for what it is. They may think they have returned to an earlier stage of the mourning process, making it necessary for them to thread their way through it one more time. "Clinically, it is not uncommon for mourners to be unaware of the precipitant of a STUG reaction or to be oblivious to its connection to the loss until it is pointed out" (Rando, 1993, p. 66). Unfortunately, many caregivers do not understand the STUG grief response either and, therefore, are not able to pass this information on to the co-victims. Other caregivers may understand but may not appreciate the importance of sharing this knowledge with co-victims. The triggers will vary with different co-victims, depending on the circumstances, and may include the following: (a) sensing (seeing, hearing, touching, smelling, or tasting) something akin to something that one was acutely aware of at the time of the trauma (e.g., witnessing the murder or the death notification); (b) media coverage of the murder or accounts of other murders or violent crimes; (c) cyclical events (e.g., anniversaries of the murder and birthdays); (d) criminal justice or civil proceedings; (e) rituals (e.g., weddings, bar mitzvahs, communions, and graduations); (f) the actions of others (e.g., the second wound); (g) onetime occurrences (e.g., the "first" anniversary); and (h) seasonal factors.

The existence of traumatic grief is evident in the recurring reports of co-victims that they "find long-term solace in continuing interaction with the inner representation" of their deceased loved one (Klass, 1993, p. 345). Klass defines *inner representation* as (a) those aspects of the self that are actualized in interaction with the deceased person, (b) characterizations or thematic memories of the deceased, and (c) emotional states connected with those parts of the self and with those characterizations and memories. Co-victims often report sensing the presence of their deceased loved one (i.e., hallucinations in any of the senses) and believe in the person's continuing active influence on thoughts or events. One mother, whose daughter was brutally murdered 24 years ago, states,

> [I] smelled Dolores' perfume wafting though a room and sometimes felt her walking by. One night . . . her organ started playing when no one was there. It was driving me crazy. . . . We had to move. . . . I feel that I have to run away. . . . I go on vacation . . . and I couldn't even get away there because I see her in front of me. (Terry, Colimore, & Gibbons, 1996, p. R3)

Figley (1992) asserts that a strong case can be made that traumatic and post-traumatic stress reactions are usually present in all bereavement. This implies that the murderous act of a person exacerbates the impact on the co-victim. In the case of survivors of murder victims, he further asserts that PTSD "should be viewed as a form of grief reaction and that therapy should be to resolve the task of grieving" (p. 8).

Currently, there are increased recognition and awareness by caregivers of the duality of the experience faced by the co-victims in the aftermath of a homicide and the need for innovative resolutions. Unfortunately, this interest has not given commensurate rise to the development and research of adequate, new treatment models.

❏ The Emotional Experience of Traumatic Grief

Traumatic grief evokes many strong emotions. Co-victims of homicide experience the same emotions as other mourners but often in the extreme. The range of trauma-based emotions includes anger and rage, which can encompass feelings of revenge; fear; and guilt and shame. A great deal of available literature adequately speaks to the basis of these emotions and offers methods for managing them. They are addressed here within the context of their unique aspects as experienced by the co-victim of homicide.

ANGER

Anger is the most obvious emotional reaction experienced by a co-victim of homicide but also the least understood. Anger and rage can be quite upsetting to all who witness it, but the co-victim may be the most frightened by extreme outbursts and accompanying feelings. For a co-victim who has never expressed such reactions before, the feeling of loss of control that accompanies anger is difficult to handle. Additional research is indicated; for example, how will a person who prior to the homicide exhibited hostile tendencies react after the homicide? Experience shows that such individuals are going to become even angrier after some serious life trauma. In dealing with a co-victim who presents intense rage, it is helpful to find out how this person dealt with anger before to put the reactions into the proper perspective.

> Anger has always been a difficult thing to deal with. In this case, it is so overwhelming, it is impossible to address and deal with. I have just learned to live with it. (Mother of murder victim)

Functions of Anger

Anger has a number of functions; primarily, it serves as a defense by blocking stress.

It does this by discharging or blocking awareness of emotional or physical arousal. There are four kinds of stress that anger serves to dissipate:

1. *Painful affect.* Anger can block off painful emotions so that they are literally pushed out of your awareness. It can also discharge high levels of arousal experienced during periods of anxiety, hurt, guilt, and so on. [Loss and depression and the need to escape them also create a tension that is painful and are included under this heading.]

2. *Painful sensation.* Stress is often experienced as a physical sensation, the most common of which is muscle tension, but stressful arousal may also stem from physical pain or sympathetic nervous system activity.

3. *Frustrated drive.* Anger can discharge stress that develops when you are frustrated in the search for something you need or want. It functions to vent high arousal levels that inevitably grow as drive activities are blocked.

4. *Threat.* Any perceived threat, either to your physical or psychological well-being, creates immediate arousal. The arousal mobilizes you and generates a very strong push for some stress-reduction activity. (McKay, Rogers, & McKay, 1989, p. 46)

In examining the above anger model within the context of homicide bereavement, it is understandable how anger can serve the co-victim to stop any pain that is being experienced. It is less painful to feel the anger than to face some of the alternative emotional reactions. The problem is that blocking painful feelings prevents an opportunity to deal with the actual problems that have caused the feelings in the first place. The more that a co-victim employs anger to avoid painful arousal, at least in the short term, the easier it is to continue to follow this course of avoidance. Thus, anger becomes a coping mechanism of first choice.

My anger makes me tired, but I cannot sleep through the night. Oh, to have eight hours of sound, restful sleep! (Mother of murder victim)

Revenge Fantasies

Co-victims may be shocked to realize that they are capable of having disturbing fantasies concerning the person or persons responsible for murdering a loved one. Other individuals, on hearing words of rage, may also be concerned and provide the co-victims a myriad of reasons why not to carry out such horrific thoughts. Co-victims are usually well aware of all the reasons why the anger should not be acted out. They are often more afraid of the existence of the fantasy than of acting on it. Co-victims with extreme anger will likely question whether they have the ability to perpetrate the act of revenge. Under all circumstances, acting out rage or an act of revenge is unacceptable and must be prevented.

> At a homicide support group meeting, a stepfather of a co-victim, his face distorted with pain and rage, stated, "When I find the man that murdered my stepdaughter, I am going to take my shotgun, after I saw it off, and I am going to put the man on the ground and hold him down with my foot. Then I am going to put the shotgun right in his face and shoot. And I am going to watch him die." A number of other members of the support group nodded in agreement as he spoke. When he finished, several of them said almost in unison, "I know what you mean. I have thought about doing that, too." The change in the co-victim's face was instantaneous as the anger and rage was normalized for him at that moment as the others validated but did not condemn his strong feelings of outrage. (A service provider)

Co-victims commonly experience such outrage that they do indeed want to take their own private revenge on the murderer. Again, caregivers, especially victim advocates, find it surprising that more individuals do not carry out such revenge fantasies. This concept has been played out in some recent movies, leading people to believe that it happens more often than it does in reality.

Normalization of Anger

Anger as a normal aspect of the mourning process, regardless of the cause of death, is frequently directed toward the deceased as the mourner questions, "Why did you have to die and leave me?" In a homicide, the surrounding circumstances may intensify this anger because the co-victim may feel rage toward the victim for the trauma and pain that the co-victim now must endure. If the victim's behavior made the person more vulnerable to the fatal violence, the anger toward the victim can be intense and long-lasting. This anger can be confusing for the co-victim because it becomes mingled with guilt and shame. Strong emotional reactions can also be self-directed, which may be intolerably painful for the co-victim.

It is also quite common for co-victims to direct their anger toward those around them. This anger can be misdirected toward family, friends, the criminal justice

> *Feeling anger or rage does not make co-victims "bad."*

system, and caregivers. Caregivers may often be the target of angry outbursts by co-victims. If there is an arrest in a murder case, the defense attorney may be on the receiving end of the outrage in court. The direction of the anger can easily shift within a short time from one person or object to another. If there is no arrest in the case, anger often remains unfocused.

Anger is a normal emotion, and co-victims need to understand that feeling anger or rage, no matter how intense, does not make them "bad." Thinking or fantasizing acts of rage and revenge can be horrifying enough for co-victims without having these feelings compounded by further judgmental responses from family, friends, and caregivers. Caregivers have to understand the function of anger and not exhibit discomfort or fear in the presence of displays of strong emotional reactions. If caregivers do not understand or are not empathetic to co-victims by allowing them to articulate their anger, the co-victims may have no other appropriate outlets and turn their anger inward. Caregivers can be supportive by encouraging and accepting co-victims' presentation of anger as well as assisting with concealed emotions and teaching anger management techniques.

FEAR

Fear is an almost universal response for co-victims of homicide. There may be fear of the unknown, fear for safety of surviving family members and self, fear of loss of control, fear of loss of the assumptive world, and fear of the perpetrator. These fears are connected with each other, and one may feed on the other. Intellectually, any of these fears can be deemed irrational, but to co-victims, they are quite real. Redmond (1989) reports, "Survivors express a pervasive sense of fearfulness and apprehension, feeling vulnerable to further psychological or physical assaults" (p. 34).

In the extreme, these fears make it impossible for co-victims to lead a normal life and can lead to chronic phobic reactions. Co-victims may need to totally change their daily routines to feel safe again.

One of the fears that is uniquely tied to the co-victim experience is fear of the perpetrator. This is the least understood of all fears because it may appear to be groundless. This fear can exist even if there is no prior connection to the perpetrator, especially if the co-victim is a witness to the crime. Unless a real threat has been made, the police often do not understand the co-victim's apprehension and may not be empathetic if the co-victim articulates this fear. While the perpetrator is in jail, the co-victim may continue to check on the perpetrator's whereabouts. After the perpetrator is released, the apprehension of the co-victim may increase even if there has been no contact. This fear can last a lifetime.

There has been little research into the fears of co-victims, especially as this subject pertains to fear of the perpetrator. More investigation will have to be conducted before specific interventions can be designed to help reduce the anxiety associated with this emotion. Normalizing the fear by allowing co-victims to speak about it in a supportive and nonjudgmental environment, such as with victim advocates, with other caregivers, or in peer support groups, may help assuage some of the apprehension.

GUILT AND SHAME

The murder of a loved one can elicit both guilt and shame in the co-victim. The terms *guilt* and *shame* are often applied interchangeably. Many caregivers are confused about the definitions and have difficulty differentiating between them; consequently, they are often misused.

> "The gross difference between the two states," said the late Helen Block Lewis, . . . "is that shame is about the self. We say, I am ashamed of *myself*. I am guilty *for something*. Guilt is out there in the real world, something you thought that you shouldn't have thought. Shame is only about the self." (Karen, 1992, p. 47)

The solution to guilt is to make amends, but dealing with the issue of shame is much more complex.

Guilt

For the co-victim, the issue of guilt seems to present itself early in the mourning process. Guilt, like anger, can be used by the co-victim to hide other feelings and issues and can delay the mourning process. Guilt in the extreme can be a precursor to destructive behaviors including suicide and severe depression (Rando, 1993).

> I should have warned them somehow. I should have called and relayed my premonitions. I was the mother, I should have taken care of them better. (Mother of murder victims)

Regardless of the circumstances of the murder, the co-victim often falls back on a recitation of a list of "if only's." The litany of items could include acts that the co-victim did or acts of omission.

> If I hadn't let him move to Houston, then he would never have gotten into that fight and gotten killed. (Mother of a murder victim)

Self-blame has been shown to have some adaptive purpose in that it may make some sense of the event and restore some control back to the co-victim. As previously mentioned, the homicide co-victim may initially internalize guilt as a result of the blaming from others.

> Traumatic events, by definition, thwart initiative and overwhelm individual competence. No matter how brave and resourceful the victim may have been, her actions were insufficient to ward off disaster. In the aftermath of traumatic events, as survivors review and judge their own conduct, feelings of guilt and inferiority are practically universal. (Herman, 1992, p. 53)

Survivor guilt is another important issue for co-victims of homicide. In cases in which several victims are killed and the survivor was a witness to the murder, the issue is more clear-cut. The issue of survivor guilt, however, is complex and can be a concern for co-victims who are parents or siblings. It is a common reaction for parents to wish they could have given their own lives for those of their children. Children often believe that a murdered sibling is their parents' favorite child or "good" child. All these situations can add to the guilt of the survivor for having been spared.

The guilt of homicide co-victims bears an analogy to the guilt felt by the survivors of suicide. The guilt seems to dissipate more quickly in co-victims of homicide, however. An acknowledgment and acceptance of the role of volition in the act of homicide seems to dispel or lessen the guilt. Efforts to normalize the guilt reaction and other emotions aid the co-victims in recognizing and accepting feelings as well as encouraging a better perspective on the situation.

Shame

The shame and inhibition of the grief process may lie in the mourner's perception, rather than in the actual beliefs of others. Kauffman (1988) points out, "A person may disenfranchise himself or collaborate in his own disenfranchisement—that is, the source of the disenfranchisement may not necessarily be societal but may arise from within the self" (p. 26). Grief that is buried in shame may have implications in mourners' ability to relate to others, as well as to themselves. In many grief-related situations, shame is elicited, including the display of one's own grief. Kauffman further notes that the element of shame is a dominant issue for the homicide co-victim but is not well understood, articulated, or acknowledged by the co-victim. Shame comes into play particularly in cases in which the events of the murder may appear to be or may actually have been related to questionable behavior of the victim. Fowlkes (1990) reports that "stigmatized loss, shrouded in secrecy or shame, leaves the mourner scandalized by or destitute in grief, actually at odds with the social milieu . . . and [leads him] to distrust the very legitimacy of grief itself" (p. 651).

A mother on learning that her murdered daughter may have been one of 17 prostitutes who were victims of a serial killer grieved over the old wounds rubbed raw again, and over the labels that people place on "poor dead girls" like her daughter. "Prostitutes," Ms. Alonso said with a bitter half-laugh. "It hurts a mother's heart. Why not call them victims of circumstances? He killed 17 daughters, you know. He killed 17 sisters to somebody. That's who he killed. . . . I want to show that these girls, these prostitutes, have families who care. They were probably alone on the streets, but not in the world." (Richardson, 1993, p. B6)

❏ Cultural and Gender Influences

In dealing with traumatic grief, it is necessary to take into consideration the individual differences of each co-victim as well as the basis of these differences. Cultural and gender influences may serve as the foundation of the co-victim's experience or as only one factor in the way that a co-victim is perceived and responded to regarding the murder.

CULTURAL INFLUENCES

Caregivers should familiarize themselves with the different cultural characteristics concerning death and the issue of violence of the various cultural groups that they serve. Caregivers must be attuned not only to the ethnic observances of death, which include the rituals and the role of family and friends, but also to the different emotional responses of co-victims on the basis of their cultural and religious background. Caregivers should be careful to avoid being judgmental about the manner in which co-victims exhibit grief. What may appear to be evidence of complicated mourning may be cultural or religious in nature. If others are unaware of the unique differences among various ethnic groups, co-victims may be wrongly labeled and misunderstood.

Remembering that each person is a culture of one—with unique experiences, family relationships, and personal history—I have highlighted several cultural groups, individual values, and personal observances of death.

Native Americans. Native Americans or American Indians are in every state in the United States—more than 400 tribal groups, each with its own language, customs, and traditions. The values of these groups, however, are often similar. Some common values are

> sharing, cooperation, non-interference with others, time orientation towards the present, extended family relationships given priority over nuclear family, harmony with nature, and the belief that life is inter-twined with the other life and the world; therefore, behavior in this world is important. (Young, 1994, pp. 15:13-15:14)

Observances of death among tribes vary considerably but usually have a strong focus on the natural world—the earth, animals, trees, the natural spirit—emphasizing the reunion with nature that occurs with death. The belief that the spirit of a person never dies and may be associated with a particular facet of nature—animal, bird, plant, water, and so forth—is especially important for caregivers to recognize. This belief may be an integral part of the grieving process for Native American co-victims.

Asian Americans. Americans of Japanese, Chinese, Filipino, Vietnamese, Khmer, Laotian, and Hmong descent constitute the largest percentage of Asian Americans. Among this population are at least 29 subgroups that are distinct in language, religion, and values. Common to most Asian American cultures are the following: focus on interdependence and community, discreetness and nonimposition on others, harmony with nature, reference to cosmic forces, and a fatalistic view of the world with reliance on God or ancestry for assistance in coping (Young, 1994).

One of the first lessons Asian children learn is to restrain emotion. They have a superstitious general avoidance of the taboo subjects of death and dying because of fear that misfortune might be attracted (Halporn, 1993). In Chinese Americans, depression is manifested more commonly through psychosomatic rather than affective symptoms, a strategy that provides a defense against guilt and shame by displacing symptoms to the body. Halporn notes that the result of these influences is an extreme reluctance to seek help, despite distress. This provides a continuing challenge to caregivers.

Black or African Americans. Estimated at more than 23 million people, the African American population has the highest rate of crime victimization of all ethnic groups. Common values that have been identified from this diverse group of individuals include time orientation toward the future, belief in duty, religion as a source of strength, family connections as important (with a matriarchal connection), distrust of the judicial system, and a split between the middle and lower class (Young, 1994).

"Mourning among African Americans is as diverse as the multiple hues of skin color and as rich as the brilliance of a rainbow" (Henry-Jenkins, 1993, p. 14). Traditions have evolved from many cultures, ethnicities, and religious backgrounds. One ritual observed by many Christian African Americans is the "home-going" service. This is a worship service, not a memorial for the dead, celebrating that the victim will be reunited with relatives and friends (Henry-Jenkins, 1993; Young, 1994). Many African Americans believe in the concept of the "living dead," which refers to people who have died but whose spirits live on in the memories and thoughts of those still living. These are the entities who will help the victim move to the next world (Young, 1994, p. 15:23).

Hispanic or Latino. Estimated to be the largest minority population in the United States by the year 2000, Hispanics or Latinos are of Mexican, Puerto Rican, Cuban, and Latin American descent. The dominant values of the culture include time orientation toward the present and past; strong extended family relationships; harmony with nature; fate as determined by God; strong religious beliefs, primarily Roman Catholic; and a belief that sacrifice in this life may lead to salvation in the next (Young, 1994, p. 15:23).

Hispanic observances related to death often include a funeral service and mass. Traditionally, in times of crisis, Hispanics contact their local clergy before seeking outside support services (Gutierrez, 1993). The rosary is said by surviving loved ones, often at the home of the deceased. Among some groups, the rosary is said for 9 nights after the death. Some families say the rosary every month for a year and then repeat it on each anniversary of the death (Young, 1994).

Jewish Americans. As with other cultural groups, observances of members of the Jewish faith vary according to membership in one of the three major groups—Reform, Conservative, and Orthodox. By tradition, Jews respect life, and an autopsy and embalming of a body are prohibited. When a homicide occurs, an autopsy is required by law; these required autopsies may be extremely distressing to Jewish families. Flowers are not a Jewish custom; it is best to honor the loved one with a gift to charity (Weinfeld, 1993).

GENDER DIFFERENCES

Male and female co-victims are treated and viewed quite differently. There is a widespread tendency for family members, friends, criminal justice personnel, and professionals alike to diagnose and pathologize female co-victims. This bias is rooted in the issues of gender power and politics and complicates the grief of all female co-victims. A second wound may be caused by this prejudice, one that is so profound that their ability to cope is severely undermined. It also influences the types of interactions, assistance, and support offered by those who come into contact with co-victims.

Research suggests that men have a fear of being overwhelmed by intense emotions, as well as a fear of expressing emotions in a social context. Men's emotional lives are marked by this dual pressure between repressing emotions and the fear of the results of expressing them (Cook, 1988). Much of what is required in mourning, "review of the relationship, emotional expression, sharing of the memories, being vulnerable, asking for and receiving support, appropriate regression, is incompatible with traditional male upbringing and runs counter to the training to act, do, produce, and problem-solve" (Rando, 1993, pp. 621-622). Men are socialized so differently from women in American society that it is not surprising that many men find the expression of grief so problematic.

Men react differently from women in many aspects of the expression of grief: The ability to ask for or seek help is one area in which there is a marked dissimilarity. Having to ask for help or support makes many men anxious or uncomfortable. How many people know men who will drive around lost for hours, rather than ask for simple directions (Wolfelt, 1992)? As a result, many men suffer silently as they deal with their grief and anger.

The studies of male grief indicate that the findings need to be reexamined from the perspective of male emotional conceptualizations and not viewed in comparison with grief strategies employed by female mourners. Cook (1988) asserts that "male behavior typically is seen as inferior or deficient to the female standard" (p. 287). Most of the strategies that men employ to handle their painful emotions involve not revealing them to others. A man's "mourning may be characterized by an emotionally controlled, privatized expression of grief" (p. 291). Women often display their grief through crying. Society accepts this as a stereotypical feminine response, and most men regard this expression of feelings as embarrassing. Men report that they do cry but that they do it in private.

Some of the other grief management strategies that men have described using include thinking about something else, reason and reflection, and involvement in some other activity (Cook, 1988). A bereaved father who attempts to suppress his grief and pain may not exhibit many outward symptoms, but his struggles to control his feelings could be characterized as profound grief work.

Literature on male grief after the death of a child is sparse. Available research tends to focus on the death of a child from illness, rather than from violence. This is another area in which the grief process is exacerbated by the circumstances of the death, and simply generalizing from one set of data does not provide sufficient information. To do so presents the caregiver with a limited knowledge and resource base to assist in understanding and supporting a male co-victim. Unfortunately, the caregiver may then rely on female-oriented grief models. The caregiver needs to acknowledge each person's approach to grieving as unique and to understand other grieving processes, without placing a higher value on one or the other. This is especially germane when dealing with the parental dyad after the homicide of a child.

The gender differences in male and female grief after a homicide can be illustrated by anecdotal information and observations garnered at peer support group meetings. Perhaps the best evidence of such differences is that women far outnumber men in attendance.

Some of these women are single parents or have other familial relationships with the deceased, but many women who have spouses also attend alone. Women report that husbands often are resistant to attending the meetings and say to their wives that they "don't need any help" or "don't need to wash dirty laundry in public." Yet when men, especially fathers, do attend a support group for the first time, they often are unsuccessful in maintaining control and break down and cry more quickly than do their wives. Initially, they may feel sufficiently comfortable in the safe and nonjudgmental atmosphere of the meeting to let go of some of their pain and grief. This can be humiliating, however, and they may never again come to a meeting. The experience of emotional outbursts in public is so foreign to many bereaved men that they report that they "felt sick" when they got home and, therefore, did not find attending the support meeting helpful.

Gender bias bears a definite relationship to the issue of prescribing medication to co-victims in the aftermath of a homicide. Doctors tend more frequently to prescribe or overprescribe medication to female, rather than to male, co-victims—another example of helping systems revictimizing female co-victims. Male co-victims, especially fathers, are usually less verbal about their grief and pain, often because of cultural expectations, and are more likely to self-medicate with alcohol and with illegal drugs. Dysfunctional behaviors and self-destructive activities are more likely to be employed by men as coping skills even while their overt grief symptoms remain hidden. These behaviors may even be acceptable by some and so are ignored or denied. Taking prescription drugs may be considered a sign of weakness for the male co-victim as well as to those who are close to him.

❏ **Mental Health Implications**

Traumatic grief makes the co-victim vulnerable to a number of a mental health and emotional problems, in addition to triggering preexisting or unresolved ones. These issues may further complicate the mourning process. Although a number of mental disorders may be implicated in the wake of a homicide, anxiety and depression are probably the two most common diagnosed mental disorders. Other significant issues for co-victims include changes in life philosophy, obsessive-compulsive thoughts, and somatic complaints. PTSD, a mental disorder previously discussed as part of the framework of traumatic grief, may also be an issue for co-victims.

Traumatic grief makes the co-victim vulnerable to mental health and emotional problems.

ANXIETY AND DEPRESSION

Anxiety plays an important role in bereavement, although its influence tends to be downplayed. Anxiety may also be a long-term stress reaction. Rando (1993) believes "that anxiety is just as logical a consequence and is, in fact, more common in bereavement than depression and actually paves the way for it" (p. 212). More co-victims do present evidence of anxiety, but it is often confused with other manifestations such as depression. The two conditions can occur simultaneously. Much of the anxiety seen in the aftermath of homicide arises from issues of separation anxiety, but more generalized anxiety can also be involved. Correct diagnosis and treatment of anxiety may help the co-victim avoid developing full-blown anxiety disorders.

More co-victims are diagnosed as depressed than as anxious by physicians or mental health workers. The co-victim often forms this determination by virtue of the self-diagnosis, "I'm so depressed." This may be accepted as a normal outcome of the murder and is not questioned by the caregiver. Caregivers should be able to differentiate between sadness, mourning, and depression for both their own edification and that of the co-victims. This requires an in-depth investigation of many factors, rather than just accepting the co-victims' report of their mental state. Sadness and grief are normal reactions to the murder, but not every co-victim will necessarily experience clinical depression.

An important concern for the caregiver in attempting to make the correct diagnosis is that depression can be physically and emotionally debilitating. If the depression includes suicidal ideation, it can also be dangerous. It is not unusual for co-victims to report having suicidal ideation. These thoughts can be frightening to co-victims, especially if they have never had suicidal thoughts before.

An in-depth assessment should include a mental health history to determine if there has been any previous history of depression. A co-victim, especially a male, may not readily self-disclose feelings of anxiety and depression.

> I felt suicidal. I felt myself being sucked back into blackness and confusion, this time not caring if I found a way out. (Significant other of murder victim)

Sufficient research data are not available to determine how many suicide attempts are made as the result of a murder of a loved one, or how many attempts end in the death of the co-victim. Service providers who work extensively with this victim population are surprised that there seem to be so few co-victims who actually commit suicide as the direct result of the murder. Nevertheless, all suicidal ideation or threats offered by co-victims, even those seemingly made in jest, should be taken seriously and addressed immediately. If a caregiver is not prepared to deal with the issue of suicide and has to turn to an outside referral, the co-victim should not be left to follow through without supervision. The co-victim needs to be told that there may be times when it is necessary for caregivers to call the police to take immediate action, with or without the co-victim's permission.

> I went through the kitchen to the garage and found a piece of heavy, rubber-encased wire with which to hang myself. I'd been thinking about it each and every day for several weeks. In fact, suicide was all I thought about. I kept putting it off. Every day I told myself to wait until tomorrow. Maybe tomorrow the pain would go away. Maybe tomorrow I'd want to live again, have a reason to live. (Spungen, 1983, p. 5)

Anxiety and depression may be diagnosed more frequently than other mental health problems seen after a homicide because of the availability of appropriate medications and ease in prescribing them by physicians. Antianxiety medication (e.g., Ativan, Xanax, and Valium) and antidepressants (e.g., Prozac, Wellbutrin, and Effexor) are routinely dispensed by many primary care physicians in the immediate aftermath of a murder in a mistaken attempt to help co-victims deal with the pain. Before dispensing medications, prescribing physicians often make little or no attempt to do an in-depth evaluation of co-victims or to give any consideration to their mental state, physical health, and coping skills prior to the homicide. Any assessment of co-victims by caregivers should include information on any an-tianxiety or antidepressant medication co-victims may be currently taking. This will assist the caregivers in better evaluating the needs of co-victims, their current state of mind, and whether these are influenced by medication (see Chapter 6, "Interventions and Advocacy").

CHANGES IN LIFE PHILOSOPHY

An individual's outlook on life can undergo major alterations in the post-trauma period. Caregivers and co-victims tend to view these post-trauma changes as falling only within the negative sphere. This is not necessarily true because positive alterations can occur as well.

Positive changes can include (a) redefinition of life goals, (b) in-creased flexibility of life goals, (c) increased flexibility in coping strategies, (d) development of new understandings of spiritual or religious issues, and (e) increased ability to communicate emotional responses and to express situational reactions (Young, 1994).

Negative changes can include revisions to the co-victim's lifestyle and personality. Examples are (a) becoming overcontrolling and rigid, (b) permanent regression to traits or life patterns central to previous life stages, (c) faulty management of tension or stress, (d) inability to retain or initiate relationships, and (e) avoidance or withdrawal from new challenges (Young, 1994).

OBSESSIVE-COMPULSIVE THOUGHTS

Another mental health problem that is present in many co-victims but that does not receive the recognition and attention that it should is obsessive-compulsive thoughts or ruminations. Technically, these may be classified as a reaction, rather than a disorder. In the earliest phases of grief, obsessive-compulsive thoughts are a normal response for co-victims, and such ruminations may be unavoidable. This can be partially explained as an attempt to replay the event to make it come out differently. In the first few weeks to months, these constant ruminations may drive out almost all other thoughts, putting severe limitations on the co-victim's ability to focus or concentrate. Co-victims may forget simple things such as where they put their keys or find that they are unable to concentrate on something as mundane as a book or television program.

Initially, the obsessive thoughts are generally focused on the murderous act itself and all the surrounding details, including the death notification. In one study of bereavement after homicide, in which only one of the participants had actually witnessed the homicide, all but one person experienced an intense and terrifying identificatory reenactment of the events of the murder (Rynearson & McCreery, 1993). In a sudden violent death, the loss of an opportunity to say goodbye to the deceased may also be a theme of the co-victims' obsessive-compulsive thoughts. According to the "theory of paradoxical intentions," it is almost impossible for individuals to will themselves not to think about something just because they want to.

These ruminations are direct indications of traumatic grief; they emanate from the trauma but adversely affect the grieving process. Through time, the thoughts generally dissipate on their own. Co-victims may feel uncomfortable with the constant ruminations and search for some relief. Generally, medication is not helpful or necessary, and relief of symptoms can be achieved by choosing from a number of effective techniques (see Chapter 6). Unfortunately, some co-victims remain consumed for years by these obsessive-compulsive thoughts, particularly those who suffer from PTSD. This state may cause grieving to be delayed.

> I used to look upward toward heaven and plead with no one in particular, "Please let me think of something else besides my daughter, let me think about something else for just five minutes." (Mother of a murder victim)

SOMATIC DISTURBANCES

A co-victim can expect to exhibit increased physical symptoms in the aftermath of a homicide. Any previous physical symptoms and illnesses will certainly be aggravated. Some of these symptoms may be attributable to the impact on the immune system of the co-victim, but without further data, the exact nature of the connection is difficult to determine. Little or no conclusive data are available that draw a clear correlation between any specific physical symptoms and homicide bereavement. On the basis of reports from co-victims and their physicians, however, a list of possible symptoms can be prepared. This list is not to be considered conclusive in nature. Some of the more common presenting physical symptoms are (a) headaches, (b) gastrointestinal complaints, (c) insomnia and other sleep disorders, (d) unusual weight loss or weight gain, (e) somatic complaints, (f) dental problems, and (g) increased respiratory illnesses.

Many of these symptoms may be dismissed by caregivers and co-victims as a normal function of the pain and grief. Without further investigation, serious illnesses may be overlooked, and symptoms that could be successfully treated may turn into chronic physical disorders. Whether a co-victim reports physical symptoms to a mental health provider or to a primary care physician, a complete examination should be conducted to rule out the presence of any disease. Questions about physical symptoms should be included in assessments conducted by caregivers to minimize the risk that a co-victim may not self-disclose physical problems.

❏ Summary

There has never been a systematic attempt to construct a model that specifically addresses the co-victims of homicide. It has taken some time for caregivers to realize that theories and interventions that apply to other victim populations cannot be simply generalized to co-victims. As more interest and subsequent research have been focused on co-victims, there has been increased recognition of the need to respond with a new paradigm. Until recently, the theories of grief and bereavement presented in this chapter dominated when it came to designing interventions and providing service delivery for co-victims. With the development of the trauma field came the realization that there was a missing component to be recognized in the grief experienced by a co-victim.

The co-victim's grief is different—not just complicated, but different: a traumatic grief. Once this is understood, it becomes necessary to respond with a new model that encompasses all the aspects of traumatic grief—the emotional experiences, cultural and gender influences, and mental health issues—resulting in new strategies for treating the co-victim of homicide.

The traumatic grief paradigm is a developmental one and is still evolving. Much research is still needed to operationalize the new model of traumatic grief into fostering the best possible techniques for delivering services to co-victims. As data become available, it will be possible to routinize these methods and procedures, and the field will necessarily become more precise.

3

Murder and
the Family System

This chapter reviews the special factors relating to the family system of someone who has been murdered. In general, caregivers and researchers have offered little recognition of such situational factors that affect co-victims. There is, for example, an insignificant body of research and literature that differentiates among the various influences on family members in the aftermath of a homicide. It is important, therefore, to look more in depth for the commonalities, the similarities, and the differences that situational factors within the family suggest and to consider *all* members of a co-victim's family in plans for recovery.

Common responses of co-victims and generalizable themes exist, although in varying degrees of intensity, regardless of the circumstances of the murder. The most frequently reported responses include isolation, grief, loss, stress, anger, blame (for both victim and self), guilt, denial, need for revenge, shock, betrayal, and emotional regression. The most important themes that need to be considered include feelings of being ignored and excluded by the criminal justice system and victim advocates, the infliction of second wounds, and disenfranchised grief.

In most murders, any extenuating factors will elicit significantly distinct responses from co-victims concerning each person's experience of trauma, grief, and ability to cope. Situational factors do not fit into discrete categories and may even overlap, putting co-victims into a number of different categories at the same time. The more situational factors that affect co-victims, the more difficult it becomes for caregivers and service providers to help them reconstruct their lives.

❏ The Uniqueness of Family Loss

After a murder, the family unit undergoes permanent changes that are hard for the surviving members to accept. Family dynamics will obviously be affected if for no other reason than that there is now a different number of people in the family. For example, after a murder, it is often confusing when someone asks, "How many children (or siblings) do you have?" Many people say that they hesitate while they search for the right answer and often do not know what to say.

Some co-victims may wish to protect other family members. This role of the family protector usually falls to the father, although not exclusively so. The bereaved one who assumes this role may not pay attention to his or her own pain and grief while trying to assist with and even divert other family members' pain and grief.

> My family had suffered a wound almost as mortal as my daughter's. Yet I was in no position to offer more than a Band-Aid. My family was drowning and so was I. (Mother of a murdered child)

Unfortunately, the members of the family network—parents, children, cousins, aunts, uncles, and so on—are usually incapable of providing each other with emotional support because they all have varying degrees of exposure to the murder and closeness to the victim. Possibly, one witnessed the murder, another found the body, and yet another barely knew the victim. Therefore, the time frames for grieving and recovery vary accordingly (Pynoos & Nader, 1990).

How a person copes with the murder of a loved one can be highly influenced by family rules and coping mechanisms. Haran (1988) has noted a number of typical family patterns: (a) death and conversations about death are taboo, (b) someone must be to blame, (c) things must go on as before, and (d) all must function with openness and a sharing of feelings.

To provide appropriate interventions, caregivers will need to understand distinct familial subsystems—parents, spouses, children, siblings, significant others, and extended family—within the context of the unique victim to co-victim relationship of each. The issues of intrafamily homicide, including pedicide and domestic violence, are also important.

PARENTS

Parents represent the largest group of co-victims by relationship. The term *child*, as used here, refers to a relationship, not an age. The death of a child is rated as the most stressful life event (Sehnert, 1981) and puts parents at high risk for complicated mourning. Rando (1993) states that "when compared to other types of bereavement, parental mourning is particularly intense, complicated, and long-lasting, with major and unparalleled symptom fluctuations occurring over time" (p. 611). The sudden, traumatic, and arbitrary nature of a child's murder even further complicates the grieving process. Being the parent of a murdered child predisposes the co-victim to posttraumatic stress responses.

The death of a child is outside the natural order of life.

The death of a child is outside the natural order of life. Children are supposed to outlive their parents; parents are not supposed to bury their children. As Rando (1993) points out, there is no word in the English language to define a parent whose child has died, as there is to describe a person whose parents have died (orphan) or whose spouse has died (widow/widower). The issues and emotions are the same whatever age the child because they revolve around the loss of the relationship. Regardless of the age of the child, the parents' role vis-à-vis the victim is abruptly broken. Parents can feel that they have lost their legacy and their immortality. The grief and mourning process must be examined in light of any developmental issues that were present in the parent-child relationship at the time of the murder.

When told of the murder of their child, irrespective of the victim's age, parents cry out, "My baby! My baby!" Many parents have reported seeing the image of their newborn or very young child in their arms, rather than a picture of the child at the time of the murder. To many parents, the vision of the baby symbolizes the responsibility they felt, often in the form of a silent or whispered promise to care for and keep the child safe from harm. This can lead to self-blame and guilt.

> Fairy godmothers are not distributed equally, but the same witch appears at every birth. Her gift is vulnerability: once delivered into the world no child is ever safe again. Parents know this. That's why they're forever yelling: "Don't touch!" and calling the pediatrician and fretting when the baby doesn't finish his bottle. That's why they turn deaf ears when their children beg to walk to school alone, go to the store alone, play in the vacant lot on their way home. That's why parents are such terrible pests. ("The girls who had everything," 1986, p. A30)

Parents often fear for the safety and innocence of their surviving children. In certain inner-city neighborhoods, it is not uncommon to find that some families have had several children murdered in separate incidents. Parents may become overprotective, causing friction as children wish to become more independent.

> After our 8-year-old son was abducted and murdered, we educated Christie at home from the time that she was 10 years old until she went to college. We couldn't bear to let her out of our sight. (Parents of a murdered child)

When an adult child is murdered, many may negate the level of the parents' grief. Others may verbalize thoughtless and cruel comments such as, "At least you must have a lot of good memories to comfort you." The toll on the parents' emotional state is even more complicated if a child's actions are perceived by others to be contributory to his or her death, such as if the child is a prostitute or drug dealer.

Parents of a murdered child are often demoted to the outsider circle of mourners, with the spouse and children of the victim being the primary recipients of attention from family, friends, and the criminal justice system.

> The parents of a 33-year-old man read about his death in the local newspaper the morning after it occurred. Their daughter-in-law was arrested for killing their son. Even though the two families only lived five blocks apart, the police never notified [the parents] of their son's murder, telling them later that they considered his wife to be the next-of-kin. (A victim advocate)

Stepparents

In today's society, the duties of parents may often be shared with stepparents. These individuals may be ignored, or their anguish may be assumed to be less. Many stepparents have had long-standing relationships with and feel deep affection for a murdered child. They, too, will grieve. On the other hand, because they are not the biological parents, the relationship has likely existed on a different plane. The stepparent is often able to step back and offer a level of support to a spouse that the birth parent is not capable of providing. Having to deal with former spouses can greatly increase the stress of parents who have divorced and remarried. Some caregivers feel that reunions should be encouraged, but this may also add to the anguish of the spouses.

Grandparents

Grandparents constitute another group of family members whose feelings are often overlooked and ignored. In the contemporary United States, an increasing number of grandparents are raising grandchildren whose own parents are unavailable because of divorce, illness, drug use, or other family problems. Rando (1993) states, "When grandparents have been involved intimately in family life, they are like bereaved parents of a second order" (p. 181). Many grandparents feel that they suffer two losses. "They not only lose the grandchild they loved, but many feel the loss of their own child, the parent who is changed so radically by the murder" (NOVA, 1985, p. 4).

Seeking Justice

Life's parents said that they "were very pleased" with the death sentence but had mixed emotions. "I feel sorry for the [defendant], I feel sorry for his family. But I feel sorry for my family," said Theodore Life. "I miss my son. I wish he was here."

"This was the ultimate justice. But it's not going to bring back my son," said Renee Life. "The pain is going to last for a long time, for the rest of our lives." (Loyd, 1994, p. B5)

Many parents are prepared to go forth—each in his or her own way—and do battle against the murderer of their child. They may even work together, attempting to bring some control back into their lives.

From a demographic standpoint, women outnumber men in the bereaved parent group, and mothers are more likely to become the family member who is responsible for calling or visiting the police, the prosecutors, or the media in the search for answers or justice. The majority of police and homicide detectives are men, however, and there are more male than female prosecutors. The result is that mothers often receive a second wound from the system, a gender-related wound that does not extend to fathers. The insensitive, and often patronizing, way some individuals are treated by the system may deter some, but this treatment often has the opposite effect on mothers by making them more resolute in their efforts.

Implications for Research

The new class of bereaved parents of young victims will have responses that are not typical of other parental bereavement. The lack of an appropriate model that addresses both the variables affecting the mourning process and specific interventions for caregivers increases the likelihood that co-victims will receive assistance that may be more hurtful than helpful. More research is also needed to determine the long-range implications of the murder of a child. This has not been explored to any great extent because only in the last 20 years have bereaved parents of homicide victims been recognized.

SPOUSES

The death of a spouse is rated by many sociologists as one of the most stressful changes that one can experience in life (Sehnert, 1981). When this death is also sudden, traumatic, and violent, the surviving spouse faces many additional issues that are not usually well understood by others, including caregivers; furthermore, the new class of spousal co-victims is predominantly young, female, and African American, not the traditional widow or widower whose spouse has died after a long illness. In addition, co-victims of all ages and socioeconomic backgrounds, including common-law partners, have had spouses who were killed during another crime, such as a robbery.

> It was supposed to be their first Christmas together and David Atlas wanted to make it memorable for his new wife, Mary Rose. . . . But for everyone who knew Atlas, this Christmas has turned into a tragedy. . . . "It's unbelievable that something like this can happen so quickly," said Mary Rose Atlas, 25, as she wiped away her tears. . . . "I never got a chance to be by his side and say goodbye. And then to hear that he died so violently . . . ," she said, her voice trailing off. (Laker & O'Dowd, 1993, pp. 4, 5)

Caregivers need to fully understand the grief process, the isolating nature of widowhood, and the unique stresses surrounding the violent death of a spouse that add to the great void in a person's life. First of all, the recently widowed spouse must learn new tasks and skills, regardless of the cause of death. There might also be a significant loss of identity. As Rando (1988) states,

> For most of us, our relationship with our mate is . . . a central part of our self and our being in the world. As a result, one of the major roles your spouse had was as someone who affirmed your identity. (pp. 127-128)

The loss of identity seems to be more problematic for women than for men, even if they are employed outside the home. If the spouse died violently, the interactions with the criminal justice system and the media will add greatly to the list of a widow's responsibilities, which unfortunately cannot be found outlined in a how-to book.

> We were building our life together. We were working to get a mortgage and everything. (Daughen, Costantinou, & Sheehan, 1994, p. 22)

Often, a spouse is considered a partner's best friend as well as lover. On the other hand, if a marital relationship is troubled at the time of a murder, there may be residual feelings of guilt and anger. If the co-victim blames a murdered spouse for certain behaviors that the co-victim feels may have contributed to the murder, the anger is exacerbated. This blame can be extended to behavior as innocuous as being in the wrong place at the wrong time or working late.

The anger associated with blame often covers up other emotions that may be too difficult to deal with, especially in the early stages of the grief process. Anger may be present in any case—anger at being left alone to deal with all the responsibilities, such as child rearing, that were formerly shared in the marriage and that are now greatly increased as the result of the murder.

CHILDREN AND TEENAGERS

Children who are the co-victims of homicide are the most forgotten co-victims. Their needs tend to be overlooked because they cannot always speak for themselves. Reliable statistics are not readily available regarding the numbers of these children, but on the basis of the demographics of murder, there seems to be agreement that the number is growing. This discussion refers to co-victims under the age of 18 as children, unless their developmental stage is of particular interest to the discussion at hand.

There are two main categories of child co-victims: (a) those who are indirect victims because a parent, sibling, friend, or classmate has been murdered, but the child was not a witness; and (b) those who have directly witnessed the homicide of a relative, friend, or stranger.

Indirect Co-Victim Issues

The extent to which violence reaches U.S. children can be seen in a study of inner-city elementary and high schools, in which more than 70% of the students reported having witnessed the robbing, stabbing, shooting, or killing of another person (Bell & Jenkins, 1991, p. 2). Today, with the increase in the homicide rate of young African American men in the inner city, African American children in the inner cities are most likely to have had a sibling murdered, with the murder of a parent being the second most murdered relative. It is not unusual for children in the inner city to have had more than one family member murdered.

Parents may feel ambivalent about whether to discuss the death and their own feelings with their young children. They also wonder whether to allow a child to attend the funeral. Many researchers believe that well-developed children aged 3 to 4 are able to understand the basic meaning of death. Parents or primary caregivers should decide whether the child will attend any services but with the child's input regarding the decision. In later years, children who were not included in the funeral often carry a great deal of resentment and feel that they missed a significant passage in their life. Children can and should be included in activities such as creating a memory book and planning memorial services or special commemorative events (e.g., a

Children and teenagers may feel isolated and withdraw from the family unit.

school assembly and planting a tree or flower garden for their loved one). These projects allow them to get involved and feel a part of what is going on.

Children, especially the younger ones, who have had a parent murdered may have an overriding concern about who is going to take care of them after the murder. This fear may be profound if the murder leaves a child an orphan. It is important for adults to allow children to vent their feelings. Because children tend to talk sporadically about the event, adults need to be ready to give their attention when children bring up the subject of the murder. Such discussions should not be put off until some later time because children may stop talking about it altogether. Adults need to give them permission to do this without being judgmental. As Beckmann (1990) notes, conversation between parents and children is important because it gives children permission to grieve.

Both young children and teenagers tend to feel isolated after a murder and may withdraw from the family unit as a result. When parents talk about what they themselves are going through, children are apt to feel left out. Some children pull back because they do not wish to see their parents further upset. But parents need to be aware that a flat affect coupled with the avoidance of any discussion of the deceased could indicate a problem. They should not assume that the child is doing fine and does not need any special help or support.

Teenagers typically do not want to talk about the murder. Adolescent children often feel their parents are not willing to talk about what happened, while, at the same time, the parents may feel their teens simply do not care.

> Whenever we mention Lloyd's name, both our children [aged 13 and 15] either make faces or get up and walk out of the room. They don't ever want to talk about him; it's as if they never had another brother. So we've stopped mentioning Lloyd's name in front of them. (Parents of a murdered child)

Direct Co-Victim Issues

Children who witness violence directly may be particularly traumatized. They frequently exhibit post-traumatic stress symptoms and other extreme reactions. Such stress may actively interfere with children's ability to reminisce or otherwise reduce the emotional resources available to them throughout the grieving process. The extent of stress largely depends on the type and amount of support available to these children and the ways in which the family interacts as a result of the murder. Traumatized children are typically haunted by intrusive images of the violence, recurring traumatic dreams, and a preoccupation with revenge fantasies. They may withdraw socially, act emotionally constricted, lose interest in their normal activities, and perform poorly in school. These children are also at greater risk to perpetrate violence as they grow older (Pynoos & Eth, 1985).

Child co-victims must be provided with assistance and services regardless of whether they are exhibiting symptoms or signs of distress. Children who witness a murder *will* be affected by this event throughout their lives, and it is best to address the issues as soon as possible. The potential costs of the multigenerational legacy of trauma that could occur if this group of co-victims is neglected are staggering in both the short-term impact on the children and the long-term impact on society.

ADULT CHILDREN

The homicide rate for older adults is much lower than for young people—67% of murder victims are younger than the age of 35, whereas only 33% of the victims are over 35 (MacKellar & Yanagishita, 1995, p. 4). Nevertheless, this category of co-victims is no less important. Yet this group receives insufficient attention because of the presumption that older adults are experiencing part of the natural order of life and, therefore, that the situation is more acceptable and easier to bear. Research relating to the violent death of a parent and the resultant impact on an adult child is almost nonexistent.

Regardless of many erroneous assumptions, the death of a parent is still a critical life passage. If married, adult children may have mistakenly assumed their primary emotional relationships would be with their own family. Many adult children are surprised at the intensity of the emotions they feel at the death of a parent. In addition, sufficient support may not be forthcoming from other family members and friends who may not recognize the degree of pain and grief that is experienced by the bereaved.

A number of factors will affect the grief and bereavement of an adult child when the parent dies, regardless of the cause of death. Rando (1988) provides a good overview of problems that adult children face when a parent dies. The violent, sudden murder of a parent, however, does not comfortably fit within those parameters. The shock and trauma exacerbate all the known issues and raise many additional responsibilities for which the adult child is not prepared. For example,

- Adult children may not recognize how much their identity is tied up with that of their parents and their own role as the child. They may experience a profound change in many familial relationships after the death of a parent.
- The death of a parent forces adult children to look at their own mortality.
- The quality of the adult child's relationship with the parent influences the grief process.
- The age and life circumstances of a parent affect the level of grief. If a parent is still enjoying a quality life, the death of the parent will always seem untimely.
- An adult child's age and period of development are also important to consider, along with whether the parent was the first or second parent to die.

I am left feeling like an orphaned child, although my father is still alive. My mother was my "constant." I'm left without a place to belong. My mother was the person that held my family together. Without her, all seems unbalanced. The most important person in my life is gone!! The loss and pain are so deep. I feel like I [am] drowning, like eventually I'll just lose consciousness and die. I've never felt so alone. Even in a room full of people who love me I feel alone. (Daughter of a murder victim)

Not only must adult children deal with the ramifications of the untimely death of a parent, but also they may take on significant new responsibilities such as going to the medical examiner's office, dealing with the criminal justice system and the media, and taking care of a surviving parent and other family members. Adult children may also have many competing interests and obligations that greatly add to their stress level. The combination of these factors and insufficient support and acknowledgment can make them question their own capacity to tolerate this event.

SIBLINGS

When a sibling is murdered, the most common emotion is guilt.

When a sibling is murdered, the most common emotion is guilt. The surviving sibling's guilt is especially strong if there was an argument immediately preceding the murder. Young children think that somehow their thoughts have caused the murder. In addition, because their bereaved parents are grieving so intensely, some children may believe that their parents loved the deceased sibling more than themselves.

Adult Siblings

Many adult siblings cannot remember a time when their other sibling was not there. Some adults consider that their sibling is their best friend. Even if they are now grown and living in different households and no longer maintain a close relationship, these siblings are still connected by strong familial ties.

Adult siblings often find themselves serving as a buffer between other family members, the system, and even society. The trauma and grief they experience after a murder can be quite devastating and may go unrecognized by family and friends. For example, bereavement leave from work may be minimal, certainly less than might be allowed the parents of a victim. Or the spouse of a co-victim may not understand the depth of grief for a sibling because the spouse did not have the same bond with the deceased. As a result, the need of adult siblings for help and support is rarely met.

Because of the high rate of homicide of those aged 15 to 24, increasing numbers of young adults have had a sibling murdered. Although they share the same emotional responses, adult siblings are often more ignored and forgotten than younger siblings. Their pain and confusion compounded by lack of acknowledgment, adult siblings perceive that they are relegated to a secondary role as mourners and do not receive the permission they need to fully experience their grief (Doka, 1988).

In the aftermath of a homicide, a sibling may often be asked, "How are your parents doing?" Condolence cards, notes, and memorial contributions are usually directed to their parents, and rarely does anyone inquire about the sibling.

> After Danny was killed, everyone flocked to my parents. I felt very alone. At night my parents got to go to bed together; if one of them cried, the other was there to hold them. I went to bed by myself. It was

the most lonely time in my life; I can't imagine ever feeling that lonely again. (Sibling of a murder victim)

Many adult siblings, predominantly men, articulate their desire to take revenge for the murder of a sibling. Some of them even form elaborate plans for doing so, although few actually carry out their plans. The revenge fantasy, at least the articulation and the planning of it, seems to be most common to this co-victim group. Sometimes, plans are made in concert with other siblings and may include the father. Most parents are fearful of such thoughts of revenge, however, because they envision the loss of other children to imprisonment or death as a possible consequence.

> The defendant accused of murdering my daughter was acquitted at his trial. After the trial, my sons, Bob, 32, and Ron, 37, came and told me that they were planning to go to Florida [where the murder occurred and the man still lived] and kill him. I really wanted to see the man punished, but I didn't want my sons to have his blood on their hands. I begged them not to carry out their plans for a year and then see how they felt about it. My sons never went to Florida as far as I know, and they never mentioned it to me again, and I didn't bring it up either. (Mother of a murder victim)

Changing Familial Roles

The murder of a sibling will alter the entire family system. Parental reactions to adult children will change; this in turn changes the responses of the surviving siblings. Each may seek to protect the other, no one revealing his or her true feelings.

> I thought it was my job to protect them. They would cry when I cried, therefore I tried not to cry in front of them, then I broke out in hives from the stress. Doctors told me not to do that anymore. (Sister of a murder victim)

After the murder of a sibling, familial roles can undergo major transformations. Adult siblings can find themselves taking care of their parents, both physically and emotionally, making decisions for them as well as nurturing and protecting them. Sometimes, this role reversal is unsolicited and unwelcome, which can aggravate an already strained parent-child relationship due to stresses brought on by the murder.

> After Marlene's 20-year-old daughter, Rachael, was murdered in a holdup, Marlene requested to view the pictures of her daughter at the death scene. She wanted to see her face at the time of death. Her other son, Michael, aged 30, contacted the prosecutor who was handling the case and told him not to allow his mother to view the pictures. Michael felt that his mother would get too upset and he didn't want to have to deal with that. Marlene was in good health, understood the possible emotional consequences of looking at the pictures, and had made her decision based on her own needs. The prosecutor barred Marlene from seeing the photographs as a result of Michael's request. Marlene felt angry, frustrated, and that she was being treated like a child by both Michael and the prosecutor. Not only were Marlene's needs not met, but she was resentful of her son's intervention, which she had not requested nor did she feel was necessary. (A victim advocate)

Adult children may view the death of a sibling in an egocentric manner and feel bereft and abandoned as do young children. Feelings of anger and resentment may also surface as adult children deal with changing familial roles. It may be necessary for them to learn to reconstruct their relationships with their parents, and they may do so only with great reluctance. Most adult children prefer their parents to maintain their former roles. Looking at their parents' vulnerability or viewing them as unique individuals, independent of the parental context, can be disconcerting (Frogge & Cantrell, 1991).

> I've never seen my dad smile the way he used to—it's different now. (Sister of a murder victim)

Integrating these changes is not an easy task for parents either, especially without some form of professional guidance. The murder may trigger other family issues that have never been resolved, such as parental divorce, various configurations of family and sibling estrangement, and other issues related to loss.

It may occur to siblings that their order in the family has been affected; the middle child may now become the oldest child. The birth order has not changed, but the way they are perceived by their families may have changed. They may feel that they need to assume a new role, although other family members may not agree. For the sibling who has become an only child as the result of a murder, feelings of isolation and loneliness may be greatly exacerbated. The remaining sibling may feel, and rightly so, that no one else truly understands his or her pain, or even makes an attempt to do so.

The family system will be affected as siblings renegotiate their individual and collective roles and as unresolved issues resurface. Depending on the relationship between the sibling and the deceased sibling, both in the past and at the time of the murder, the grief process can vary greatly from sibling to sibling.

BEYOND THE IMMEDIATE FAMILY

Although the immediate family of a murder victim may feel the greatest impact from the death, others experience its effect as well: Friends, significant others, and extended family members may feel the loss as deeply or, under certain circumstances, even more deeply. The victim may have lived far from family members and learned to rely on friends and colleagues as a surrogate family. Or, perhaps, a family estrangement may have led to the strengthening of other nonfamilial relationships. Employed adults spend the majority of their waking hours at work, where they often develop strong friendships. In addition, extended family members such as aunts, uncles, and cousins may have had a special bond with the murder victim. The strength of such relationships and the great pain these people feel when their loved ones are murdered are well articulated in the following paragraph.

> It took away my friend and also part of me. Although I have a family, I miss her, I feel as though my life is empty. I still can't believe she's dead. I cry a lot even while working, or on my way to and from work. I'm alone a lot more often than I used to be, preferring to be by myself than with others. We were like sisters. She and I shared everything— dreams, plans for the future, and so forth. (Best friend of a murder victim)

These mourners are also co-victims, but their status is often misunderstood or denied. They too suffer from what Doka (1988) refers to as "disenfranchised grief," and they may not feel that they have permission to grieve (p. xv). Someone may remark to such a co-victim, "What are you so upset about?" Co-victims feel even worse when they do not receive the necessary acknowledgment and support from others around them. Caregivers, members of the criminal justice system, and even victim advocates may not think to include or invite this group of co-victims to court proceedings or support groups or to offer them any standing in the case.

Significant Others

The term *significant other* can be applied to a number of relationships, including fiancé(e)s, live-in partners, and gay or lesbian partners, who are all relegated to the position of secondary mourners. They are left to believe that their pain can be considered only after that of the more immediate family. It is often wrongly assumed, especially by blood relatives, that their relationship is less significant than that of other family members. Furthermore, these relationships may not have met with the approval of certain family members.

Friends and family may presume that because the co-victim was "only" a significant other, he or she will more easily find a replacement relationship. These loved ones, however, are unlikely to simply forget the victim and "move on" with their lives as though nothing has happened.

> There were times when I believed that I wouldn't get through it, I felt that I would never meet anyone else, I didn't want to meet anyone else. I never wanted to fall in love again. (Significant other of a murder victim)

The family of the victim may exclude significant others in the funeral or memorial arrangements. At the services, they may be left to sit by themselves. The family may even perceive the presence of significant others as an intrusion and may resent their involvement on any level.

Co-victims may have no idea where to turn for help. They may not even fully comprehend the depth of their despair, which could stem from a lack of acknowledgment. The co-victim may feel uncomfortable in going to a support group, especially if the family of the victim also attends. Mental health professionals may not be supportive either because they may not fully comprehend the repercussions of the co-victim's loss.

Socially Forbidden Relationships

Other significant others include those who are engaged in extra-marital affairs or in a gay or lesbian relationship with the murder victim at the time of the death. According to Fowlkes (1990),

> In the socially forbidden relationship of an extra-marital affair, special stigma is attached to the "other woman [or man]." . . . Secrecy obscures the ending of such a relationship socially just as it obscured its existence. There is no satisfactory outlet for the expression of loss and grief. (p. 645)

The trauma, the loss, and the grief are thus complicated, which makes the mourning "perhaps the loneliest and potentially most destructive grief of all" (p. 644).

The co-victim of a gay or lesbian homicide victim is affected in a similar way. Whether or not others know, the relationship will still be stigmatized by some, which will affect the co-victim in the aftermath of the murder. If the relationship is a secret, the partner may be excluded from the funeral—and from interactions with the criminal justice system, which may seriously impair the criminal investigation. If the victim was killed in a violent incident related to sexual orientation and the blame placed on the victim, and through the victim to the co-victim, the empathy and support offered to the co-victim will be lessened.

> "I always believed that it was a matter of harassment, not life and death, that it was something that happened to gay men, late at night, outside of seedy bars," she said. "I always thought that life-endangering oppression happened to people different than [sic] me. To heal, I had to acknowledge the world as a place that includes the possibility of getting shot and killed at any moment." (Lesbian lover of murder victim, quoted in Weiner, 1995, p. G4)

If the relationship is not publicly acknowledged or condoned, then public mourning will not be condoned either. These co-victims may be expected to continue their daily lives as if nothing had transpired.

Coworkers

In many instances, employed adults consider their coworkers as surrogate family members. Today's workplace environment, which includes the extensive use of work teams, fosters the formation of close relationships. Grief in the workplace has received little attention from human resources departments and employee assistance programs. Developing protocols to deal with the problem is not considered a priority, although mourning after a loss must occur for a person to heal. The emotional ups

The murder of a fellow employee triggers many strong emotions.

and downs of mourning may be considered verboten in the workplace, particularly if it negatively affects job productivity, increases sick leave, and leads to increased workers' compensation claims. Stein and Winokuer (1989) state that

> the vision of man as a machine is diametrically opposed to human needs. This kind of work experience fosters an environment in which the expression of feelings is taboo. In the norms of the world of work, all losses then become disenfranchised because emotions and feelings are discounted, discouraged, and disallowed. The exception to this unstated rule is loss due to death. However, even mourning as it relates to death is severely constrained by narrowly defined policies that govern acceptable behaviors. (p. 93)

When a violent death of a colleague occurs, whether in or out of the workplace, most employers are clearly not prepared to deal with it. The murder of a fellow employee triggers many strong emotions in the other employees, including past issues that have not been resolved.

> If I was working . . . I would have hit the murderer with a chair or grabbed her from behind. I wouldn't have let her take my friend away

from me. If I had gotten shot also, well so be it. (Friend and coworker
of murder victim)

A murder in the workplace, whether or not coworkers have been
actual witnesses, is certain to lead to an increase in workplace problems. In this worst of all scenarios, it is important to provide special
services, for example, the creation and training of a team to conduct
a critical incident stress debriefing. This fairly new intervention
model allows caregivers to respond quickly whenever a coworker is
murdered, regardless of whether the event occurred at the work site
or elsewhere (see Chapter 6, "Interventions and Advocacy").

Because there are few mechanisms within the work setting to
acknowledge and deal with emotions, the granting of time off for
bereavement may be left to the discretion of a supervisor. Any
policies on bereavement leave are usually qualified by relationship,
which does not often cover absence from work for coworkers or
colleagues of the victim. An exception may be for coworkers to attend
the funeral or to pay a condolence call to the family of the victim.

Whether formal or informal bereavement policies are in place, they
do not begin to take into account the manifestations of grief that
appear later in the continuum of mourning. In addition to group
crisis intervention, coworkers, who are co-victims, will benefit from
services such as peer support groups, referrals to victim advocate
agencies and other community resources, and participation in memorial services or scholarship funds.

Companies need to provide training in grief to both managers and
employees. For managers this training will provide the information
necessary to understand the grief process. . . . For employees it can be
a road map through a difficult time. (Stein & Winokuer, 1989, p. 99)

In dealing with a homicide in the workplace, the manager or supervisor may also be grieving and may not be in a position to be helpful.
Education in the grief process will need to be offered so that both
employer and employee can better understand the added dimension
of the trauma of a homicide as well as the grieving process.

❑ Intrafamily Homicide

Intrafamily homicide is quite complicated for all parties concerned: the co-victims, the criminal justice system, and the caregivers. The majority of intrafamily homicides involve domestic abuse and child homicides, leaving behind many co-victims. In 1993, 12% of all victims were known to be related to their assailants (Bastian, 1995, p. 3).

COMPLICATIONS OF HOMICIDE
IN THE FAMILY SYSTEM

The murder of a loved one by another family member exacerbates all the issues that affect co-victims of homicide. Furthermore, the stresses of an intrafamily homicide may destroy any semblance of family, at least as it existed before the murder. In addition to the trauma, grief, and bereavement issues, there are many other complex family system and legal issues, such as custody, property matters, and concerns with social security payments. It is not uncommon for the family to end up in criminal court, civil court, or both, locked in an adversarial stance.

Each of the many co-victims within any given family has experienced a different relationship with the victim and the perpetrator. The family is often sharply divided by individuals' responses to the event and the manner in which they grieve. Thus, familial relationships may be irreparably damaged.

> Stephen Raymond, a 72-year-old retired physician, murdered his 33-year-old daughter after a family argument. He had a wife and nine other grown children. Mrs. Raymond and eight of the children took sides against the father. Only one of the children maintained contact with Dr. Raymond in prison. When the question of bail came up, he was the only family member to be supportive of his father and offered to let his father come stay with him if he were to be released on bail. A number of the siblings went for counseling together in an attempt to work through the issues raised by the murder. (A service provider)

Families may be forced to make some hard decisions regarding their relationships after the murder. In the case above, Mrs. Raymond faces multiple losses: (a) her daughter who was murdered, (b) perhaps a son who is siding with his father, (c) her husband who is in prison, and (d) the family as it existed before the murder. Each decision may leave co-victims with an increased feeling of loss and new mourning issues. They are often left to grieve not only the loved one who was murdered but also other family members who are now estranged, perhaps forever—as well as the loss of the family itself. Co-victims are commonly overwhelmed by intense feelings of anger that may be directed at different targets in rapid succession—the murderer, the victim, the other members of the family, and even themselves.

The question of whether to forgive the defendant also plays a prominent role in intrafamily homicides, possibly further dividing the family. Because of strong ties, some co-victims may be aware of extenuating circumstances and feel compassion for the murderer. This feeling of forgiveness may not be shared by family members who still feel only betrayed by and anger toward the defendant.

Because of the amount of denial often exhibited in intrafamily homicide, co-victims may not seek helping interventions; they may eschew the very notion of assistance such as counseling. Furthermore, even if the co-victim agrees to it, a homicide support group may not be an appropriate intervention, particularly if other family members attend the same group. Such groups rarely prove helpful and can lead to a potentially volatile situation. Under the right circumstances, however, counseling can be effective, especially if the sessions get beyond personal issues and assist the co-victim to work on healthier relationships. Experience shows that support groups with this same focus may be an even better choice than either homicide peer groups or one-on-one counseling.

The court setting can be an arena fraught with difficulties and perhaps violence as tempers flare and anger escalates among family members. Court administrators may often need to put extra officers on duty in an attempt to quell verbal and physical confrontations.

Sherwood Gease, brother of the victim . . . had just testified and was passing the defense table when he directed an insulting gesture at his nephew [the defendant]. The defendant returned the gesture and followed with a stream of obscenities. Within seconds, the two lunged at each other but were quickly stopped by the three sheriff's deputies in the courtroom. As they wrestled onto a bench, Sherwood Gease picked up a chair to hurl at him. (Paik, 1995, p. B7)

In 1994 and 1995, two prominent intrafamily murder cases received worldwide attention: Susan Smith's murder of her children in Union, South Carolina, and the O. J. Simpson case in which Mr. Simpson was accused (and later acquitted) of murdering his former wife, Nicole, and Ronald Goldman, her friend. These cases are prime illustrations of the pain and anguish generated by an intrafamily murder.

PEDICIDE

Pedicide, the killing of children aged 1 through 16, and infanticide, the killing of children under the age of 1, is an increasing problem in the United States. At least half of all such cases are perpetrated by parents (Marzuk, Tardiff, & Hirsch, 1992, p. 100). As child abuse rates increase, the number of child homicides also increases.

Studies have implicated teen pregnancy, drugs, and poverty as among the primary causes contributing to the increase in child abuse. In a growing number of these cases, the perpetrator among the nonparent group is not a stranger but the stepfather, paramour, or live-in boyfriend. Researchers point to this presence in the home as one of the greatest risk factors. In addition, when the boyfriend is placed in a position of trust and responsibility as the baby-sitter, the child's vulnerability increases.

When a child is murdered by the boyfriend, the mother may react in surprising ways. Although the mother may exhibit shock, anger, and guilt, there may also be denial of the boyfriend's culpability. Many mothers, while grieving for their children, continue to have ambivalent feelings toward the boyfriend. Some mothers maintain their loyalty, even to the extent of refusing to testify against the boyfriend in court. Blame is often directed toward the mother as well as the perpetrator, especially if there was evidence of prior child abuse and the mother was aware of or witness to it and did not intervene.

"He never told me," she said. "He never told me he hurt two other
kids. If I would have known. . . . I trusted him." . . . Now, she trusts no
one. "I mean, I've talked to guys, but that's it," she said. "I tell my
girlfriends they have to be careful, because you never know." (Mother
of child murdered by her boyfriend, quoted in Woodall, 1995, p. A17)

The circumstances of pedicide and infanticide have tragic consequences for everyone involved, including the community. Members
of the criminal justice system, victim advocates, and other caregivers
may feel incapable or frustrated in their attempts to offer any significant assistance to the mother. Grandparents, who are also the co-victims, find their pain and grief compounded by the confusion over
their daughter's role and subsequent response to the murder. They
may not be offered any support in managing their own grief nor be
in a position to offer any assistance to their own daughter.

DOMESTIC VIOLENCE

The term *domestic violence* refers to persons related by blood or legal
ties and to others having an intimate past or present relationship with
the victim. This can include any number of combinations of relationships and encompasses parents and children as well.

With her bruises captured in photographs and her fear echoing on a
911 audiotape even after her death, Nicole Brown Simpson has un-
leashed a wave of support for battered women and firmly anchored
domestic violence in the American psyche as a problem that must be
dealt with, experts say. (Jones, 1995, p. A28)

Domestic violence has always been part of the fabric of our society.
The "dirty little secret," as it is often referred to, has contributed to
recent high-profile cases in the criminal justice system. These cases,
as well as new legislation, such as the 1994 Violence Against Women
Act of the federal crime bill, have helped legitimize the issue. Beating
one's spouse or partner is no longer considered a private matter and
is now widely regarded as a criminal act.

Recent statistics document the extent to which domestic violence
has touched U.S. society:

- An estimated 8 to 12 million American women are at risk of being abused by their current or former intimate partners (Flitcraft, Hadley, Hendricks-Matthews, McLeer, & Warshaw, 1992, p. 40).
- Each year, more than 1 million women seek medical treatment for injuries inflicted by husbands, ex-husbands, or boyfriends (National Clearinghouse for the Defense of Battered Women, 1995, p. 217). Battered women may account for 22% to 35% of women seeking care for any reason in emergency departments (Flitcraft et al., 1992, p. 40).
- The Bureau of Labor Statistics reports that an estimated 4 million women are battered each year by their partners (English, 1995, p. A20). Many in the field consider this number to be grossly underestimated because many cases of domestic abuse go unreported.
- Domestic violence occurs across all socioeconomic lines.

In the last 20 years, as a result of the women's movement, human and social services for domestic violence victims have greatly increased in both quality and quantity. Lawmakers—federal, state, and local—have been increasingly supportive in passing and funding legislation to benefit the victims. The criminal justice system has finally begun to make positive strides in its response to domestic violence, but there is still much to improve.

Domestic Violence and Murder

Domestic violence and murder are often strongly connected. The incidents of domestic violence put the victims at risk for increasing and potentially more lethal violence. There is no question that the family unit can be a violent place.

An estimated 1,432 females were killed by intimates (husbands, ex-husbands, boyfriends, or ex-boyfriends) in 1992. Female victims represented 70% of the intimate murder victims. Out of *all* female murder victims, about 33% were killed by an intimate compared to only 4% of male murder victims. (Zawitz, Klaus, Bachman, Langan, Graziadei, & Harlow, 1994, p. 2)

Spousal and partner homicide is well documented in a number of excellent resources that look at both men and women as the perpetrators of domestic violence. In-depth information is easily accessible and focuses on demographics, causes, prevention, intervention, and

sociolegal responses, concentrating on the victims of domestic violence and how best to protect them, as well as how best to promote
healing after the violence has occurred.

Few, if any, formal follow-up programs track the effects of the
aftermath of domestic violence on the victims. This reflects the lack
of systems for data collection that are reflective of family relationships, although plans are under way to make sweeping changes that
should remedy this situation. There is also little to document the
experience of, and the response to, the other set of victims of domestic
abuse—the families and friends of those killed by homicide among
intimates.

Issues Leading to Blame

There are certainly times when the man is a victim of battering and
may even seek a restraining order. It is more common, however, for
the victim to be a woman, and the degree of injury sustained during
an incident is likely to be far worse for her. Experts in the field of
domestic violence agree that a woman with a history of being battered by her partner will find her life most at risk when she seeks to
end the relationship: an informal or formal separation, filing for a
restraining or protection order, or filing for divorce.

The issue of restraining orders offers some troublesome concerns.
A restraining order is only a piece of paper. Although it has the
enforcement power of the court behind it, it cannot stop bullets. A
family member may be thwarted by an unwieldy criminal justice
system in assisting a domestic violence victim to obtain a restraining
order. In the meantime, someone may be killed by a partner. Or, after
a woman has been granted a restraining order, she may ultimately
be killed by her partner. In either case, co-victims may feel angry,
resentful, and frustrated, blaming the criminal justice system and
domestic violence agencies.

In response to their anger, co-victims have sued agencies that they
felt were negligent in providing protection for a loved one who had
been a victim of domestic violence. One of the substantive provisions
under the Violence Against Women Act of 1994 provides the first
federal civil rights remedy for gender-based violent crimes. The law

allows victims of such crimes, as well as their estates, to bring civil actions in federal court for damages and other relief.

> Last Saturday in Yuba City, California, a man was arrested for stabbing his estranged wife and reportedly telling her, "O. J. got away with it, and so will I." (Jones, 1995, p. A28)

Domestic violence occurs between two people who have a prior relationship. This is not a crime between strangers. If it were, the law would be considerably less lenient in its approach toward response and intervention. In most cases, co-victims also have some previous knowledge of, or even relationship with, the perpetrator. These issues can greatly add to co-victims' grief and loss. They may feel that they have to choose sides in the aftermath of murder. This can be especially difficult if the victim leaves surviving children who are also the perpetrator's children.

The dual issues of anger and forgiveness, which are a possibility for all co-victims of homicide, are intensified in many domestic violence cases. As is often the case, a battered woman may obtain a protection order and then return to the relationship. This can happen numerous times. The reasons are myriad and have been examined in other literature. If the woman is ultimately murdered by her spouse or partner, the co-victims may experience a great deal of anger and frustration with her because she is no longer available to respond to their doubts and questions. These emotions are often shared and articulated by the criminal justice system, the media, and family and friends. Blaming the victim, not an uncommon attribute, is certainly present in many domestic violence murders. Lack of understanding of the escalating process of domestic violence is usually the source of the blame. Co-victims may find that they cannot adequately mourn before they forgive the victim, but without a fuller comprehension of the victim's plight, this may be difficult to achieve.

Battered Woman Syndrome

Battered women may also kill their batterers; men represent 30% of the intimate murder victims (Zawitz et al., 1994, p. 2). In recent years, the increased credibility of the battered woman syndrome has enabled it to be used as a homicide defense. This plea maintains that a woman has killed her abuser in self-defense and, at the time of the killing, had been a victim of abuse. In a recent study of such cases, 9% to 12% of the women had their cases diverted, rejected, or dismissed before trial because of evidence of past abuse (National Clearinghouse for the Defense of Battered Women, 1995, p. 1). The claim of self-defense is the most frequent reason for the acquittal of a woman, but it is not an irrefutable defense. Women who were previously convicted and incarcerated prior to the understanding of the battered woman syndrome, however, are now in the position of being pardoned or having their sentences commuted after evidence is presented that attests to their having been abused.

On the other hand, the use of this defense is frequently contested by a co-victim who tends to deny or disregard the history of abuse and still seeks justice in the form of a conviction and incarceration of the perpetrator. Many victims' families are more accepting of the woman's claim, however, and agree not to prosecute. These complex factors of domestic violence can be quite distressing and override familial connections. Co-victims are often faced with confusing emotions and lack the normal support of family and friends who may now be their adversaries.

Considerations for Caregivers

Caregivers have many factors to consider when planning assistance to a co-victim of a domestic violence murder. Not only is the relationship of the co-victim to the victim important, but the caregiver should determine whether the co-victim was privy to any knowledge of previous domestic violence. The co-victim may experience guilt or anger at not recognizing the signs or having ignored or denied the existence of violence. The use of post-incident analysis can help the co-victim to better understand what has happened; tackle the question "Why?"; dissipate some of the anger, guilt, and frustration; and restore a level of control.

The purpose of a post-incident analysis is not to obsess over what has happened or fix blame. Co-victims often initiate a post-incident analysis by asking what they can do so "no other family has to go through this pain." Ideally, participants should include members of the criminal justice system, both police and prosecutors, advocates from domestic abuse and homicide victim witness units, and family members who want to attend. If various factions of the family are antagonistic, it may be inappropriate to have them at the same table. All who attend the session must be willing to abide by preestablished ground rules so that the process can be healing and informative. The criminal justice system and advocates, for example, may be able to apply any new understanding toward making positive changes in policy regarding issues such as protection orders and new legislation.

Victim advocates and other caregivers may encounter difficulties in providing assistance to co-victims in domestic abuse cases. First of all, caregivers may themselves have unresolved issues concerning domestic violence—conscious or unconscious—that interfere with their ability to help clients. Second, caregivers may not always be knowledgeable about domestic abuse. For example, advocates and other caregivers are also capable of blaming the victim. The role of agencies is to provide services for the co-victim. They may find themselves in a dilemma, however, when their sympathy is directed toward an abused woman who is also the defendant. Thus, many issues can severely hamper the proficiency of caregivers who pride themselves as professionals.

Caregivers should learn as much as possible about domestic violence and understand their own feelings. If they cannot manage their beliefs in such a way as to provide services that benefit the co-victim, they may need to refer the case, when possible, to another advocate. In any event, they will need a great deal of sensitivity in their interactions with co-victims of intrafamily homicide.

❑ Summary

Almost every homicide will have some effect on the entire family system. It is not enough to view the impact of homicide on individuals as if they exist in a vacuum. The importance of family dynamics should not be overlooked.

Parents constitute the largest group of co-victims, and the short- and long-term ramifications of the murder of a child, regardless of age, will alter the family dynamics forever. The parental relationship serves to complicate all the grief and bereavement issues in the aftermath of a homicide as family roles undergo irrevocable changes. Stepparents and grandparents often play a parental role as well and should be included within the family system.

Other family and close relationships, such as spouses, children, siblings, significant others, friends, and coworkers, may not receive the acknowledgment and assistance that they need. Not being accepted as co-victims may leave them feeling alone, isolated, and bereft.

The complex issues of intrafamily homicide—pedicide, domestic violence, battered woman syndrome, and blaming—create dilemmas for everyone involved. Service providers should be especially attuned to family members who have experienced an intrafamily homicide, assisting each member in the attempt to process and rebuild the family system.

As a situational factor of homicide, the family system has not received the attention that it demands. Viewing co-victims as single entities, rather than as part of a larger system, results in an incomplete approach to intervention and caregiving. Research needs to continue to seek out and develop innovative service delivery strategies, models, and practices that address family issues.

4

Circumstantial Influences

Several unique circumstances cause complications in the aftermath of a murder. This chapter explores co-victims of homicide in the following situations: (a) a murder of a police officer, (b) an alcohol-related homicide, (c) a case in which there is no arrest, (d) a bystander or random killing, (e) a community disaster or multiple murder, and (f) a murder-suicide. The following review is by no means exhaustive but introduces some major situational factors that can add to the problems co-victims face.

❏ Co-Victims of Police

In the United States during the last decade, 740 police officers were killed in the line of duty (Clines, 1993, p. A1). This number does not include off-duty law enforcement officers who were killed while acting in an official capacity or officers who died in accidents while on duty.

DISENFRANCHISED GRIEF

Anticipated death. Doka's (1988) work in disenfranchised grief (see Chapter 2, "Traumatic Grief") can be applied to co-victims of police murders. The killing of a police officer is considered an "anticipated death" by the co-victims, both family and fellow police officers. No one disputes that law enforcement is dangerous; therefore, everyone assumes that these professionals have a high risk of injury or death as a result of violence on the job. The expectation that one might be killed before the day is over is held by officers and colors the way a police killing is viewed by families, friends, and members of the general public.

> *The killing of a police officer is considered an "anticipated death."*

The spouse of a police officer who is killed may be somewhat prepared, but it appears that most children of police officers are not. Many of them have been shielded from this type of anticipatory grief and experience a difficult time. Although police departments may provide special services for children of slain officers, these services and other necessary follow-up procedures are seldom sufficiently long-term.

Loss of respect. In recent years, the lessening of respect accorded police officers by many segments of society also speaks to the issue of disenfranchised grief. Although a high level of communal grief is experienced by the police department when an officer is killed, this may not be shared by the community at large. This situation can strongly affect the mourners' ability to fully grieve the death.

Nomenclature of the killing. Law enforcement and the media have a unique set of descriptive buzzwords for the killing of a police officer. In a survey of newspaper accounts covering the violent deaths of 10 officers, the term *murder* was never mentioned. Instead, words such as *shot, killed, assassinated, slain,* and *dead* were used. Often, the phrase *in the line of duty* or *fallen hero* was included to describe the cause of death. A veteran police reporter stated that the word *murder* is omitted because of legal reasons. Even after an arrest has been made and the suspect charged, however, the word *murder* almost never appears in newspaper accounts, nor is it used by fellow police officers or co-victims. This unique practice seems to apply only in the death of a police officer and not to any other violent death. Only the spouse of a police officer may, on rare occasions, describe the perpetrator as a murderer.

> Philadelphia police officers embrace as they attempt to console one
> another after grave side services for Lauretha Vaird at Ivy Hill Ceme-
> tery. Vaird, the first woman Philadelphia officer to be slain in the line
> of duty, was killed January 2. Her funeral was attended by more than
> 1,000 people, including Governor Ridge, Mayor Rendell, and Police
> Commissioner Richard Neal. (Valbrun, 1996, p. A1)

The root of the exclusion of the word *murder* may be found more in the societal perceptions regarding the implied risk in the job description of a police officer than in police culture. This phenomenon is not explained in any research or literature. Not using the word *murder* to designate the actual event that takes place, a term that is applied in other settings when an individual has died violently, has great implications for co-victims and their ability to cope with the death.

FAMILIAL ATMOSPHERE

Police departments consider themselves a close-knit family. The killing of a police officer creates a large class of co-victims, the fellow officers in the department. This group is comparable in size only with the number of primary victims created in a large-scale community crisis. Many officers work with a partner and on a squad or team, making them even more susceptible to feelings of vulnerability when a fellow officer is killed. The murder of a police officer is a serious blow to all officers, within their own department as well as in other police departments. Police funerals are well attended by thousands of officers from many departments, some of whom travel great distances. Below, the partner of an officer killed 3 years earlier discusses the jury's decision of life imprisonment for the convicted killer.

> Howard, who was shot in the chest during the holdup, stormed angrily out of the courtroom. Later, he cried while telling reporters that the jury's decision pained him. "I told myself it wouldn't hurt. I told my sarge it wouldn't hurt. But it hurts," Howard said, in a choked voice. "I wanted the death penalty for him." (Loyd, 1995, p. B1)

Police officers use words and phrases such as *stunned, devastated, upset,* and *shaken* to describe their feelings after a fellow officer is killed. Yet within hours after the death, officers have to put aside their emotions and go back out on the street.

> We've lost family members. . . . We can't even express the way we feel. Everyone's in shock. . . . We get paid by the City of Philadelphia, and we're here doing our job. . . . The phrase we use is "The show goes on." If we don't show up, who's going to? (Gammage, 1993, p. A1)

At court proceedings, the courtroom is packed with so many officers that there is rarely room for outside spectators other than the officer's family. The family of the victim is usually surrounded at all times by large numbers of officers. This protective circle of blue is intended as a support system for family members, but it also tends to isolate them from outside sources of assistance. In addition, the special kinship within the police force affects all its members so much that the needs and emotions of the slain officer's spouse and children may be neglected.

Many spouses of slain police officers report that once the case has been completed in the criminal justice system, they feel forgotten, as the outpouring of emotional support and assistance from the police department and coworkers tapers off. Perhaps the co-victims' presence invokes an unpleasant reminder of just how vulnerable each officer is. There is a new awareness in some departments—officers plan special events to include spouses and families, such as memorial services or anniversary luncheons in honor of slain officers.

CLEARANCE RATE

Police departments consider it of paramount importance that no police killings remain uncleared, and they routinely deploy vast resources with a great sense of urgency to solve such crimes. The public often receives the impression that a police killing takes precedence over other murder cases, although officers deny this is so. Nevertheless, an unsolved police killing is taken as a personal affront to all officers, serves to increase

The Philadelphia police department has only one unsolved police killing.

their feelings of vulnerability, and affects the morale of the entire police department. In addition, police maintain that if the killer has no regard for the life of a police officer, then what does this say about the killer's regard for the individual citizen?

For all the above reasons, police go after "cop killers" with a vengeance and are almost always successful in arresting those responsible. In Philadelphia, for example, there is only one unsolved police killing in the history of the police department. The yearly unsolved rate for all other murders in Philadelphia is more than 35%. Nationally, the FBI's *Uniform Crime Reports* (1993) includes dispositions of 1,003 persons identified in connection with officers' murders from 1980 to 1991, whereas the number of pending cases was only 12 (p. 4). Not only do police departments have a high clearance rate in solving police killings, but also the conviction rate in these cases is almost 100%. As a rule, prosecutors seek the most extreme sentences allowed under the law for killing a police officer, and juries tend to comply.

IMPLICATIONS FOR CAREGIVERS

Proven techniques that are used to respond to violent incidents in other workplace settings such as crisis intervention, critical incident stress debriefing or group crisis intervention, counseling, and support groups are underused in police departments. If a police department employs a crisis intervention program to assist the police, it is usually activated in the immediate aftermath of the killing. Some police departments bring their officers together to make the death notification of a fellow officer and to provide some debriefing of the event. Counselors from within the department may make themselves available on request to provide further assistance. As in most workplace crisis situations, the rate for self-referral is quite low.

Police officers, at any level, do not easily give permission to grieve and mourn or to acknowledge that such feelings exist. This denial is universally shared by both officers and their superiors. Many police believe that any display of emotion may negate their ability to function in their job. Police officers consider it a weakness to show their feelings and to ask for or receive help to ameliorate the effects of such trauma. On the other hand, these same officers may experience feelings of abandonment as a result of the police department's attitude and lack of proactive outreach.

Spouses and children of slain officers may view other co-victims who are not co-victims of police homicide as having a dissimilar experience to theirs. They feel uncomfortable at the prospect of sharing their grief and pain in a regular homicide support group. Although the counseling offered by most departments is usually short-term, the spouses often feel that even professional caregivers may not understand the situation and do not seek outside help. There is no question that the co-victims of a slain police officer have to deal with specific and complicated issues. Many mental health providers and victim advocates, however, are adequately equipped to handle these problems.

Support groups are available throughout the United States under the umbrella of Concerns of Police Survivors (COPS), formed solely to address the special needs of families and coworkers of slain officers. Initially, the slain officer's partner may have an interest in attending the group, but it is widely reported that the partner may quickly drop out. Many families find the groups to be a safe haven in which they can share their pain and grief with others who understand. Every spring, COPS sponsors a national memorial ceremony in Washington, D.C., which is well attended by families and police officers.

As more women join the police force in this country, there will undoubtedly be more female police officers killed in the line of duty. There is little experience in providing assistance to the surviving male spouse, who may also be a police officer.

The killing of a police officer causes great pain within the police community, as well as to the immediate survivors. The isolation that the police department imposes on itself and the families can be a real impediment to the healing process for all concerned. The dual perspective of isolation and denial fosters an environment, both within and outside the police department, that is ill prepared for the planning and implementation of programs to help co-victims.

❏ Alcohol-Related Vehicular Homicide

Victims of drunk drivers have been recognized as victims of violence only through the efforts of Candy Lightner, founder of Mothers Against Drunk Driving (MADD), whose daughter was killed by a drunk driver in May 1980. MADD was founded the following September. Prior to the inception of MADD and the organization's advocacy on behalf of the victims of alcohol-related crashes, the involvement of the criminal justice system was minimal; in many jurisdictions, homicide perpetrated by drunk drivers was not even considered a felony. By recognizing the victims, co-victims received a much needed acknowledgment. In 1995, 17,274 victims died in alcohol-related crashes. This number represents a 24% decrease from the number of drunk driving deaths in 1985 (S. Frogge, personal communication, February 7, 1997). These statistics reflect a shift in the public's perception of the problem of drinking as well as a change in the attitude of law enforcement.

NOMENCLATURE OF THE KILLING

Perhaps the most pertinent issue affecting a co-victim whose loved one has been murdered by a drunk driver is the terminology used to characterize such a death. In this circumstance, the word *murder* is seldom used by the criminal justice system, the media, and other members of society; *accident* is more often appended to the term *drunk driving*. This lack of acknowledgment of the circumstances of the crime adds greatly to the co-victim's distress (S. Frogge, personal communication, January 2, 1997).

CRIMINAL JUSTICE RESPONSE

Another issue with serious ramifications for the co-victims is the manner in which the criminal justice system deals with the event. If the victim is killed by a hit-and-run driver who is never identified or apprehended or by a perpetrator who is impaired but still under the legal blood alcohol limit, the criminal justice response is limited. If the offender dies in the same incident, a situation that warrants no criminal investigation, the co-victims may have feelings of ambivalence. They may feel a sense of relief as well as a sense of disappointment that the case will not be dealt with in the criminal justice system.

When a drunk driving case is successfully prosecuted by the criminal justice system, the penalty may be considerably less than that meted out in other types of murder cases. In recent years, under the leadership of MADD, there has been a positive change in the manner in which the system responds to the issue of drunk driving and to its victims and co-victims. Much still remains to be accomplished in this area, however.

COMPLICATIONS OF GRIEF

The physical violence involved in a drunk driving death may be so extensive that co-victims may not be able to identify or view their loved one. This mutilation of the victim's body is more common in drunk driving cases than in other types of murder; this is a significant factor that may further complicate the co-victim's grief.

Being involved in the same accident and witnessing the violent death of a loved one is another difficult issue that is common to co-victims of drunk drivers. The role of witness may exacerbate the co-victim's feelings of guilt and shame at not having had the power to change what happened or save the life of the loved one. Many times, the co-victim feels guilty just for surviving.

IMPLICATIONS FOR CAREGIVERS

Caregivers can address the needs of co-victims of alcohol-related homicides by understanding their special circumstances. They should be prepared to refer co-victims to organizations such as

MADD for support, education, and information. Co-victims of drunk driving murders may feel more comfortable being involved in a support group that is specifically designed for them. Organizations such as MADD can offer these co-victims an opportunity to become social activists—working to decrease drunk driving incidents and influence the criminal justice treatment of these crimes—which can be an important part of the healing process.

⊐ No-Arrest Cases

Statistics indicate that approximately one third of homicides committed in the United States are never solved. According to the *Uniform Crime Reports* (1993), an arrest was made in 65.6% of all homicides (p. 208). The clearance rate for homicide is higher than for other violent crimes, and some police departments within large cities can rate 75% or better. Most homicide arrests are made immediately after the crime or within a few days. With each passing day, *About one third of homicides in the United States are never solved.* the opportunity for an arrest declines. No-arrest cases are never closed because there is no statute of limitations for homicide. A no-arrest case presents the co-victim with a number of complicated issues that are difficult to resolve or may never be resolved.

> An arrest would make a big difference to me. It would answer a lot of questions, and I would feel safer. (Daughter of murder victim)

NAVIGATING THE SYSTEM

No-arrest cases usually fall into one of two categories: (a) There is a suspect but not enough evidence to make an arrest, or (b) the police have no clues regarding the identity of the suspect. The former situation seems to be more difficult for co-victims to accept because they usually do not understand why an arrest cannot be immediately effected or more evidence gathered. Often, the police and the prosecutor may disagree about the strength of the evidence, or lack of it, needed to make an arrest. The police and the prosecutor have different agendas, despite a common goal of achieving justice. The police are looking, first and foremost, to clear a case and then, ultimately, for a successful prosecution. The overriding concern for prosecutors is not just in clearing a case by making an arrest but in bringing the case to a successful prosecution. The final arbiter in this scenario is usually the more conservative prosecutor. Co-victims may not always understand or appreciate this process even when they are fully informed of what is going on.

LONGING TO KNOW

No matter how many years have passed since the homicide, most co-victims never give up the belief that an arrest will be made. For many years, they may live thinking that they have come to some resolution about the case. Then some external event may serve to trigger all their earlier hopes and anxieties.

> My 11-year-old son was murdered more than 20 years before, and an arrest had never been made in the case. One of my coworkers was murdered as he walked back to his office after lunch. Although he worked in a different division of the company where I was employed, I immediately got back on that emotional roller coaster that co-victims are destined to ride every so often. I realized that although I thought that I had made peace with my son's murder, I was ready and willing, once more, to do everything I could to see if the case could be finally solved. (Mother of murdered son)

Identity

A no-arrest situation presents co-victims with two unforgettable issues: discovering who perpetrated this heinous act and getting justice. For some co-victims, an arrest is built up unrealistically in their thinking as the panacea that would restore life to the victim and return their own world back to normal. Even when co-victims understand the true implications of making an arrest, they usually feel that whatever it takes is a small price to pay for getting a modicum of closure. Many families in no-arrest cases feel it is incumbent on them to call the police repeatedly and periodically, sometimes for years, to ask if there is any new information that might lead to an arrest. Police, especially homicide detectives, tend not to understand the need to return telephone calls if they have nothing new to report. Co-victims, however, would rather hear "I'm sorry that I have nothing new to tell you" than to receive no return call.

Typical comments of co-victims in no-arrest cases are, "It's the not knowing who it is that makes it so difficult," and "I wonder when I go somewhere, is the murderer out there watching me or someone in my family?" Many co-victims also want to know all the details about what happened—how their loved one died, and perhaps, most important, why. It is important for co-victims to realize that such information is not always available even when there is an arrest, and, if the details of the death are forthcoming, they may become privy to information that is even worse than what they imagined.

LONGING FOR JUSTICE

> What I want now is revenge for that poor girl who is lying in Wood-lawn Cemetery in the Bronx. . . . I want justice done. Perhaps then she can rest in peace. (Fried, 1990, p. B4)

A co-victim often labors under the misunderstanding that if there is an arrest, then justice will automatically prevail. Because justice can be elusive, co-victims may discover that an arrest is not what they thought it would be. The arrest is only one more step in the process, and it has no greater power to bestow.

In no-arrest cases, co-victims often feel that no one cares about their deceased loved one. There may be an element of truth to this thinking if the victim's lifestyle was considered a contributing factor to the murder or, in large cities, if the victim was an African American male. Other issues such as race, gender, and the good victim-bad victim syndrome also contribute to such a perception, influencing police to be nonresponsive or appear nonresponsive and uncaring to this group. These co-victims tend to exist in a void, fraught with uncertainty, frustration, helplessness, and confusion. Being ignored by the police only exacerbates these feelings.

On the other hand, police often feel that a no-arrest co-victim is, at the least, an annoyance to be avoided. This is not necessarily mean-spirited or uncaring but may be a reflection of their frustration, stress, and workload.

> In a city with over 2,000 murders a year and fewer cops, it stands to reason there is less time to investigate all kinds of cases, including murders. . . . Some people are doing it themselves, some are hiring private detectives, and, worse, some of it is just not getting done. (Blumenthal, 1990, p. B5)

Some homicide detectives do get inexorably involved in a specific no-arrest case and maintain contact with co-victims, often for years, even beyond their retirement. A detective may actually become obsessed with a particular case and continue to work on it at every opportunity, following up anything that looks like a lead. More progressive jurisdictions have a special unit that handles only un-solved cases after the regular detectives have exhausted all their leads.

Doing Justice

Many co-victims take on the quest of making an arrest happen in the case with the same fervor as those who pursue the Holy Grail. Taking an active role in the case can give co-victims some direction in life, allowing them to work out their anger and frustration and providing an avenue for taking back some control. All victims of violence experience a feeling of powerlessness, but lack of control is intensified in a no-arrest murder case. The co-victims' persistence in contacting the police and prosecutor may even initiate action in cases in which not much attention is being paid. In larger jurisdictions, the police may need something to make the case stand out among all the other unsolved murders. In addition, the co-victims may have knowl-edge of certain facts that could be helpful to law enforcement.

> King [the prosecutor] praised the victim's family for relentlessly urg-ing investigators and prosecutors to keep working to identify, and to later convict the murderer. "What a family!" King said. "They were

persistent. And that persistence made us persistent." (Goodman, 1995, p. A1)

Co-victims may feel some comfort in knowing that they have done everything in their power by hiring a private detective or pathologist, often working in cooperation with the police to uncover some new and pertinent information in the case.

> It's one thing if people die of natural causes, but when a person is murdered, you feel like you were robbed and the person who did it is out there. . . . I can't go on with my life until everything that can be done is done. (James, 1992, p. B5)

Co-victims can also contact an international organization called the Vidocq Society, a volunteer group of forensic experts who meet to solve unsolved crimes, especially murder. Although the group has no legal standing, it operates by team approach to bring together victims' families and law enforcement agencies in a search for truth (Levy, 1996).

Family and friends of the victim, as well as other concerned parties, may raise money to be offered as a reward for information in the case. Reward money does not always work in the way that people expect, and the police do not necessarily consider rewards helpful toward making arrests. Furthermore, the amount of money offered has little or no correlation with creating the type of leads needed by the police department. No-arrest co-victims may also turn to the media to bring their story to the public's attention (see Chapter 8, "Facing the Media").

IMPLICATIONS FOR CAREGIVERS

Victim service agencies and advocates—whether nonprofit, independent, or affiliated with a prosecutor's office—often provide no special services or outreach to no-arrest co-victims, who may fall through the cracks as more active cases take precedence. If agencies are involved, it is usually because the co-victims have initiated the contact. Victim service providers should reach out to co-victims on a regular basis. An effective technique is sending a special introductory or condolence letter (that includes a reference to the no-arrest status) 4 to 6 weeks after the homicide. Service providers may also assist co-victims by offering to make telephone calls on their behalf to obtain information or arrange meetings with various detectives or prosecutors.

Support groups. A 6-week intensive format was established through the Families of Murder Victims (FMV) support group in Philadelphia to address the no-arrest co-victims' unmet special needs. The tone of the group was more informational than that of the regular monthly format, both in educating about the emotions as well as in explaining the criminal justice process in no-arrest cases.

After several meetings, a number of participants dropped out. It was clear from the follow-up responses that the co-victims had expectations that attendance would soon lead to arrests. When no arrests were made, they were disappointed and felt no reason to return to the group. The desire of the co-victims for an arrest to be made in their case was so strong that they heard only what they wanted to hear and were deaf to the true purposes of the group.

The goals of such peer support groups should be made explicit. This might be accomplished by preparing meeting guidelines, putting them in writing, and sending them to members in advance. The group could review this information at the first meeting to see if it is in agreement with the guidelines. An alternative procedure is for the support group members, aided by the support group facilitator, to prepare these goals and objectives together at the first meeting. In either case, to lessen the chance of miscommunication, co-victims should sign a copy of the guidelines to signify that they have read and understood it.

Individual counseling. No-arrest co-victims live on hope and expectations that should not be taken from them. Others are not in a position to judge the co-victims' need to know. Counseling can assist co-victims in formulating realistic expectations and in learning to accept the actuality of the situation—an arrest may never be made, and the co-victims may never know what happened. The achievement of these goals is part of the grief work for no-arrest co-victims, and without an arrest, this part of the work will never be completed.

Eventual arrest. A no-arrest case may be cleared—within days, weeks, months, or even years. This is sometimes a result of good police work or luck but more likely a combination of both. In the immediate aftermath of an arrest, co-victims may experience feelings of elation. But when this surrealistic glow wears off, co-victims may often experience an emotional letdown. They may feel confused because the arrest did not provide them with the expected relief from their pain. It also opens a new door to additional and difficult experiences. Co-victims may find it difficult to comprehend and handle these new feelings. At this time, assistance in the form of a support group or professional counseling is beneficial to co-victims.

❑ **Bystander and Random Killings**

Random murders of bystanders can be defined as

> shootings of persons with bullets not intended for them as individuals—either with bullets aimed at someone in particular, with bullets aimed at no one (as in bullets fired into the air), or with bullets aimed at a crowd of persons or stream of automobile traffic without individual targets. (Sherman, Steele, Laufersweiler, Hoffer, & Julian, 1989, pp. 299-300)

Perpetrators often refer to innocent bystander victims of a random shooting as *mushrooms* because they pop up in the line of fire. The term is apparently derived from the mushrooms that are depicted in the "Super Mario Brothers" Nintendo video game (Sherman et al., 1989).

AN INCREASING TREND

Although still rare, bystander and random shootings are increasingly portrayed by the media and others as a disturbing trend (Sherman et al., 1989). Data collection is difficult in these cases because the usual methods of reporting homicides by the police departments and medical examiners do not always take into account the circumstances of the murder. Even so, media coverage provides a method for documenting such murders. In a study of newspaper coverage of random shootings in four cities, Sherman et al. found a significant increase in the number of bystanders killed and wounded by stray bullets between 1977 and 1988. Although the trend is increasing, national statistics show that fewer than 2% of victims of homicide are bystanders (Matza, 1991, p. A10).

The increase in random shootings has been attributed by authorities to four factors:

> An explosion in the availability of firearms; increased use of guns as the weapon of choice; brazen crossfires over turf and market share in the illegal distribution of drugs; and a growing capacity for otherwise law-abiding citizens to inflict lethal damage when they settle disputes violently. (Matza, 1991, p. A10)

These events not only result in more fear and outrage among the public but also may cause some residents to alter their habits and lifestyles. In many urban neighborhoods in which random shootings are reported as a regular occurrence, children are instructed to fall to the ground and roll away if they hear the sound of gunshots, even if they are inside their own homes.

> Car one stops at a traffic light. Windows open. Radio playing inside. Car two pulls alongside. Passenger in Car two aims pistol at driver of Car one, a complete stranger, and kills him. Why? "I didn't like his music," murderous passenger tells the police. (Baker, 1993, p. 21)

THE "INNOCENT" VICTIM

Key to this type of murder is that the murder victim can be considered to be innocent in a way that does not apply to other murder victims. Bystander murders occur because the victim was in the wrong place at the wrong time.

Many victims of random shootings are young children. The picture of a young child, the innocent victim of a bystander shooting, is often placed prominently in the daily newspaper. The media may cast such a victim into a universal symbol of urban violence and the ills of present-day society. The same picture may be shown time and time again as the case progresses through the criminal justice system and as other random murders occur. The child's face and eyes, frozen forever in time, stare out at the reader in mute testimony to a world that has become too dangerous. Innocence can also be characterized by the random bullets that penetrate a car or the home. The safety of these spaces is violated by such an act.

"I'm not one of those frightened little old ladies," Mrs. Green said, "but I was terrorized." She said her six grown children recently persuaded her to move . . . when they realized she was sleeping on the floor. (Gross, 1990, p. 18)

IMPLICATIONS FOR CAREGIVERS

The literature and limited studies regarding bystander shootings focus on the causes and ramifications of such events. For example, individual co-victims are usually not mentioned, even in a peripheral manner. The definition of a bystander murder and the scope of the problem are integral to understanding the unique situational factors that affect co-victims. The issue of the innocence of the victim is paramount to sensitizing caregivers and preparing them for their work.

"The hurt doesn't go away," said Yates, whose 5-year-old son, Marcus, was killed by a drug dealer's bullet on a July afternoon in 1988. "People say that time heals all wounds. But it doesn't. This kind of thing never leaves you." (Phillips, 1991, p. B2)

Besides being traumatized, these co-victims may experience deep rage at the randomness of the death of their loved one. They feel especially impotent because of their inability to have prevented the event. The issues of trauma, helplessness, and anger are so important that they need to be recognized at an early stage and warrant precedence over most other treatment issues.

Caregivers need to be sensitive not only to individual co-victims but also to the impact of random murders on the entire community. Schools and workplaces are forever affected by such killings. Critical incident stress debriefings or group crisis interventions that are used following multiple murders and community disasters are effective after random killings as well.

❏ Community Disasters and Multiple and Serial Murders

Many of the trauma and grief issues experienced by individual co-victims of homicide can be applied to co-victims of community disasters, multiple homicides, and serial murders. The scope of the event and the number of victims, however, are primary factors that should take precedence over other circumstances.

LOSS OF VICTIM INDIVIDUALITY

One of the unique and difficult issues that co-victims must face is that the individual victims tend to get lost in the scale of the horror. This blurring of identity exists along the entire continuum from multiple murders involving three or more victims to large-scale disasters such as the bombing of the federal building in Oklahoma City in 1995, in which 169 people were killed. These events are usually forever afterward referred to by a title or euphemism such as "the Dahmer case" or "the Oklahoma City bombing," rather than being connected to the name of any victim. This situation is problematic for the co-victims and may not be given sufficient weight and consideration by caregivers, the criminal justice system, and the media.

In multiple murders, individual victims tend to get lost in the scale of the horror.

> My brother was one of eight people who were killed in an arson fire. I looked to see how accurately his death was reported in the media. I was offended by the mistakes that were made; they didn't even get his age right. He achieved such a little bit of prominence in his horrible death, and he will now never achieve any prominence in his life. Nothing showed that our loss was worse or different. The reporting was so impersonal. Our family wanted to share the loss with other

people, to differentiate his death from the others. But he was only one of the people who died; there was no hope of singling him out from the others. (Sister of a murder victim)

Initially, victims, such as the children in the Oklahoma City bombing, may be given significant coverage by the media, but usually most of the other victims are folded into the larger picture. This may be less true on a local level as the differentiation between victims can remain more distinct because of the community connections.

The "chosen" victim. Certain victims, because of special attributes they possess or that are ascribed to them, may often seem more important than the others. The media, in their rush to put a face on the story, are often responsible for the creation of a victim's special identity to serve as the pictorial representation of the event, in other words, as the anointed "poster child." For co-victims who feel that their loved one has been ignored or forgotten, there are often feelings of resentment and frustration at seeing the chosen victim's picture displayed over and over again at every mention of the event. On the other hand, co-victims who have had a loved one selected for the role of representing other victims may experience feelings of reluctance, exploitation, loss of control, and anger.

Becoming "a number." The tendency to lose sight of the individual victim is exacerbated as these cases unfold and traverse the criminal justice system. Many co-victims report that they wish the system could be changed so that victims' names would at least be mentioned. The *bills of information,* known under different terms in various jurisdictions, list the particular charges in the case as well as the victims' names. They are referred to in a sentencing by an assigned number, however, rather than by the reading of the names. To many co-victims, this is society's final way of dismissing the recognition of their loved ones.

At the sentencing, my brother's murderer received eight life sentences, five were to be served concurrently and three were to be served consecutively. When they read the bills of information, they never mentioned in which manner each victim's case was to be served. The system took away my brother's identity and his individuality. (Sister of a murder victim)

IMPLICATIONS FOR CAREGIVERS

One of the major techniques for intervening in an event with multiple victims is the critical incident stress debriefing. These debriefings were held, for example, in the Dahmer case in Minneapolis and in the Oklahoma City bombing (see Chapter 6, "Interventions and Advocacy"). In addition, ceremonies and services that memorialize the victims are a significant adjunct to the healing process of both the individual co-victims and the community.

Victim advocates, crisis responders, mental health professionals, other caregivers, the media, and the criminal justice system face difficult decisions in the planning of responses to multiple murders. The creation of an atmosphere that equalizes the victims as much as possible should be foremost in planning procedures and policies. Currently, there is no general agreement on how best to accomplish this goal.

❏ Murder-Suicide

Murder-suicide is a situational factor that involves a multitude of complicated issues. The event may contain elements of other situational or relational factors such as spousal or partner homicide, suicide, and mass murder. The occurrence deserves attention because of the pain and trauma that it visits on the lives of families, friends, and communities.

WHAT IS MURDER-SUICIDE?

There is considerable confusion about how to categorize this phenomenon. Marzuk et al. (1992) state that "one may ask whether murder-suicide more closely resembles a suicide with a homicidal component or a homicide with a suicidal component. . . ; [however,] many of these events are planned as a unified two-stage sequential act" (pp. 100-101), suggesting that murder-suicide should be treated as a distinct phenomenon. Co-victims do not seem to fit comfortably in both the homicide and the suicide co-victim classification at the same time. Often, depending on their relationship to the deceased, they may feel that they are more firmly in one category than the other. Nevertheless, co-victims are still affected by the phenomenon as a whole.

There is no national database or classification system for this occurrence. The term *murder-suicide* is most widely used, although *suicide* is not a legal term. There is no standardized definition for the phenomenon; the most commonly accepted one refers to a person who has committed a homicide and then commits suicide within 1 week of the homicide (Marzuk et al., 1992). Most suicides, however, occur within a short time relative to the murder, a half hour to an hour afterward.

FREQUENCY

Although murder-suicide is considered a rare phenomenon, the exact numbers are not known. The CDC, the National Institute of Justice, Justice Statistics Clearinghouse, most local police departments, and the FBI *Uniform Crime Reports* do not provide or keep statistics for the combined category of murder-suicide. Annual incidence reports reflect only the numbers of murder and suicide separately.

Statistics may be extrapolated from sources such as local police reports. The Philadelphia Police Department classifies murder-suicide under the category of "exceptionally cleared," along with some other types of murders that do not ever come to trial, including self-defense cases that the district attorney's office decides not to prosecute. There are between 8 and 10 cases of murder-suicide in Philadelphia each year, which represent a little more than 4% of all the murders committed there annually (Lieutenant M. Kelly, personal communication, September 14, 1995).

The data that do exist do not take into account the number of co-victims that remain in the aftermath of such an event. There may be a larger number of co-victims after a murder-suicide than after a single homicide because of the dramatic and violent manner in which at least two people have died. If the event occurred in a public place, such as a work setting, there will be a wider circle of impact that may include coworkers and other witnesses.

The high-profile media treatment of murder-suicide may create the perception that the rate of such occurrences is actually higher than the statistics show. Media coverage of murder-suicide often leads to an immediate increase of cases, with the possibility of a copycat effect. The role of the news media in precipitating this phenomenon, however, has never been assessed.

PROFILES OF MURDER-SUICIDE

Despite the lack of a national database on the murder-suicide phenomenon in the United States, certain information can be inferred from sources such as newspaper articles, anecdotal information, and statistics kept by some local police departments and other organizations. Murder-suicides most often occur within the family.

Spousal

Murder-suicides span the range of relationships between the victim and the perpetrator, but the most common profile occurs among spouses or partners. This is the most common type of murder, with numbers varying from one half to three fourths of all murder-suicides in the United States (Marzuk et al., 1992). There may be a strong history of previous domestic abuse. These murder-suicides are most likely to occur at the time that the female partner attempts to leave the relationship or during custody disputes. Although the spouse or partner is the primary victim, the children and other members of the family may also be victims.

The predominant perpetrator or suicide victim in these cases is a young adult white male with a strong likelihood of a history of alcohol or other substance abuse. A firearm is most often used, although the victim may be stabbed, strangled, or set on fire (CDC, 1994, p. 2).

Suicide rates increase with age and are highest among Americans aged 65 years and older (CDC, 1994, p. 1). Older men are known to suffer from a high incidence of depression. When they make a decision to commit suicide, they often kill their spouses or partners first.

Many of these men have spouses who are ill, and they may be serving in a caretaker capacity. Even when the spouse is in relatively good health, an older man may decide that he does not want to leave his spouse alone as a result of his suicide. A number of experts maintain the view that these events are not necessarily a result of a suicide pact between the couple because evidence at the crime scene often indicates that the wives struggled before being killed (C. Hartshorne of CDC, personal communication, September 7, 1995). There appears to be a trend toward an increase of murder-suicides among this age group (D. Cohen, personal conversation, September 7, 1995).

Pedicide

Pedicide, the murder of a child aged 1 through 16, followed by suicide is another intrafamily type of this phenomenon. In the United States, the parent is the perpetrator in at least half the cases of pedicide, and "16% to 29% of mothers and 40% to 60% of fathers commit suicide" (Marzuk et al., 1992, p. 100). In some cases, more than one child is murdered. The mother of the child may also be a victim. The co-victims, especially the surviving parent, need a great deal of support from family and friends as well as assistance from caregivers. Pedicide followed by suicide is one of the most tragic deaths for a co-victim to deal with in the aftermath.

> When she was pregnant, she said, he choked her until she passed out. Later, in front of their baby son, he beat her with a potty chair until it broke. A judge ordered him to stay away from her . . . but he was permitted to continue to see him [his son]. The last of those visits came to a grim end Sunday night, when Harris shot Tivon, 2½, and then himself . . . as the boy's mother listened in horror from the street. (Barnard & Henson, 1996, p. B1)

Revenge

One category of murder-suicide falls outside family relationships but generally targets a victim or victims with whom the perpetrator is acquainted. In these cases, the perpetrator is usually seeking revenge for real or imagined acts. Such murders may also occur as a result of interpersonal problems and conflicts. Most extrafamilial homicides occur in or adjacent to the workplace. The perpetrator usually targets a specific individual or individuals, but many other people may be killed before the perpetrator commits suicide.

Some of these cases may stem from domestic violence, especially if the spouse or partner has been issued a protection from abuse order. A partner with a stay-away order cannot legally have contact with the spouse or partner at home and may instead target a spouse or partner at work, but other workers may also be wounded or killed in the incident. Again, the perpetrator is usually a male, and the weapon of choice is a gun.

When such incidents occur, employee assistance personnel and human resource administrators need to respond quickly and should have a written plan to follow. The services offered should include critical incident stress debriefings, followed by individual counseling, referrals, and grief support programs.

IMPLICATIONS FOR CAREGIVERS

The co-victims of murder-suicide have to deal with a number of extenuating circumstances that complicate the grieving process. They are the co-victims simultaneously of two of the most horrific traumas that a person can suffer in one lifetime—homicide and suicide.

Murder-suicide victims should not be excluded because of a lack of involvement on the part of the criminal justice system. This is even more reason to consider their distress and to provide services in an appropriate and timely manner.

Most victim advocate agencies report that they offer few proactive or formal outreach efforts directed to this group. As a result, few co-victims receive any qualitative or quantitative service or assistance unless they seek it out. In response to this need, FMV automatically sends a special condolence letter to these co-victims, noting their unique situation and offering support services.

The use of post-incident analysis may be helpful, although somewhat restricted because the case is closed when both victim and perpetrator are dead. A post-incident analysis, or psychological autopsy, includes interviews with family members, friends, teachers, social workers and other mental health providers, and/or coworkers. This process is used to elicit information to assist caregivers in designing prevention strategies. Co-victims also need to understand that they are not responsible for what happened and that no reasonable interventions would have changed the outcome. Co-victims may derive some comfort if they can better understand the antecedents of the event and how this information can be used to help others by providing a basis for intervention. A post-incident analysis can also serve a purpose similar to that of a trial by resolving some of the co-victims' questions and concerns.

Some co-victims feel angry that they will not have their day in court. They may have many questions that they want to have answered, and there is no one to answer them. This seriously inhibits their ability to reconstruct their life. On the other hand, some co-victims are relieved that they will not have to be involved in the court process because of the circumstances that surround a murder-suicide.

> What was initially viewed as the fire death of a father and his teenage son was ruled a murder-suicide yesterday, leaving relatives and friends with more questions than answers. (Sabatini, 1996, p. R3)

Co-victims may feel forgotten by friends and family because of the embarrassment, shame, and stigma that most individuals experience in the wake of a murder-suicide. Co-victims may also need to cope with the strong emotions that they feel toward the perpetrator or the victim or both. Yet these co-victims may find themselves so paralyzed by grief and pain that they are unable to ask for the help that they need.

The co-victims of a murder-suicide may provide caregivers with the most difficult challenges. There is still insufficient information and available training to draw on for helping co-victims reconstruct their lives. The demands of serving these co-victims may be so overwhelming for caregivers that they are reluctant to even take them on as clients.

❑ Summary

The categories presented in this chapter relate to the circumstances by which a person becomes a co-victim or to situational factors in the aftermath of the crime. It is not sufficient to look at all co-victims as having the same issues and problems. The circumstances that influence and complicate the impact of the murder on co-victims must be given full consideration by caregivers. As discussed in the chapter, co-victims of police officers have a far different experience from that of murder-suicide co-victims. Caregivers must understand the commonalities, the differences, and the nuances that these factors suggest. This area needs further research to determine optimal service delivery for each situation and to design innovative practices to respond to co-victims on the basis of their uniqueness as individuals as well as the uniqueness of the situational factors.

5

Death Notification:
The Long-Term Impact

Two detectives came to my house and said they had found Gail. I asked
if she was O.K., and they said she was dead. I asked them a second
time if she was O.K., and they said she was dead. Then I asked them
a third time, and one of the detectives grabbed me and said, "Bob, she
is dead." ("Man tells," 1995, p. B4)

One of the most defining events for a co-victim, other than the
murder itself, is the death notification. For many co-victims, their
odyssey begins with the ringing of the doorbell or telephone followed
by those awful, terrible words, "This is the police. I'm sorry to have
to inform you that your son (husband, daughter, father, mother) has
been murdered." That message changes lives forever; co-victims are
suddenly and traumatically plunged into a netherworld from which
there is no reprieve.

The cornerstone of the recovery process after a homicide rests on
this initial interaction. Unfortunately, most caregivers and service
providers are unaware of the important role that the death notifica-

tion plays for the co-victim. The consequences of the death notification are so pivotal, yet scant attention is given to it in the literature,
and training of emergency responders is
often neglected.

The cornerstone of the recovery process is the initial death notification.

In exploring the concepts underlying
death notification, this chapter provides
caregivers with an understanding of how
and why the death notification protocol
was formulated. This chapter discusses
why service providers should be knowl-
edgeable about the death notification process, specifically, how death
notification information and training can be integrated into their
work. The consequences of death notification for co-victims and for
those who deliver the death notifications, as well as techniques to
deal with these effects, are included. Finally, a protocol specifically
designed to meet the needs of a homicide death is presented. This
protocol offers the caregiver key techniques and tools to deliver
homicide death notifications, train others in appropriate death notification procedures, or both.

❏ Role of Caregivers and Service Providers

All caregivers who serve co-victims of homicide, even if they do
not actually deliver death notifications, need to be familiar and
comfortable with the death notification model. There is no way to
completely eradicate the negative effects of an improperly handled
death notification. There may be an opportunity, however, for caregivers to ameliorate any harm done by performing those portions of
the notification that were initially not provided or left incomplete.

Caregivers, especially clinicians, should attempt to elicit information about the death notification from the co-victim to assess the
individual's experience. This can then be used to understand feelings
related to the death notification and the murder. This knowledge will
be significant in assessing the level of the trauma response and in
planning appropriate service delivery and treatment plans.

After he was taken to the hospital, I was confined to a trailer where I was being "watched" by a state trooper. I felt like I was under arrest. I wasn't allowed to go to the hospital and the trooper wouldn't give me any information. (Girlfriend of murder victim)

Whether or not caregivers are involved in the actual delivery of the death notification, they need to be aware of who delivers death notifications and endeavor to see that they are adequately prepared for the task. Service providers may consider developing a training program for interested agencies in their jurisdictions.

DEATH NOTIFICATION TRAINING

There are several models for death notification training. Mothers Against Drunk Driving (MADD) has developed a widely used program, and the National Organization for Victim Assistance (NOVA) also has developed a protocol. Victim advocates are the primary persons who seek out and receive death notification training. As previously mentioned, there is an appalling lack of formal training in death notification for police, emergency room and other medical personnel, and medical examiners' and coroners' office personnel. The death notification protocol, which follows later in this chapter, was specifically designed to use with homicide co-victims. It is intended to introduce caregivers to the various components of the model for use as a training protocol.

Training techniques. In planning a training for in-house staff or for outside agencies, the following techniques are helpful:

1. Allow approximately 4 to 6 hours for the training if it is to be completed in one session.
2. Provide a handout of the model.
3. Introduce the training by showing a video on death notification or by presenting a short (15 to 20 minutes) panel composed of homicide co-victims to tell their death notification experiences, both positive and negative.
4. Include as much experiential and participatory material as possible in the training session. This includes using role plays and small-group exercises. Break the group into teams of three or four persons, with one

member taking the role of the victim, one or two members taking the role of the notifier, and one person acting as the observer. If time permits, roles can be switched until everyone has had an opportunity to act out all the parts.

5. Include a debriefing section in the program. Participants may take the role of a debriefer and move around during the small-group exercises, or this technique can be demonstrated as a role play in front of the entire group.

6. Take 5 to 10 minutes at the end of the program to debrief the group and to incorporate some stress management exercises. This material may be emotional and powerful to some of the participants.

7. Hold a short booster training session on a 6-month or yearly basis to strengthen skills and discuss any problems or issues that may be impeding a participant's ability to carry out the protocol.

WHO PERFORMS THE NOTIFICATION?

First, determine who should make notifications. This varies from area to area, but in most larger urban areas, it is usually law enforcement, hospital emergency room personnel, or medical examiner offices. In some neighborhoods, co-victims may be informed of the murder by neighbors, friends, or witnesses. Professional notifiers should recognize this fact and continue with the notification as planned because misinformation or little information may have been given by the initial notifier. Victim advocates and clergy are sometimes involved in the process, either to work on a stand-alone basis or in a team with other official personnel.

Death notifications may be delivered by police, medical examiners, victim advocates, clergy, hospital personnel, funeral directors, or a multidisciplinary team. The optimal situation is to create a multidisciplinary team composed of at least one representative from law enforcement and a victim advocate or other human service provider.

The formation and implementation of multidisciplinary homicide death notification teams have not yet come into widespread use. In most jurisdictions, death notification is made by homicide detectives or other police personnel. Unfortunately, the police are often the least prepared to do the job. Some police do a fine job with death notification, but by virtue of their training as law enforcement officers, police have been taught not to feel or show emotion when performing in their professional capacity. The resultant flat affect may work well for most police work, but this same attribute makes police less than ideal candidates for delivering death notification. Typically, most police departments do not offer adequate formal training in the appropriate techniques of death notification, nor do they routinely provide crisis response debriefing. In many urban areas, the sheer quantity of homicides also diminishes the police officer's capabilities to perform this function.

PREPARATION FOR DEATH NOTIFICATION

In preparation for the death notification, several steps need to be taken. First, personnel making death notifications should have the following characteristics: immediacy, availability, authority, information, compassion, sensitivity, training, and objectivity. The last four requirements—compassion, sensitivity, training, and objectivity— are not routinely fulfilled.

> Compassion is the key. The officer that informed me just seemed cold. I think he needs a different line of work or sensitivity training. (Daughter of a murder victim)

Second, the notifier should ascertain the co-victim's needs. Common needs include, but are not limited to, ventilation of emotions, calm reassuring authority, restoration of control, and prediction and preparation for possible future events.

Third, the person performing the death notification needs to have clear goals regarding the purpose of the process. Some realistic goals for notifiers include (a) making a clear statement about the death; (b) providing pertinent information; (c) obtaining medical help (if needed); (d) guiding the bereaved and assisting with managing details (e.g., notification of other family and friends and calling the funeral home); and (e) making referrals to other service providers (i.e., through brochures or pamphlets because the co-victim will probably not remember verbal information given at this time).

Finally, in preparation for the death notification, the notifier must obtain as much information as possible about the deceased: what, when, where, and how it happened and the source of the identification. The notifier should attempt to ensure that the most appropriate next of kin is notified first. This may be a parent, a sibling, or a spouse. If possible, it is helpful to get information, including medical information, about the person to be notified.

> It would have helped if they would have told us all of the information, the painful truth, sparing nothing, as we wished. Instead we learned a lot of information at the trial, that was difficult. (Mother of murder victim)

PERFORMING THE DEATH NOTIFICATION

Table 5.1 details the protocol that should be followed in performing all death notifications.

NOTIFICATIONS IN SPECIAL SETTINGS

Hospital notification. If the notification takes place in a hospital setting and family or friends have been notified to come, they should be met by police, medical personnel, or a hospital social worker. Family members may arrive at different times. It should not be assumed that family members will inform each other. They might not be physically able to do so. In addition, because of divorce or other reasons, family members may be estranged from each other. Every effort must be made to inform *all* family members.

Whenever logistics permit, the family and friends should be placed in a quiet room or area to wait. If a death notification must be made, the co-victims will already be seated and not standing in a crowded waiting area or hallway. If the victim is still alive, the co-victims need to be told as much accurate medical information as possible and given timely updates. They may want to see the victim. If this is not possible, they should be told why they cannot see the victim at that time.

TABLE 5.1 Death Notification Protocol

1. Go in person. Do not call unless it is logistically impossible because of geographical or jurisdictional limitations to do otherwise. With some effort, it is almost always possible to make the death notification in person.

2. Go in pairs. Decide who is to be the lead person. The lead person will make the actual notification. The other team member should assist by monitoring survivors for danger signs to themselves or others, preparing to care for children if needed, and so forth.

3. Talk about your feelings with your partner on the way to make the notification (e.g., fear, anger, frustration, sadness).

4. If no one is at home, wait for a reasonable time.

   • If you are noticed by a neighbor or you ask a neighbor about the whereabouts of the co-victims, do *not* inform the person of the true meaning of your visit. You can simply tell him or her that there has been a medical emergency and that you are trying to locate a member of the family.

   • If you are unable to make contact while you are at the premises, leave your card with a note to call you at your office. When someone calls, do *not* inform over the telephone but offer to return to the premises or ask the individual to meet you at the hospital (if that is appropriate).

5. When you arrive at the co-victim's residence, present your credentials and ask permission to enter. Make sure that you have the right person. Do not make the notification on the doorstep or through a screen door unless you cannot get permission to enter.

   • There are occasions when notifiers, particularly if they are law enforcement officers, may be met with an adversarial response.

6. Suggest that co-victims sit down, and sit down with them, preferably face-to-face.

7. Tell the information simply and directly. Do not use euphemisms such as *expired, lost,* or *passed away.* Use the deceased person's name, or at the least, the relationship to the person being notified (e.g., *your son* or *your wife*). Avoid *body* and *corpse.*

   • Come to the point quickly; do not prolong their anxiety. Most people will know from your appearance and your manner that something terrible has happened.

   • Tell them, "We have come to tell you some terrible news. I am so sorry. Your son was shot and killed by a man who came into the store where he worked." Do not leave room for doubt.

(continued)

TABLE 5.1 *Continued*

---

8. Allow time for the news to sink in. It may be necessary to repeat your notification several times using the term *dead* or *died*. Do not be afraid of silence. It is all right not to talk and to let the co-victims sit quietly for a few minutes as they try to process what you have told them.

   • If a person insists that there must be a mistake, say, "There is always a slight chance of mistake, but I think that it is very remote in this case." In the face of denial, be ready to present confirming evidence that is clear and convincing.

9. Avoid blaming the deceased in any way even if the person may have been at fault.

10. Answer all questions honestly and tactfully, but do not give more information than is necessary. It may be necessary to repeat certain information because co-victims may ask the same questions over and over again.

11. Do not discount feelings—yours or theirs. Expect the full range of reactions such as anger, hysteria, physical violence, or no reaction. Remember that all feelings are acceptable, and refrain from being judgmental about the resulting reactions, words, or thoughts.

    • Sometimes, the person will exhibit anger toward the death notifier. Try not to take it personally; the person needs to vent at somebody, and you just happen to be there.

    • Do not to try to talk co-victims out of their pain or try to force them into regaining control. Do not say "I know how you feel" or "I understand" unless you have truly walked in their shoes. "It is understandable . . ." is a more acceptable response. Saying "I'm sorry" and letting the co-victim know that you care may be the best you have to offer.

    • The only thing to be restrained is destructive behavior.

    • Intense reactions are normal; they are healthier than a flat affect, but they are difficult to deal with and to witness.

    • If the person goes into shock or faints, help to get the person safely to a place where he or she can lie down with feet elevated. Call for medical help.

12. Offer to make phone calls to family, friends, neighbors, employers, clergy, and so on. Ask co-victims if they want you get someone to stay with them.

13. Do not leave the person alone. Respect the person's privacy but also ensure the person's safety.

(continued)

TABLE 5.1 *Continued*

14. Give pertinent written information and instructions because verbal information may be forgotten.

- Provide co-victims with the names and telephone numbers of a victim advocate, prosecutor, medical examiner, or hospital. Provide crime victim compensation forms and any brochures or other written information that might be helpful. Try to consolidate all written information onto one sheet.

15. Explain to the co-victim what will happen next (e.g., the autopsy, police investigation, criminal justice response, and facing the media).

- Give co-victims as much information as they ask for without overburdening them. Again, you may have to repeat this information several times.
- If the case appears to have a high profile, warn co-victims that members of the media may be calling or coming to the house. Let them know that they do not have to talk to anyone unless they want to.
- Determine if the co-victims have a way to get to the medical examiner's office, hospital, or police station.
- If co-victims do not have any means of transportation, are alone, or are not physically able to get somewhere on their own, offer to drive them or to arrange transportation.
- If you are providing transportation to one of the above destinations, be sure to check if they have someone to take them home or if they have money to take some form of public transportation.
- If the notifying team is made up of police personnel and a victim advocate, the victim advocate may remain with the co-victim after the police leave.

SOURCE: Adapted from Eth, Baron, and Pynoos (1987); Lord (1993); Young (1994).

The death notification protocol described in Table 5.1 should be followed. It is helpful, however, to arrange for a physician to be present to answer any medical questions. If possible, the doctor should be asked to meet with the family in clean clothes.

Arrangements should be made to allow the family to see the deceased. The room or cubicle where the deceased is should be cleaned up as much as possible. The co-victims should be prepared before the viewing if there is anything special to know (e.g., disfigurement). If the victim must be covered with a sheet because of the condition of the body, the co-victims may be satisfied just to see and touch the victim's hand. The co-victims should be given a reasonable time to remain alone with the deceased if they so request.

> The doctor was young and uncomfortable. I told him that Lewis was dead and all he could do was confirm my feeling. (Mother of a murder victim)

If the case is high profile and the media are already outside, the family should be escorted out a different exit, unless they prefer to talk to reporters. Especially in the case of a police shooting, it is common for the media to be waiting at the hospital, often even before the family arrives.

Notification in the workplace. If the death notification must be made to the co-victim in the workplace, the notification team should first contact the supervisor or manager and ask to speak to the co-victim. It is not necessary to explain the purpose of the visit. The notifiers should request a private place for the meeting and follow the death notification protocol. If necessary, transportation should be arranged for the person to go home or to identify the deceased. The co-victim should be allowed to decide what to tell the manager or supervisor and if the notifiers should speak on the co-victim's behalf.

Telephone notification. If co-victims live out of the jurisdiction, immediate contact should be made with their local law enforcement agency. The police should be given as much information as possible and asked to make the death notification. If this cannot be arranged and there are no viable alternatives, the death notification may have to be made by telephone. Under such circumstances, several additional items must be considered. If possible, without breaching confidentiality, arrangements should be made with someone (neighbor, friend, or clergy) to be there with the co-victim. The notifier might say, "I'm calling to inform you that an emergency has occurred involving your (neighbor, friend, etc.). Will you please sit down while I explain to you what has happened?" If the co-victim is alone, permission should be asked to call a clergy, relative, or friend to come to the home.

Over the phone, the general death notification protocol should be followed regarding answering questions and providing information, remaining nonjudgmental, and predicting and preparing the co-victim for possible future events. Before hanging up, the notifier should ask if there is anyone else to notify for the person. If a number of family members and friends who know each other are being notified, each one should know who else has already been told.

Death notifications from other sources. Some co-victims hear the news of their loved one's death in the media or are told by someone else who has heard it first. When reporting a homicide, reporters may often say, "The name of the victim is being withheld until the next of kin can be notified." There are many exceptions, however, to this unwritten rule.

> A mother received a call from a newspaper reporter in the city where her 20-year-old son attended college, asking her, "I am calling to verify the spelling of your son's last name as I am writing an article about his murder." The mother had no previous knowledge of her son's death. (A victim advocate)

OTHER ISSUES OF CONCERN

Identifying the victim. If the co-victims are going to identify the victim at the location of the medical examiner, coroner, pathologist, or morgue, they should be informed of what will transpire there and the general procedures for viewing the murder victim. The guidelines in Table 5.2 will be helpful.

> Letting the family make choices is important. Others should not decide what is good for us. (Mother of murder victim)

Cleaning the crime scene. Another important issue regards who is going to clean up the crime scene, especially if the murder occurs in the victim's residence. If the victim or the family has a homeowner's

TABLE 5.2 Guidelines for Identification of the Victim

---

1. Give co-victims the opportunity to make a choice whether they want to view the deceased, although some medical examiners' offices may not allow co-victims to make this decision. Many co-victims are too upset or intimidated by the process to volunteer or articulate their needs and wants. Ask them!

2. Some medical examiners' offices allow viewing of the deceased only on closed-circuit television and have no other provisions for viewing. This is not acceptable to many co-victims.

3. Medical examiners may not be well informed or understanding about co-victims' needs and may not be supportive of their requests or decisions. Educating medical examiners in these matters is important. If the person making the death notification is not capable of making the co-victim's needs known, it may be helpful to invite a victim advocate along.

4. Do not be judgmental about co-victims' reactions or make decisions for them. Do not discount a co-victim's request, choice, reaction, or action. Do not make decisions for the co-victim on the basis of gender or relationship to the deceased. Female, as well as male, co-victims should be asked if they want to view the deceased. Women should not be excluded from performing this task.

5. A co-victim may want to touch the deceased. This is not sick or maudlin. For some people, this is a way of beginning to accept the reality of the death; this may be their only chance to do so. They should be informed that the person will feel cold to the touch.

6. If the deceased's body is mutilated, burned, or decomposed, then identification may be made by dental or other medical records. Explain to the co-victim why this is necessary. As MADD states, "The issue is informed choice" (Lord, 1993, p. 21). Most family members know what they can handle.

7. It is not necessary to give all the worst details and descriptions of the condition of the deceased's body. It may be necessary to involve the family in the identification process, particularly when a victim has been missing for a lengthy time. If there is doubt about the victim's identity, inform them honestly and ask for their assistance. If an identification is delayed or cannot be made, keep the family informed.

---

insurance policy, the crime scene cleanup may be covered. An outside company that specializes in cleaning up after a fire or flood can be called in, with the cost assumed by the insurance company. Commercial maintenance and janitorial companies and housecleaning services may also be available to provide this service. In addition, a few companies specialize in crime scene cleanup. In some jurisdictions, if there is no insurance coverage and the family cannot afford to hire a commercial service, the fire department may be available to perform this service.

> Crime Scene Clean-Up, Inc., a company that specializes in disposing of blood, body fluids and decomposed remains . . . [reports that] business is so good that four months ago, they opened a second office in Fairless Hills, Bucks County. (Cipriano, 1996, p. A3)

In a commercial establishment, an office, or a school, on-site maintenance personnel may be called on to do the work. This can be problematic if the staff knew the victim. It may be helpful to bring in outside personnel in such situations. In any case, debriefing of these personnel should be done after the cleanup is completed.

Photographs. Photographs are usually taken of the deceased at the crime scene. These are for use by the homicide detective, prosecutor, and medical examiner and may be used as evidence at the murder trial. A co-victim might ask to view these photographs immediately or at a later time. This can become an area of contention, especially between the police, the prosecutor, and the co-victim. The request may be denied in an effort to protect the co-victim or because there is no understanding of why the co-victim may want to see the photographs. The co-victim should not have to justify this request. If the photographs cannot be shown until after the trial, then this should be explained and any decision to show them postponed until after the criminal justice proceedings are complete. This issue can be handled in a kind and sensitive manner. Officials can retain control of the situation while allowing co-victims to feel that they still have some control. Some description of the photographs should be given so co-victims can decide if they still want to view them.

The photographs should be viewed in a quiet, safe, and private place. Everyone involved needs to understand that co-victims will become upset on viewing the photographs. For this reason, co-victims may wish to have other family members, a victim advocate, or a mental health professional accompany them, or at the least, provide transportation. The best way to present the photographs is to show them one at a time, not all spread out. In this way, the co-victim can be asked after each photograph, "Do you want to see another one?" The person may find that it is sufficient to see only one or two photographs. Co-victims are more likely to make this decision if they have been informed that the photographs will still be available for viewing at a later time and will not be destroyed.

Crime scene visits. The crime scene often plays an important role to the co-victims as they begin to process the event. Some co-victims want to view the location of the death. This request is usually made to law enforcement personnel in the immediate aftermath of the homicide or even days or weeks later. Opinions vary from one jurisdiction to another about allowing these visits. In one place, the police may ask co-victims if they would like to go to the scene and offer to transport them. In another jurisdiction, the police may be reluctant to sanction such visits. Sometimes, the police do not understand the co-victim's need to see where a loved one was murdered. Often, it is the victim advocate who intercedes and goes with the co-victim. Again, this is a matter of choice, and co-victims should have the right to make this decision without being judged by others.

There has been a growing practice for a crime scene located in a public place to be made into a shrine. Friends, family, neighbors, and community members may stop by to leave a flower, a candle, a card, a stuffed bear, or other mementos. Or they may pray or stand in quiet contemplation of the scene. For most co-victims, this activity can be quite beneficial.

FOLLOW-UP TO DEATH NOTIFICATION

Within the next day or two after a death notification, the notifier should call the co-victims to see how they are and let them know that someone cares. A personal visit is better, but it may not always be possible, especially in a large urban community. Law enforcement personnel are the least likely to comply with this part of the protocol for a number of reasons: (a) The importance of the follow-up visit has not been stressed and, therefore, it has not been made a priority; (b) there is no official sanction for the visit; and (c) there is a lack of time.

> After we were notified, the doctor and nursing staff avoided us for whatever reason. I suppose we were a wake-up call that this could happen to any one of them. (Mother of a murder victim)

The family may have additional questions and will need to talk about what happened again and again. This is a good opportunity to make referrals to a victim witness agency or to other mental health, social service, or legal agencies. Police, in their official capacity, may have given papers and forms to co-victims (e.g., crime victim compensation forms and victim witness information and pamphlets) in the immediate aftermath of the death notification. During the emotional turmoil and confusion at the time, these items may have been misplaced or lost. If the co-victims do not have this material, it should be mailed or delivered to their home.

Consequences of the Death Notification

> I guess it's a little different because I wasn't notified for over a day that she was murdered. I was just notified that she was dead. . . . My aunt went to the coroner's office to identify the body and when she walked in someone handed her a packet and said "You know your friend was brutally murdered." So then she had to drive home and tell me that. I remember I couldn't breathe and I felt sick to my stomach. (Daughter of murder victim)

Death notification becomes intertwined with the trauma of the event.

An ill-conceived and poorly delivered death notification predisposes the co-victim to later complications in the area of trauma and grief. Whatever co-victims remember, or do not remember, about the ensuing days immediately after the murder, they can usually recall most of the details of the death notification. They may not remember every word, but the essence of the words and the manner in which they were delivered will stay with them forever. The death notification becomes intertwined with the trauma of the event and resurfaces with the other traumatic memories of the murder.

COMMON CO-VICTIM REACTIONS

> I felt dizzy, then dazed. My first thought was how I was going to tell my 8-year-old sister that Mommy was murdered. (Daughter of murder victim)

A co-victim can experience many immediate physical and emotional reactions after receiving a death notification. Knowledge of some of the common reactions will prepare the caregiver to better respond to the co-victim's needs. Having a plan may also lower the caregiver's anxiety level.

> I screamed because I couldn't believe she was dead. Then I started to cry, and I haven't stopped crying yet. (Friend of murder victim)

Family members, on learning of the murder of their loved ones, may experience psychic numbness, but a high level of arousal can also exist at the same time: "The world became soundless"; "I screamed, but no sound came out." Some co-victims do not accept the news at first, whereas others can become angry and react with strong emotions. Most are distraught with pain and confusion.

> A lot of people don't believe it when you tell them. . . . The most uniform thing that we get up front is, "Are you sure?" or "I don't believe it!" (Homicide detective)

Co-victims often experience a flooding of their senses. Both physical and sensorial reactions become indelibly engraved in the co-victim's memory. This may include what is seen, heard, or even smelled at the time the news was delivered.

On hearing the news of the murder of a loved one, the co-victim may not be able to intellectually process the news but instead will experience a strong visceral reaction. This will usually be accompanied by a wide variety of physical responses including a flushing of the face, a feeling that the person's head has separated from the body, nausea, light-headedness, weakness in the extremities, and faintness.

> After I hyperventilated and passed out, I felt intense pain in my heart. Also, I broke out in hives all over my body and developed a lump in my throat. (Sister of a murder victim)

> I felt like I was floating, my head up somewhere near the ceiling. (Spungen, 1993, p. 344)

EFFECTS OF PERFORMING
DEATH NOTIFICATIONS

The person performing the death notification is delivering possibly the worst news that a person may ever hear. This role is not an easy one and, for the bearer of the terrible news, one fraught with stress and the potential for negative consequences. All service providers who deliver death notifications are predisposed to stress-related problems that can adversely affect their job performance.

Service providers who deliver death notifications are predisposed to stress-related problems.

In their research study on death notification, Eth et al. (1987) examined the attitudes and feelings of 50 homicide detectives. Although this study is only a small sample, it is illustrative of the situation in police departments throughout the United States. Of all detectives who had delivered death notifications, 44% said they had experienced the task to be from moderately to extremely stressful, 64% found a major source of their distress was concern about the possible reactions of the co-victim, and only nine officers had received some formal instruction or training in how to deliver death notifications.

Even when death notification training may be offered, there is often a great deal of resistance by police officers to take the training.

I've never had training in how to do a death notification, but I'm comfortable about doing it—I could probably teach it. I don't know what they would say to change my mind about the way I do it. I'd say that I'm more or less hardened. (Homicide detective)

Many officers felt that although death notification was part of their job, the difficulty of routinely performing such an arduous task was not appreciated. They felt that they received little or no recognition by anyone, including the police department, the media, and even the co-victims.

That's all I am is the equivalent of the angel of death. (Homicide detective)

The officers did not engage their colleagues in discussions about their feelings about death notification because of self-imposed taboos about the issue and concerns about losing face in front of their peers or supervisors. Eth et al. (1987) found it "remarkable" that the homicide detectives in the study had never been in contact with any police mental health professionals.

Debriefing of notification personnel. Individuals making death notifications need to avail themselves of some form of critical incidence debriefing to address the stress that results from the experience. Notification does not seem to get easier with repetition, and the level of stress may even increase with subsequent notifications.

There are two parts to delivering a death notification—the professional and the personal. Most people have little trouble assuming their professional role and are able to set aside the personal aspect while they are performing their job. The personal aspect, however, must be dealt with in fairly short order and not be buried to deal with later at some nebulous time. By postponing management of these issues, there is a high risk that they may never be handled. Through time, layer on layer of unresolved issues can build up to the professional and personal detriment of the death notifier. The negative consequences to avoiding such issues include burnout and other psychological problems as well as becoming so inured to the procedure that the caregiver is no longer helpful and may actually be hurtful to the co-victim.

Debriefing may be either formal or informal, but it should be done as quickly as possible—if not the same day as the notification, within the next few days. Debriefing is best carried out by the individual's supervisor. Unfortunately, supervisors are not always trained in debriefing techniques; in larger urban settings, there may not be time to debrief all personnel who provide death notification. Partners can learn the skills to debrief each other, or it can be done among coworkers. Debriefing should be considered an integral part of the death notification protocol and routinely performed.

Formal death notification training and techniques for critical incidence debriefings should be included as a regular part of the curriculum for police and other service providers. In-service training programs can help prevent the vicarious traumatization of caregivers. Police departments and other agencies need to make a conscious effort to erase any stigma that may prevent personnel from openly discussing death notifications. Only then will peer support and critical incidence debriefing be considered acceptable and routinely used (Eth et al., 1987).

❏ Summary

The death notification process has been vastly misunderstood and underplayed. Developing and delivering sensitive homicide notifications cannot be accomplished until there is greater recognition of existing problems. To realize this goal, factors that need to be addressed include (a) more effort directed to research that will demonstrate the short- and long-term impact of homicide death notification on co-victims; (b) additional study relating to the development and efficacy of homicide death notification protocols; (c) increased attention directed to training and debriefing all service providers, especially police, who regularly perform this task; (d) a greater appreciation by supervisors of the consequences to service providers of delivering death notifications; and (e) an agency environment that encourages and gives permission to death notifiers to openly discuss the process.

6

Interventions and Advocacy

No theoretical models have been in use long enough to yield sufficient data to conclude that one particular intervention is the "best"
or "correct" model to use with co-victims of homicide. Nevertheless,
service providers cannot afford to wait for the development of new
models and the accompanying research to serve co-victims. Nor is it
sufficient to rely on the treatment of grief and bereavement issues as
basic to intervening with co-victims of homicide. There are many
innovative, often interdisciplinary, treatments to consider.

The paragraphs below explore the role that caregivers play in
understanding and integrating the concept of traumatic grief in their
work with co-victims. Further, this chapter provides a number of
techniques for these caregivers. First, trauma should be considered
as the introductory stage of dealing with the grief process. Recognition of the important elements of interventions for both trauma and
grief is required. Whatever the role of the caregiver, it is essential to
have an informed and accurate perspective of the co-victim as well

as of traumatic grief. This knowledge will also alert the caregiver to potential problems to be able to make appropriate and timely referrals. An informed caregiver not only will offer services that most closely meet the specific needs of the co-victim but will avoid perpetrating the second wound of inaccurate referral.

This chapter on interventions for co-victims of homicide will be presented on two levels. It will first define the intervenors, including the range of services provided to co-victims, the skills needed to assist co-victims, legal concerns, and the dangers of vicarious traumatization. Then, various intervention models and techniques will be discussed, including post-trauma counseling, individual therapy, family therapy, group therapy, support group, critical incident stress debriefing, alternative or innovative therapies, interventions with children, and psychopharmacological issues.

❏ Who Are the Intervenors?

Throughout this book, the term *caregiver* has been broadly used to include any helping person who provides services, support, or assistance to co-victims of homicide, such as victim advocate or victim service provider, counselor, therapist, other mental health professional, and emergency room or other medical personnel. Caregivers may be volunteers or salaried and associated with private nonprofit, for-profit, or governmental agencies. Their services may be delivered at a single time or through a continuum.

Although trained caregivers are available to provide services, co-victims may not know how or where to get assistance. They may not understand the importance of getting support and assistance from a professional. A co-victim may ask, "What is the point of going for counseling or for help? No one can ever make it better." There is no good response to such a question because caregivers, whatever their credentials and abilities may be, cannot change the reality of the circumstances. Caregivers, however, can walk with the co-victims in their pain. That is an end in itself; nothing more is required.

THE ROLE OF VICTIM ADVOCATES

Historical Perspectives

The establishment of services in response to the obvious neglect that victims have received from the criminal justice and other "caring" systems as well as the community at large has not been without controversy. Some, such as Elias in *Victims Still* (1993), question the motivating force behind such programs. For example, Kahn (1984) has pointed out that victim and witness programs

> are motivated by the desire of criminal justice personnel to ensure the cooperation of victims and witnesses in the prosecution of cases rather than by a desire to help victims. But victims have benefited, and gradually the welfare of victims has taken on value in and of itself. (p. 8)

Even so, there are times when victim advocates may feel frustrated because they seem to be primarily serving the criminal justice system, especially the prosecutor's office and the police, and only secondarily the victims of crime. This issue must still be grappled with in both public and private settings in many jurisdictions.

Historically, victim service providers have been the primary caregivers for co-victims, having had the most contact and experience with them as both early intervenors and throughout the process of recovery. Beginning with the proliferation of victim service and witness agencies in the late 1970s and early 1980s, victim advocates have traditionally been the group of caregivers to provide specialized services to victims of violent crime including co-victims of homicide. Victim advocates, more than other types of caregivers, often work from within or alongside representatives of the criminal justice system; therefore, they are most able to act as case or system advocates for co-victims, in addition to providing support and information.

Victim advocates, who originally entered the field in the early 1970s, often came as volunteers to rape crisis and battered women's programs. These caregivers had expertise that consisted primarily of an understanding of the victims' problems and pain, often because of having been similarly victimized. As victim service agencies expanded their scope of services and types of victims, a reactive technology began to develop in response to what the advocates themselves determined were the immediate needs of victims.

Much of the early training of advocates came from experience garnered on the job. This multidisciplinary orientation was the result of the varied educational backgrounds of the victim advocates. There was no specialized curriculum or professional courses that they could take to broaden their level of expertise specific to victims of crime, although studies in psychology, social work, and counseling provided some requisite knowledge. Victim advocate agencies gradually began to set their own training guidelines and develop accompanying curriculum. This was followed by programs sponsored by various state agencies, statewide victim coalitions, and national victim organizations. Some of this training has been funded by grants through the Department of Justice, Office of Victims of Crime, and other federal agencies.

Currently, a nucleus of experienced victim service providers throughout the country is available to serve crime victims at local agencies as well as to provide training to those newly entering the field or in allied fields. Victim service agencies also have become a training ground for college students serving undergraduate and graduate internships. Despite few specific professional courses or nationally prescribed criteria for victim advocates, there is a growing interest in establishing undergraduate and graduate courses leading to degrees or certification programs. Professional organizations such as the Association of Traumatic Stress Specialists (ATSS) offer rigorous certification programs to victim advocates.

After being on the scene for more than 20 years, victim advocates have started to receive the acceptance and acknowledgment that they deserve. Nevertheless, they still run the risk of being dismissed by some, particularly members of the criminal justice system, as "volunteer do-gooders." The time has come for victim advocates to institute professional training and credentialing programs, not only to develop their own skills but also to provide a standardized model for victim services providers and agencies.

Gender Issues

One of the legacies of the early victims' rights movement (which originally focused on victims of sexual assault and domestic abuse) is the preponderance of female advocates. Unfortunately, this gender inequality has continued. Victim advocates tend to be vastly under-paid; this may account for why male advocates are underrepresented in the field. It also may have been wrongly assumed that men cannot serve co-victims of crime because so much emotional support is required. On debriefing a male graduate student who had worked for the summer with co-victims of homicide, I asked, "Do you think that men can work effectively with co-victims of homicide?" He answered, "Yes, if they know how to hug."

It has been my experience that co-victims of homicide feel as comfortable with a male, as with a female, advocate. Male advocates can work advantageously with other men by assisting them with sensitive gender-related grief issues. I hope that as the field of victim advocates becomes more accepted as a profession and salaries in-crease as a result of specialized course work and credentialing, more men will be attracted to this work.

Continuum of Services

Commonly, the advocate's involvement is initiated shortly after a murder and may continue for several years, or until the case is completed in the criminal justice system. Victim advocates can be proactive in reaching out to co-victims because they are often based in the prosecutor's or police headquarters or are otherwise present at various stages and hearings in the criminal justice process. Such intensive contact with victims of crime gives advocates a level of insight into the victim experience that most mental health clinicians are not able to achieve. Clinicians, for example, do not usually have the benefit of the day-to-day contact with a crime victim, nor do they commonly get training that is specifically focused on victimization as a result of violent crime.

THE ROLE OF MENTAL HEALTH PROFESSIONALS

A mental health professional is classically trained as either a social worker, a psychologist, or a psychiatrist. The skills needed for advo-cacy and counseling are at the same time both similar and different. The key differences are that (a) the counselor focuses on the co-victim's internal needs, and (b) the advocate focuses on the external needs of the co-victim and helps communicate these to other individuals and systems. Young (1994) identifies the similarities as follows:

1. Both counselor and advocate seek as much factual information as exists about the case.
2. Both counselor and advocate assist victims and survivors in formulating plans of action and predicting future obstacles.
3. Both counselor and advocate seek to enable victims and survivors to design and accomplish their own goals.
4. Both counselor and advocate focus on the victims' and survivors' interests and should not confuse those interests with their own. (p. 7:7)

Therapeutic Services

Formal interventions by mental health professionals are only one segment of a strategy of intervention. If formal interventions occur early in the process and prove to be effective, the necessity for future "corrective therapies may be reduced" (Kahn, 1984, p. 6). It is suggested that mental health professionals collaborate with victim advocates and members of the criminal justice system to become knowledgeable about the uniqueness of co-victims' needs and the nature of their ordeal.

Mental health professionals may need to rethink the definition of counseling and therapy to include some advocacy-oriented procedures as well. Standard assessments and treatment plans may have to be drastically altered to fit the parameters of the co-victim's circumstances. For example, the murder of a loved one has probably brought the co-victim to counseling. The co-victim is looking for a way to lessen the pain and to cope with this terrible event. This individual often reports feeling "crazy," helpless, and in turmoil. Professionals should be aware that such symptoms, if exacerbated as a result of inappropriate counseling, may cause a co-victim to prematurely terminate treatment.

In most cases, short-term focused interventions can be helpful, but this does not exclude more interactive approaches, along with innovative therapies in both group and individual settings. Rather than terminating treatment after the client has achieved a certain mutually agreed-on point in the therapeutic process, the co-victim and the therapist will need to plan future tune-up or booster sessions. These sessions may be necessitated by occurrences that have triggered the trauma and grief (e.g., subsequent temporary upsurges of grief), including events as they are played out in the criminal justice system. This recommendation may not be applicable for the therapist who is treating a co-victim already in counseling at the time of the homicide or for the co-victim who must face other mental health issues or past traumas.

Financial Considerations

In light of today's increased reliance on managed care, mental health providers will be concerned about the stringent limitations imposed by most insurance companies on mental health counseling and therapy. In many states, crime victim compensation (CVC) may reimburse the mental health professional for services rendered, although such payment can take up to a year to receive. Co-victims must meet certain criteria, which are explained in the following chapter on the criminal justice system. It behooves the mental health professional to become knowledgeable about CVC procedures, which can be accomplished by contacting a victim advocate agency, the prosecutor's office, or each state's CVC board directly.

> *Crime victim compensation is one of the few tangible rights accorded to a crime victim.*

Mental health professionals are trained not only to provide direct service but also to act as educators and researchers. Incumbent in this role is the responsibility to develop new models of treatment as well as design research. Thus, therapists have an opportunity to make significant contributions to all victims of violent crime by engaging in these activities.

SERVICE DELIVERY CHOICES FOR CO-VICTIMS

The array of services offered by victim service caregivers is quite broad and focuses on long-term supportive counseling and advocacy. Many of the services available are generalizable to all crime victims; individual aspects of such services, however, may be tailored to fit the unique needs of different circumstances—homicide, rape, children, battered women, and so on. Some of the services may represent the first and only instance in which help is offered to co-victims.

The following paragraphs highlight the key areas to be included in a training program for caregivers who serve co-victims of homicide. The skills and services described can also be easily integrated into the set of tools available to any professional. Whether the caregiver is based in a comprehensive victim service agency or in one created solely to serve co-victims of homicide, a wide variety of services should be offered, some of which may overlap.

Crisis intervention. In the immediate aftermath of a homicide, crisis response is a priority. The type of services and assistance that the co-victim receives at this time will establish the setting for the future. Crisis intervention may include support services at the crime scene, hospital, medical examiner's office, co-victim's home, police station, or court setting. Follow-up and brief crisis intervention counseling that involves providing information, nonjudgmental listening, and referrals for other services can be quite comforting and helpful.

Advocacy. Advocacy, which does not technically fall under the umbrella of therapy, can be therapeutic. As the name implies, the caregiver has the mission to act as a voice for co-victims, both individually and collectively, and to empower them to find their own voice. The criminal justice system can be confusing and overwhelming and, intentionally or not, often excludes the co-victim. *Case advocacy* provides an opportunity to work with co-victims as a guide through the criminal justice system and to intercede on behalf of individuals when problems or issues arise. *System advocacy* looks at the larger picture and involves representing groups of co-victims. This may involve legislative issues as well as changes within the criminal justice system. Case and system advocacy work in both directions because information and changes from one area will ultimately affect the other.

Advocacy is also achieved by assisting co-victims in formulating plans of action and designing and accomplishing their own goals.

Some victims are so wounded that they are never again able to take control of their lives. Thus, patience is a must. Caregivers can offer practical advice by educating co-victims in good coping skills and encouraging them to establish healthy routines.

Supportive counseling. In the aftermath of a homicide, counseling may be offered through mental health providers, but continuing emotional support is often provided by victim advocates and other caregivers. Supportive counseling is a passive process, in comparison with mental health therapy, and is often performed ad hoc, for example, outside a courtroom or at the medical examiner's office. The goal of supportive counseling is to help co-victims feel empowered and regain a sense of control in life. This is accomplished by allowing co-victims to discover their own direction in the process of reconstructing their lives. Any trauma, pain, or grief belongs uniquely to the co-victim, not to the caregiver. One of the supportive roles is to be available to offer practical information and education about the grief experience and the criminal justice experience. In addition, offering a hug or holding the co-victim's hand is often the most significant support a caregiver can offer.

Criminal justice information, orientation, and court accompaniment. This area is a major focus for victim advocates and, in comparison with other caregivers, one for which they are uniquely prepared. The advocates guide co-victims through the unfamiliar and often confusing maze of the criminal justice system. This is best accomplished by acting as liaisons with various members of the system and keeping co-victims informed about their individual cases. Orientation to the criminal justice system, whether by a formal court orientation program or with an informal introduction, is helpful to co-victims. This accomplishes two objectives: (a) By becoming more familiar with the system, the co-victims are more informed consumers and, consequently, achieve more control of the situation; and (b) proper preparation reduces the overall anxiety that clients will experience about the system and their role in it.

Court accompaniment provides the co-victim with the needed strength, sometimes quite literally in the form of an arm to lean on, during the painful and possibly intimidating court hearings. Caregivers may spend a great deal of time in court with the family and friends of a homicide victim; without such an advocate, a co-victim might be alone or may not even find the strength to be present.

Crime victim compensation assistance. Assisting a co-victim in the completion of CVC claim forms and acting as a liaison with the CVC board when problems occur are essential services. Completing a CVC form can be confusing and difficult. Generally, the victim advocate has the experience to expedite this process. Although reimbursement of costs incurred as a result of a murder can ease the financial burden and associated distress of loved ones, it cannot make up for the intrinsic loss of the deceased person. Because CVC is one of the few tangible rights accorded to a crime victim, an advocate should try to ensure that this right is fulfilled. The act of helping a co-victim complete a CVC claim form can prove to be therapeutic for the co-victim. An average of 2 hours is spent in completing a CVC form with a co-victim. The time spent completing the form is also an opportunity to offer support counseling, provide information, and make referrals to legal and mental health professionals (see Chapter 7, "Justice for All").

Referrals to other service professionals. A co-victim may require referrals to a network of outside service providers to take care of issues related to the murder: mental health counseling, social security, real estate, and custody matters, for example. The caregiver is in a position to recognize and assess health and legal problems and refer a co-victim for additional assistance that cannot and should not be routinely provided by the victim service agency.

REQUISITE SKILLS FOR
ASSISTING CO-VICTIMS

Communication

A key skill needed by caregivers lies in the area of communication. Professionals may be experienced in their field but may not be able to communicate information in a way that facilitates the processing and integration of that information for the co-victim. In addition, good communication enhances the ability to understand, establishes trust, and promotes dignity for both the speaker and the listener. Communication skills are often neglected as a component of professional or continuing education courses but are a necessity for victim advocates. Adults often assume that they are proficient in communication just because they can speak effectively. They cannot be more mistaken; communication is a two-way street, and a competent communicator must also be adept at listening as well as speaking. Unfortunately, listening is one of the most neglected and undervalued communication skills.

Listening to co-victims is an important communication skill for caregivers.

For many co-victims, the telling and retelling of their story is the only way they actually can begin to believe what has happened. Unfortunately, not many people are willing to listen to co-victims, at least not for long. Some who try to listen may deal with their own discomfort by changing the subject, talking about the weather, or talking about their own experiences. Caregivers can be guilty of the same behaviors. This tends to shut down the co-victims, leaving them with no one else to talk to, or, more important, to be a listener. As professional caregivers, it is not necessary to make it better or to fix it, to have the answers, or to take away the pain. In and of itself, the act of listening is profoundly healing. Caregivers should remember that silence is also a communication skill. Additional communication tips are shown in Tables 6.1 and 6.2.

Cross-Cultural Awareness

The second skill of cultural competence is invaluable for intervenors. A caregiver is asked to respond on several levels: (a) to the unique differences of the emotional makeup of each co-victim; (b) to the influences of each co-victim's personal history; and (c) most important, to the caregiver's *own* cultural identity, values, and references before interacting with co-victims. Young (1994) developed a "matrix of cultural influences" that allows personal and professional assessment of culturally shaped attitudes, beliefs, and behaviors along a spectrum of cultural identities, such as nationality, income, education, residence (rural or urban), gender, ethnicity, religion, age,

TABLE 6.1   Active Listening Guidelines

- Watch body language—yours and theirs.
- Use nonverbal cues, facial expressions, eye contact, posture, and gestures to show that you understand and accept what the person is saying.
- Give nonverbal encouragement—a smile, a hug, a nod, or a touch.
- Use verbal encouragements such as "okay" or "uh-huh."
- Use a nonthreatening tone of voice.
- Take time to just listen. Do not interrupt, give suggestions, offer advice, bring up your own feelings or problems, or think ahead to your own response.
- Check to make sure that you understand. Restate or say in your own words the person's most important thoughts and feelings.
- Put yourself in the other person's place to understand what the person is saying and how she or he feels.
- Focus on feelings without judging them right or wrong. "How did that make you feel?" "You seem angry. Want to talk about it?"
- Use encouraging phrases that communicate how much you care. "Tell me about it." "Then what happened?"
- Ask questions when something is not clear. "Can you tell me more about that?" "Am I intruding?" "What do you need?"
- Avoid "why" questions, which tend to blame and put people on the defensive. "I'm not sure I understand—what happened first?"

TABLE 6.2   Useful Phrases When Responding to Co-Victims

It is helpful to say

    It is understandable that . . .

    I'm sorry that . . .

    It must have been upsetting to . . .

Rather than

    I understand.

    You should . . .

    That's wrong.

    Everything will be okay.

sexual orientation, mental or physical abilities, profession, and geographic reference (p. 15:32).

In working with co-victims, a caregiver may want to determine the level of ethnic identification of an individual or family. Young (1994) provides a checklist to aid caregivers in this assessment with these suggestions:

1. Determine the extent that the ethnic language is spoken in the home.
2. Determine how well the dominant language (in the United States, English) is spoken.
3. Assess the stresses of migration of the ethnic group as a whole and how long the individual or community has been in the United States.
4. Determine the community of residence and the opportunities for linking with people of similar origin.
5. Determine the educational attainment and socioeconomic status of the individual and community.
6. Determine the degree of religious faith of the individual and whether that faith reflects the religion of the ethnic group.
7. Determine the nature of political affiliations because in some countries, class, values, and culture are reflected through political orientation.
8. Determine the presence of intermarriage for the community, the individual, and the individual's family. (pp. 15:4-15:5)

Several recommendations will increase the effectiveness of caregivers who are providing services in cross-cultural contexts. A caregiver should have a general knowledge about as many of the cultural groups in the agency's service area as possible. A good place to start is to understand the culture's routines, traditions, and impact on family relationships (Young, 1994). In many agencies, one worker becomes the "expert" on a particular cultural group because of continuing interaction with certain co-victims and becomes a valuable source of information for the agency. It is also helpful to have bilingual workers, to publish all written materials bilingually, or both. Awareness of spatial relationships, or proxemics, often makes cross-cultural connections easier. Four distinct zones—intimate, personal, social, and public—vary greatly from culture to culture. One pertinent example is demonstrated in the following scenario:

A conversation between two acquaintances, one of Latino and one of Anglo-American culture, begins at one end of a room and finishes at the other as the Latino tries to move closer to the personal zone where he feels most comfortable, and the Anglo-American draws away, feeling uncomfortable in his intimate zone. The Latino invariably goes

away thinking that Anglos are stand-offish, and the Anglo leaves with
the perception that Latins are pushy. (McKay, Davis, & Fanning, 1983)

Caregivers should observe the comfort zones of the cultures with
which they will be intervening.

A final recommendation is that caregivers address practical problems first. As is often the case in human service, providing clients
with concrete needs often paves the way to trusting relationships.
The same principle applies to cross-cultural service delivery. Depending on the time frame in which a caregiver is intervening with
co-victims, there may be a wide variety of needs to meet, such as
funeral expenses, financial support, and the victim's hospital bills.
Helping co-victims file CVC or public assistance forms, locating a
funeral home that will defer payments, or simply informing co-victims
of their rights regarding the debts of the deceased will go a long way
toward building a supportive and trusting relationship with co-victims
of any cultural background.

In an ideal world, the racial and cultural experience of caregivers
would always match that of the co-victims. Because of the small
number of workers and the heavy reliance on graduate school and
college interns at most agencies, this goal is difficult to achieve. It is
beneficial if agencies can recruit caregivers and volunteers from the
community, in an effort to provide increasingly community-based
services by caregivers whose cultural experience and reference are
most like those of their clients.

Ability to Support

A caregiver's role is not to encourage the co-victim to "get over it."
This goal can be detrimental to both the caregiver and co-victim
because it is unrealistic. Co-victims will never "get over" the murder
of a loved one and will continue to think about it for the rest of their
lives. Advocates should not make co-victims feel that they "should
be doing better by now" or "should be able to stop thinking about
the person already." This thinking can be nonproductive; it sets
co-victims up to fail because they can never achieve the nebulous
goal "to get better" that others have imposed on them. Caregivers

also are faced with an impossible task if they share these unrealistic aims.

Supporting co-victims' strengths and validating their pain go a long way toward helping them in their lifelong process of recovery. Professionals assist co-victims best by helping them achieve a new "normal" life, albeit a different life from what they had in the past.

Supporting co-victims' strengths and validating their pain helps in their lifelong process of recovery.

LEGAL ISSUES

Two key legal issues affect professionals in their work with co-victims of homicide. The first deals with the issue of confidentiality. Throughout the United States, domestic violence and rape advocates have almost universal protection from subpoena; this protection, however, does not commonly extend to advocates who serve the co-victims of homicide. If advocates have already gone through domestic violence or rape training and work with an agency that provides services to those crime victims, there is more likelihood of protection from subpoena. Agencies will need to obtain legal advice on this matter. In any case, careful attention should be paid to avoid discussing the actual details of legal cases against an accused perpetrator of homicide with co-victims because of the danger of being subpoenaed by the defense counsel. Professionals should also understand that written material concerning the legal issues of the case that are entered into the caregivers' case records can be subpoenaed as evidence.

Another issue revolves around the "duty to warn." If a co-victim makes a threat to harm another named individual, and the victim advocate is privy, firsthand, to this threat, the matter should be discussed immediately with a supervisor to determine if someone should be warned. In situations such as these, personal and agency liability can be at stake. The California case of *Tarasoff v. Regents* (1976) was the origin of liability for agency workers. Duty to warn is a statute in some states but not in others. Victim advocate agencies and the advocates employed there should be informed about the statute in their state and its applicability to their professional situation. If there is no statute, liability issues may still exist. Again, an attorney is the best person to provide such information.

VICARIOUS TRAUMATIZATION

Empathizing with co-victims' experiences can have an effect on caregivers who work with homicide co-victims. Caregivers' feelings need to be attended to, not only for their own well-being but also to better enable them to continue serving in a productive manner.

Insufficient attention has been paid to the possible long-term consequences for caregivers resulting from exposure to victims' experiences. This lack of concern can be equally shared by all involved—the researcher, the supervisor, and the caregiver. McCann and Pearlman (1990b) describe a process called "vicarious traumatization [in which] persons who work with victims may experience profound psychological effects, effects that can be disruptive and painful for the helper and can persist for months or years after work with traumatized persons" (p. 132). They go on to explain that "just as PTSD is viewed as a normal reaction to an abnormal event, we view vicarious traumatization as a normal reaction to the stressful and sometimes traumatizing work with victims" (p. 144).

If the feelings and needs of caregivers are not attended to, the resulting symptoms can adversely influence their work and personal life. Many caregivers find themselves deeply affected by the stories of the co-victims and their incredible anguish to the point at which they themselves feel stressed. Some advocates have reported feeling as though they are experiencing the death as close to home and go through shock reactions similar to those whose family member has died. Others have found themselves experiencing nightmares, low tolerance to stress, hypervigilance, and a disruption of their thoughts with vivid images of the client's trauma.

Caregivers need to take steps to prevent or combat the negative effects of their work. Coping strategies that can be helpful are shown in Table 6.3. Caregivers usually receive tremendous gratification in being able to help those in need. Co-victims will continue to live and love, and caregivers need to remember that they are privileged to witness the strength and resilience of the human spirit.

TABLE 6.3 Coping Strategies for Caregivers

- Be continuously aware of and pay attention to your feelings. Verbally acknowledge them to yourself, and if possible, take the opportunity to talk to a coworker. You may need to debrief with someone not involved in the case before you are able to pick up and start working again.
- Balance your caseload with a variety of clients representing different circumstances and presenting problems (a luxury for some caregivers, especially victim advocates who work in a program that serves only homicide co-victims).
- Be aware of limitations of your own personal issues and unresolved traumas. If you have not been in counseling yourself, particularly if you have unresolved problems or trauma in your life, it is a good idea to invest in personal therapy. If you have previously been in counseling, be aware of the times that you might need to return for a booster session.
- Supervisors should include time for debriefing during interagency case conferences. If this does not fit within the boundaries of your agency or workplace, start an informal peer group in your agency or with other caregivers who work in different settings. Meet regularly to talk about emotional issues involved in the more difficult cases you have worked on, and gather input on how to handle future cases.
- If the formation of a peer support group at work is not feasible, try to find a caregiver "buddy" to communicate regularly with by telephone, fax, or e-mail.
- Balance work with your personal activities—make sure you are able to relieve stress at the end of the day. Activities such as exercise, artistic or creative outlets, working on pleasurable hobbies, spending time with a friend, and so on are excellent stress relievers. Try being involved in a group or activity that will provide you with hope and optimism—consider an activity that has a spiritual component to it, such as yoga, tai chi, meditation, or massage.
- Schedule time every week to do something special for yourself, such as taking a bubble bath or finding a quiet place to read a book for a half hour. Include your special times and activities in your written schedule in the same way as you do for other commitments. Share your activity with another caregiver so that you can report back when you have completed it.

For further information on this subject, caregivers can see Figley (1995) and McCann and Pearlman (1990b). Caregivers have a responsibility to themselves and to their clients to familiarize themselves with these materials and to educate themselves on the impact of working with a traumatized client population.

RECOMMENDATIONS FOR SKILL BUILDING

The American Psychological Association Task Force on the Victims of Crime and Violence published a report (Kahn, 1984) that, among other items, suggested a number of recommendations for psychologists. Unfortunately, these recommendations have not received the recognition that they merit, and as a result, many of them have not yet been integrated into the profession. The recommendations are generalizable to other mental health professionals, and a multidisciplinary effort should be made to accomplish them in an expeditious manner. A synopsis of the recommendations includes the objectives listed below.

- *Objective 1:* Psychologists involved in service delivery should acquire specific, identifiable skills in direct intervention with victims. This objective can be achieved by establishing the following: (a) training courses for working with victims that are incorporated in graduate and postgraduate curricula; (b) required licensing and accreditation reviews to demonstrate knowledge and expertise in service to victims; (c) continuing education workshops that address the provision of services to victims.

- *Objective 2:* More psychologists should become involved in initiating and evaluating changes in the criminal justice system designed to ameliorate the problems victims experience in that system.

- *Objective 3:* More psychologists who are prepared to do so should actually provide service directly to victims, to indigenous helping systems, and in the criminal justice systems. The development of training modules for crisis intervention personnel and mental health providers is central to this objective.

- *Objective 4:* Psychologists should be more involved in gaining knowledge about the victim experience and helpful interventions for victims.

- *Objective 5:* There should be greater public awareness about the mental health needs of victims and the roles psychology and psychologists can serve in helping victims. (Kahn, 1984, pp. 10-13)

❑ What Are the Interventions?

When working with co-victims of homicide, caregivers should first focus on interventions that address any existing trauma. Earlier traumas, with which the co-victim may not have already dealt, will most certainly be triggered by the new trauma of the murder. Previous traumas will need to receive attention first. Other problems, such as alcohol and drug abuse, should be handled by the caregiver only if they relate specifically to the presenting trauma. Often, it is necessary to refer co-victims to other professionals for further specialized counseling or treatment.

The primary objectives in offering trauma or crisis response counseling, as the first tier of intervention after a homicide, are to lessen or ameliorate the effects of the trauma by helping co-victims establish healthy coping skills and to help co-victims prevent or overcome PTSD by early intervention. A number of standard treatment methods have been found to meet the needs of co-victims. They typically include individual and family therapy, group therapy, peer support group, crisis incident stress debriefing, and innovative therapies. Ideally, all co-victims should be given the opportunity to be involved in the spectrum of treatments. Special attention to the treatment of children and pharmacological issues may be needed, as is discussed below. There is controversy among experts regarding which type of treatment should be offered at what point in the service continuum. More research on interventions for co-victims is required to determine the answers to many questions about treatment.

POST-TRAUMA COUNSELING

In *Responding to Communities in Crisis* (Young, 1994), NOVA suggests the following guidelines for post-trauma counseling, which apply to most interventions that are used with homicide co-victims:

1. *Normalization* focuses on reassuring the survivors [co-victims] that they are not crazy and that their traumatic reactions are not uncommon.
2. *Collaboration* between the victims or survivors and the post-trauma counselor serves to reconstruct a new life for the co-victim. The counselor should be involved as a listener and a resource, not a decision-maker.
3. Supporting survivors in a *unique pathway to reconstruction or healing* is essential. Counselors should be non-judgmental, supportive and open in their response to decisions. (p. 7:2)

NOVA also outlines some general techniques to be used in post-trauma counseling. These include education, promoting general good health, humor, tears, spirituality, the integration of social support systems, and peer support groups.

A number of processes can help co-victims, especially in the first few months after the murder, and can be integrated into all treatment modalities. The co-victim needs to be educated and supported by caregivers in putting these techniques into place. Such methods as the ones below assist co-victims in externalizing thoughts that may be intruding on their ability to concentrate, sleep, and carry out everyday tasks.

Keeping a diary. Co-victims can keep a daily diary or journal and write all their thoughts about the murder and death of a loved one. The co-victim should purchase a small notebook to carry and should be encouraged to write the thoughts down as soon as they occur. If this is inconvenient, then the co-victim should attempt to write or even tape-record the day's feelings every evening before bedtime. Because the notebook is primarily for the victim's edification, the structure can be quite rudimentary, without concern for grammar or spelling. The victim need never read any of the notebook again; the writing process itself is of paramount importance. Some co-victims may ultimately fill several notebooks before they realize that they have made progress.

Behavior modification. Some clinicians favor a process whereby the co-victim wears a rubber band on the wrist. Co-victims are instructed to snap the rubber band whenever they have thoughts or images of the murder. The simple act of snapping the rubber band helps to dissipate intrusive thoughts and eventually lessens their frequency.

Thought stopping. This method can easily be taught to a co-victim to help manage repetitive thoughts that can cause increased anxiety, self-doubt, and fear. "Thought stopping involves concentrating on the unwanted thoughts and, after a short time, suddenly stopping and emptying your mind. The command 'stop' or a loud noise is generally used to interrupt the unpleasant thoughts" (Davis, Eshelman, & McKay, 1988, p. 91). Key to mastering this method is a willingness to practice it on a regular basis.

Controlled dreaming. This method assists the co-victim with being able to take control of unpleasant or frightening dreams. It entails using techniques such as suggestion to become more aware while dreaming.

INDIVIDUAL THERAPY

Van der Kolk (1987) relates that most trauma victims benefit initially from some individual therapy. Individual therapy, however, can lead to dependency on the therapist, who is seen as having all the answers. Newer models of individual treatment cast the therapist in the role of a facilitator and return much of the control of the session to the co-victim. This empowers co-victims and allows them to work on their strengths instead of their weaknesses.

It would be ideal if most co-victims had access to individual therapy, but there are many barriers to this type of service delivery. Many co-victims feel stigmatized by individual therapy and are unwilling to seek it out or attend regularly. In addition, individual counseling requires the therapist to be skilled in both trauma and grief and bereavement issues as well as to be comfortable in presenting the counseling within a short-term focused intervention model. Thus, the cost of this approach can be quite prohibitive, especially if co-victims have no recourse to medical insurance. Even with medical coverage, managed care may severely limit the number of visits to a therapist. Most important, not many therapists currently in private practice specialize in working with crime victims, particularly co-victims of homicide. Much of this is because college-level and graduate course work is rarely directed toward crime victims. As more continuing education courses in this field become available, more skilled therapists will likely be available.

FAMILY THERAPY

Family therapy is recommended in conjunction with individual treatment but tends to be the intervention method least used with co-victims of homicide. Family work helps family members reorganize their roles, understandings, and expectations. "The family must accept the death of the loved one and reorder the kinship system so the life cycle can continue" (Getzel & Masters, 1984, p. 141).

As part of this systems perspective, genograms (diagrams of all persons in the family system, living and deceased) are a valuable tool in both initial family assessment and continuing treatment. Usually created during an intake session, the genogram provides a visual record of the family history and patterns and identifies all family members, sibling positions, roles and functions of family members, conflictual relationships, and members who have been cut off. Most important, it helps define family patterns, rules, lines of communication, and the availability of a support system for the survivor (Redmond, 1989). Using the standardized symbols developed by McGoldrick and Gerson (1989), genograms depict family patterns at a glance. It is also critical to ascertain if other family members have been murdered because this circumstance will have tremendous impact on the family's current grieving patterns.

The tasks of family therapy with co-victims of homicide may be different from those needed for working with other families. Recommended tasks to use with such families include these:

- Helping the family understand and put into perspective the rage and guilt they feel about their relative's murder
- Helping co-victims examine their grief reactions and other persons' availability to them so that they regain their confidence in the social order
- Helping the family accept the death of their relative as something irrevocable yet bearable
- Assisting members of the kinship system in establishing a new family structure that permits individual members to grow in a more healthy and fulfilling manner (Getzel & Masters, 1984, p. 141)

As discussed earlier, each family member has experienced a different relationship with the deceased, and each may be exhibiting grief or trauma in distinct ways. This should be taken into account when family systems therapy is initiated.

GROUP THERAPY

I went to the group because I couldn't talk to just family anymore. . . .
I realized that I was not alone, that there was a safe environment to

talk about the murder to a group of people who understand that it is
not possible to just move on. (Daughter of murder victim)

The use of informal peer support groups was co-opted from support groups for sexual assault and domestic abuse victims and has
been widely employed with homicide co-victims. The more formalized and structured therapy groups for homicide co-victims have
never been used as much as they might have been, to the detriment
of co-victims. The concept of therapy groups for co-victims is just
beginning to receive increased attention as an important and necessary adjunct to the other interventions.

Surviving When Someone You Love Was Murdered (Redmond, 1989)
is a good blueprint for running a group for homicide co-victims. Its
focus, however, although taking into account the traumatic aspects
of the murder, remains grief and bereavement oriented. Further
exploration of this method would make it possible to develop a
therapeutic structure that incorporates all aspects of the model of
traumatic grief.

Assessment. Co-victims are often admitted to groups too soon after
the murder. Redmond (1989) states that "if survivors are still in shock
and experiencing psychic numbness from the trauma, they are unable to relate or recognize the emotional process" (p. 58). The ideal
time for admission to the group appears to be 4 to 6 months following
the murder; this must be assessed for each co-victim, however.

Redmond (1989) recommends the use of a Grief Experience Inventory, or similar instrument, for all group programs. Such instruments
measure the co-victims' experience of grief and the intensity, frequency, and duration of bereavement symptoms, but not their experience of trauma. As discussed in the chapter on traumatic grief, a
separate instrument must be used to measure trauma until one is
developed that addresses both issues.

Techniques. The goal for group leaders, who are trained counselors
or therapists, is to coordinate and lead each group member into
individual confrontation and resolution of trauma and unresolved
grief issues. During therapy, the major tasks are to create and maintain cohesion, guide and direct the focus on trauma and grief issues,

and prevent constriction of affect. Group members have the opportunity to use one another as mirrors to reflect traumatic memories and feelings, providing a shared reliving of the murder event. A sense of community develops as members share their horror and other group members do not withdraw their emotional support. Tasks are accomplished by a series of processes that may include homework.

> Individual counseling just wasn't enough. I thought a group would help me release a lot of suppressed emotion. The feeling of aloneness temporarily fades during the group session. I've met people who really know firsthand how I feel. I've actually said things that I think have helped others. (Daughter of murder victim)

Some group processes including alternative therapies, such as guided imagery, may be conducted with the complete group. The therapy group is best accomplished by a 6- to 10-week series of 2-hour group therapy sessions.

The use of the therapy group is an intervention that should be receiving increased acceptance and use as new models are explored and developed. Victim assistance agencies may well be at the forefront of this effort if funding from sources such as the federal Victims of Crime Act (1984) can be funneled into this area.

SUPPORT GROUPS

> We formed our own peer support group because we were determined to help families like ours. In the group we get support and acceptance, we learn coping skills from each other, and we learn to survive! (Mother of murder victim)

Peer support groups are provided to *support* the co-victim, not to resolve conflicted issues or deal with corrective issues as in therapy groups. The group is therapeutic but is not therapy. Support groups were the first modality available to co-victims and were modeled after the support groups offered to other victims of crime. This environment is an excellent format to acknowledge the pain of loss and to gain knowledge of other systems. A peer support group

following the therapy group provides a bridge back into social relationships and a greater sense of community.

> I attended the group because I felt like I was losing myself in my grief.
> . . . It has helped to share my grief as well as experience theirs, being
> with others who have the same feelings, depression, and confusion
> that I have, knowing that others felt the same. (Friend of murder
> victim)

Support groups specifically for families of homicide victims can
provide a safe and understanding environment for members to share
experiences. Co-victims often feel alone in their grief, anguished with
feelings that only others with similar experiences can understand.
Running a support group can be problem-
atic for a victim assistance agency because it
is difficult to sustain attendance without a
great deal of patience and effort. It is less
complicated to develop a support group
than a therapy group, however, while still
providing an excellent intervention for co-
victims.

*In support groups,
co-victims can
acknowledge loss
and gain a sense of
community.*

> After the support group meeting, I slept well that night. It is helpful
> for me to know that I am not alone in my grief. (Mother of murder
> victim)

Support group guidelines. Persons setting up or running a homicide
support group should keep in mind several recommendations for an
effective group:

- Although such groups are referred to as "peer" support groups, it is
  advisable to have a trained leader who facilitates the group either alone
  or with a co-victim. A competent victim advocate or trauma therapist
  who is familiar with the issues of homicide, grief, and the criminal
  justice system can easily run the group. People who are employed in
  other fields or are graduate students in schools of social work or
  psychology can be trained as facilitators. The facilitator's role is to guide
  the group through the process while remembering that it is the
  co-victims who are the experts in the room, not the facilitator.

- The group should be structured so that its main function is to provide support while members work through the trauma and grief. The facilitator needs to work with the co-victims to keep the meeting focused. It should not be a gripe session regarding the criminal justice system. Concerns with the criminal justice system can be addressed in another forum, such as speaking about the problem after the meeting or referring the co-victim to a victim assistance agency, police, or prosecutor's office. A special meeting can be organized to include outside guests such as a detective or prosecutor who can answer questions and explain how the system works.

- Participants should be asked to commit to attend regularly. Trust in each other is a valuable part of the group process. If co-victims make a decision not to return to the support group, the facilitator should ask them to say goodbye to the other members.

- Prospective members should complete an assessment application to help determine whether this type of group process is appropriate. This application can incorporate some of the information that is required for therapy groups but does not have to be as in-depth. Because support groups are not intended to be therapeutic in content, more general information about the event, the family, and so on is all that is needed. The assessment can be completed by mail, over the phone, or in person. If the co-victim is not known to the agency, however, a face-to-face interview is helpful. Co-victims who have experienced serious pathologies or who have substance abuse problems may be disruptive to the group. Not everyone is ready for a support group, although there is no set time frame for when to begin. Attending a support group too soon after the murder may be harmful to some people. Allowing members of a family in which an intrafamily homicide has occurred to attend the same support group may lead to an uncontrollable situation. If it is necessary to turn somebody away, for whatever reason, offer other alternatives (counseling referral, etc.) or the opportunity to call back at a later time.

Format for support groups. In planning a homicide support group, it is best to structure the group to be 2 to 2½ hours long, including a short coffee hour afterward so that members can talk informally. The suggested format is a continuing, open-ended group. If the resources are available, however, an agency might want to consider starting new members in a short-term, close-ended informational group of four to six weekly sessions before they graduate to the open-ended group. Special groups or workshops can be offered for children, families with no-arrest cases, teens, siblings, men, and so forth as the need arises.

Postgroup follow-up. Follow-up calls should be made to participants after the first group meeting they attend, especially to participants who have seemed extremely upset by the meeting and those who have attended regularly and then miss several sessions. They may be frightened or upset by feelings that have emerged, both for themselves and for others, and have decided not to return. They need an opportunity to discuss these feelings in a nonjudgmental atmosphere and to formulate a decision about returning to the group.

The purpose of the follow-up is not to pressure co-victims to attend the meetings; rather, it is to assist in obtaining the best services to meet their needs. For example, a follow-up call could reveal that the reason for dropping out of the group was merely that the time or place of a meeting was inconvenient, so a referral to another group would be appropriate. If the feelings and experiences of the other group members were overwhelming for the co-victim, then a referral to individual therapy might be in order. This follow-up procedure, although time-consuming, will go a long way toward reducing dropouts, maintaining an active and viable support group, and ensuring that optimum services are provided to co-victims.

CRITICAL INCIDENT STRESS DEBRIEFING

One of the major techniques for intervening in a crisis such as a multiple murder or community disaster is the critical incident stress debriefing, also known as group crisis intervention. For example, debriefings were held in the Dahmer case in Minneapolis and after the Oklahoma City bombing. This team approach provides group debriefings for the direct and indirect victims of any large-scale disaster. Debriefings are usually conducted, whenever possible, within the first 72 hours after the event by a team of specially trained professionals. Concurrent debriefings should be held for different categories of those affected—victims and their loved ones, injured persons, eyewitnesses, rescuers, and the community at large. Group debriefings can assist in validating individual reactions, especially if like victims are debriefed together. This approach helps defuse emotional reactions that occur after an incident as well as identifies those victims who require additional professional assistance such as counseling.

NOVA, the American Red Cross, and the International Critical Incident Stress Foundation (see Resources) have recognized programs of crisis response that are used throughout the United States for group debriefings. The NOVA trainings are generally 24- to 40-hour programs focusing on special techniques of crisis intervention with individuals applied to the needs of a large group of traumatized people. NOVA's training manual of the crisis response team, *Responding to Communities in Crisis* (Young, 1994), is an excellent resource.

The goals of a group debriefing consist of the following: (a) helping the group define the crisis reaction, (b) providing crisis intervention to group members as needed, and (c) preparing the group for possible future events. During the debriefing sessions, group members are asked to talk about their experience during the traumatic events, describe what has happened to them in the aftermath of the event, predict the possible range of emotions they will feel in the days and months to come, and think about how they will deal with nightmares, intrusive thoughts, and other such stressors (Young, 1994).

INNOVATIVE THERAPIES

There is a great deal of interest in the innovative approaches to the treatment of trauma. Dr. Charles Figley (1996), director of the Florida State University Psychosocial Stress Research Program, has stated that new paradigms of treatment should be integrated into traditional work with victims of trauma, including co-victims of homicide. He has investigated and endorsed a number of new approaches in his recent groundbreaking study, "The Active Ingredients in Efficient Treatments of PTSD." Some of these interventions are being used in Oklahoma City for victims, co-victims, and caregivers.

Until now, most approaches to post-trauma stress reduction fell into two categories: coping techniques and cathartic techniques. These techniques may help a person feel better temporarily, but they do not resolve trauma so that it can no longer exert a negative effect on the co-victim (Gerbode, 1993). The "alternative" methods operate on the principle that a permanent resolution of trauma requires more than mere catharsis or coping skills. To do this, each method takes a client-centered viewpoint and, from that viewpoint, explains what makes trauma traumatic. No one technique is favored over the others, but some work better with different traumas and at different times. These methods are at once highly focused, directive, and controlled, yet noninterpretive and nonjudgmental. In competent hands, they are powerful tools for use in the rapid and successful resolution of virtually any trauma-related condition.

Training and supervision are available to counselors and therapists who wish to integrate innovative techniques with the more traditional forms of therapy. This allows co-victims to more quickly deal with trauma issues so they can move on to the next level of treatment and deal with grief issues. These innovative methods are meant not to supplant other methods but to add to the tools available to the therapist (see Table 6.4 for examples).

CHILD-SPECIFIC INTERVENTIONS

In "Treating Children Who Witness Violence," Newberger and Newberger (1992) assert that without effective intervention, a child may establish a lifelong pattern of aggressive behavior. They give the following guidelines for managing interventions with children:

1. The specific symptoms that a child is experiencing should be assessed within the context of whether that child was a direct or indirect victim of violence.
2. A family history should be taken, particularly if the homicide occurred within the context of the family. This background information helps not only to understand familial relationships but also to appreciate the present level of functioning of the other family members.
3. How the child deals with aggression should be ascertained. Children should be given the opportunity for positive emotional experiences through interactions with the therapist and other caring adults such as teachers and mentors.
4. Treatment issues should include the restoration of control to the child and focus on self-esteem and empowerment.
5. Parents or guardians may need individual counseling and treatment. At the least, they need to be involved in a collaborative relationship with the therapist or counselor.

There are a variety of ways to assist children in this difficult and painful period after the murder of a family member or friend. The greatest

TABLE 6.4 Innovative Treatment Methods

Traumatic incident reduction: This Rogerian-based treatment method follows a carefully crafted protocol that rapidly enables the client in a humane and empowering manner to retrieve important information about the nature and consequences of the traumatic event. (Florida State University, 1994)

Eye movement desensitization and reprocessing: This has received international acclaim as a "miracle treatment" by clinicians for its rapid treatment of a wide variety of phobia and PTSD symptoms. Clients are asked to focus on a goal from the treatment that not only eliminates the unwanted symptoms but generalizes to other areas (e.g., self-confidence). Clients then are asked to address certain circumstances associated with the traumatic event while the therapist induces rapid lateral eye movement. (Florida State University, 1994)

Guided imagery: Imagery is a mental representation of reality or fantasy. It encompasses all five modes of perception (visual, auditory, kinesthetic, olfactory, and gustatory). "Guided imagery is a therapeutic process whereby an individual harnesses his or her ability to imagine and utilize all of the senses. Through the creation of a self-selected image, the person can communicate with physiological processes of the body outside of conscious awareness" (Vines, 1988, p. 56). This can be used in group and individual settings with the co-victim working on traumatic images to reduce their power and ultimately their affect.

Neurolinguistic programming: This method employs a "fast phobia trauma cure procedure" (developed by Richard Bandler) that has the client, in a manner similar to the eye movement desensitization and reprocessing procedure, focus on the causal origin of the traumatic stress. It establishes a dissociation method that enables the client to eliminate all affect associated with the stressor. (Florida State University, 1994)

Thought field therapy: Similar to the previous approaches, thought field therapy involves rapid treatment of a client's various unwanted symptoms through a procedure that asks clients to concentrate on the symptom while performing a carefully prescribed muscle relaxation and stimulation procedure that directs various "thought fields" in a way that eliminates the symptoms. (Florida State University, 1994)

---

barrier to children's receiving the appropriate help is that the caregivers and other adults do not always fully recognize their need or accept that services must be continual according to the developmental levels of the child. Successful interventions with children include rebuilding and reestablishing relationships through loving and caring behaviors by adults, counseling, support groups, and school-based interventions.

Reestablishing Relationships

It is important for children to have a loving and caring environment provided by their families. Adults need to be able to spend extra time with children in the aftermath of a murder. Children also need to see evidence that their parents will soon be able to take care of and nurture them, especially if the parents are also co-victims.

Children should not be led to believe that the dead person is "sleeping" or has "gone away." This often causes confusion and mistrust. Children may begin to fear sleeping at night because they think that they might never awaken or may believe that the dead person will come back. In this case, children may feel abandoned, wondering why the dead person has left them without saying good-bye (Beckmann, 1990). Young children may ask the same questions repeatedly until they are able to process and understand all the information. Adults should be patient because they may have to respond many times to the same questions.

Therapy and Counseling

Child co-victims benefit from therapy because of the long-term effects that the murder will have on them throughout their development. Ideally, the child should be seen by a therapist who is skilled in the treatment of childhood trauma other than sexual abuse. If a child is to participate in the trial, the therapist can help the child become a better witness as well as ensure that the child's overall emotional well-being is considered. The murder of a family member or friend involves many grief and bereavement issues, but the initial focus of any intervention must deal with the trauma.

For older children and teenagers, the major developmental tasks for adolescents should be integrated within the counseling framework. These include (a) separating from family, (b) forming a healthy sexual identity, (c) preparing for the future, and (d) forging a moral value system (Prothrow-Stith, 1991).

Children frequently feel stigmatized by counseling, which may result in their being made the brunt of jokes by friends and classmates. It has been reported that children who have had a loved one murdered are teased by their classmates about the death. Going to counseling sometimes serves to reinforce the belief that they are bad or sick.

Support Groups

The use of support groups for children who are co-victims of homicide has not been as widespread as that for adults. Several reasons hinder the development and continuity of such groups: (a) Adults have the same resistance to bringing children to support groups as they do for bringing children to counseling, (b) children may feel stigmatized in going to a support group, (c) complicated logistics are involved for adults who usually have to physically bring their children, and (d) the hectic schedules of teens create an easy rationale for missing group meetings.

Currently, there seems to be increased interest in the establishment of support groups for children and teen co-victims. As more support groups are established, there will be a concurrent need for additional research to learn the best methodology to use with such groups as well as to determine the efficacy of these groups.

Children as young as 4 or 5 years of age can benefit from a support group. Support groups for young children should be limited to four to six children and can include siblings. Parents may join in the session with the younger children or attend another group with other adults that meets at the same time.

Children's support groups need to be both participatory and experiential because some children may not be able to verbalize their feelings and will need activities or tools to initiate the dialogue (Beckmann, 1990). Worksheets, games, play therapy, role play, skits, puppets, writing, music, storytelling, and art should be integrated into a specific support group format for children.

A child's readiness for a support group needs to be assessed by the group leader in conjunction with the child's parents. Involving parents early in the process will give the group leader valuable information and will, it is hoped, enlist support in maintaining the child's attendance at every group session. Beckmann (1990) recommends from 6 to 12 months after the murder before a child should become involved in a group.

Older children and teen groups can focus on writing stories and poems using drama or physical activity to express their grief. Teens may be more interested in participating if they can get involved in a project such as developing a violence prevention program for their school. Linking teens with younger children is also a viable project.

School-Based Interventions

Workers need to recognize the dynamic interaction of the individual child, the classroom, and the school environment (Haran, 1988). Someone who is already employed within the school system may be asked to serve as a resource. Outside workers must recognize the boundaries that exist in the school and must work within this system. Collaboration with administration, parents, teachers, the classroom group, and individual students is essential for successful school-based interventions.

The classroom is a potential mutual aid system that has the ability to solve problems, make decisions, and provide mutual support (Haran, 1988). The worker's role is to facilitate and mediate the intervention process and encourage the sharing of information. The classroom itself can be viewed as a support group, encompassing all the issues and responsibilities described above.

As discussed earlier, crisis intervention stress debriefing is effective within the school setting to provide a group response to those children who have experienced a severe trauma. Recently, this form of intervention has been used to address the needs of children when a classmate or teacher has been killed. It is quite practical because large groups of children can be simultaneously involved. As more personnel get training in group crisis intervention and apply the model to schools, the use of intervention will become more prevalent. School districts should consider training crisis debriefing teams with linkages to already existing community-based teams. Established on a proactive rather than a reactive basis, this tool will be available to schools as soon as the need arises.

Memorial services can be integrated within the group crisis intervention or presented separately. The children should be included in both the planning process and presentation of memorial programs. They may write poems or stories, draw pictures, plant a tree, or create some other permanent memorial. The family of the victim may be invited to be present or participate in the program as well.

School systems may also want to consider the benefits of violence prevention in addition to intervention programs. Research indicates that violence is a learned behavior. School-based programs already in place throughout the United States, such as the Student Anti-Violence Education Program (SAVE) in Philadelphia, indicate that children can learn alternative responses to violence through special curricula and by modeling positive behavior.

PHARMACOLOGICAL ISSUES

Psychiatrists are medical doctors who are the most skilled physicians in prescribing medication for mental health problems. There are also psychiatrists who specialize in pharmacology, the study of drugs and their uses, and are referred to as psychopharmacologists. This category of psychiatry evaluates the need for medication and prescribes and monitors its use but may not be involved in providing therapy or counseling. When considering the use of medication in the aftermath of a homicide, the psychiatrist or the psychopharmacologist is probably the best candidate for referrals. The psychiatrist can do an assessment that includes the co-victim's emotional state as well as the existence of any other medical problems. If medication is indicated, the psychiatrist can arrange to regularly monitor all prescriptions. The co-victim and the psychiatrist can also discuss the need for counseling and who would be the best provider.

I began seeing a psychologist one week after the murder. I was evaluated for medication and began taking Trazadone for depression and Ativan for anxiety and panic attacks. I have been on the medication for 9 months. (Daughter of murder victim)

Pros and Cons of Medication

I refused medication from the start. I did not want to compound what
I was going through. (Girlfriend of murder victim)

Many co-victims' actions and behaviors can be attributed to the
experience of traumatic grief, but they also may be masked or exacerbated by antianxiety and antidepressant medications. It is quite
appropriate for a victim advocate or other caregiver to ask co-victims,
in the aftermath of the homicide, if they are seeing a physician and if
any medication has been prescribed. If the answer is in the affirm-
ative, the caregiver should determine whether the doctor who prescribed the medication is a general practitioner or a therapist. Self-
prescribed medication, including alcohol and drugs, is another issue
of concern to the caregiver. If the use of medication appears to be
problematic, other referrals can be suggested. Many co-victims are
prescribed medication by a primary care physician without an explanation or monitoring of the side effects and the possible interactions
with other medications or alcohol. The co-victim is rarely afforded
an opportunity to make an informed choice about medication.

Having a loved one murdered, whatever the circumstances, is one
of the most terrible events that life can present, and it is impossible
to avoid enduring the pain. Keeping co-victims so heavily medicated
that they remain sedated for long periods on antianxiety medication
does not permit the grief work to commence and can cause the entire
grief process to be sidetracked or even circumvented. Heavy reliance
on medication, especially in the early days of the grief process, can
lead to delayed or unresolved grief. The rule of thumb for many
practitioners seems to be that feelings of pain must be avoided at all
costs.

Victim advocate: Are you having any difficulty sleeping?
Mother of a murdered child: No, I sleep too much, I seem to sleep
   all the time.
Advocate: Are you seeing a doctor?
Mother: Yes, the day my son died from the beating that he got from
   those boys my husband took me to our doctor.
Advocate: Did the doctor give you any medicine?

Mother: Yes, she gave me Ativan [an antianxiety medication], and
I have been taking it ever since [6 weeks]. I just call her every
week, and she renews my prescription.

Difficult as it is to experience and to witness, there is no other way
to handle the pain but to go through it. Many of these medications,
which have numerous side effects, may cloud the issue. It is often
difficult to ascertain if the co-victim is experiencing the pain and grief
as a result of the murder or whether the presenting symptoms are
induced by the medication.

Although a co-victim may be medicated with the wrong dosages
or with the incorrect medication, there are also errors in the other
direction. There are some co-victims for whom antianxiety or antidepressant medications may be helpful, and the co-victims may not be
getting the help they need.

> "You've got to give me something," I begged. "I have to take some-
> thing. I can't stand it anymore! I'm losing my mind! Give me a pill!"
>   "No," [the therapist] said simply.
>   "Please! I've got to get rid of it! . . . I can't do it on my own. A pill
> *please!*"
>   "Your daughter is dead. That hurts. You're feeling the pain. You
> *have* to feel it! And you *have* to stand it! That's the way it is."
>   "No pills."
>   "No pills," she said. "You have to feel it sooner or later. It may as
> well be now." (Spungen, 1983, p. 408)

The use of such drugs is not without merit and may be indicated,
even necessary, in certain situations—the co-victim is suffering from
extreme and debilitating distress or anxiety or cannot sleep, or the
stress is exacerbating a preexisting medical condition. Another example of the beneficial use of medications is in the treatment of clinical
depression in co-victims. As previously mentioned, clinical depression, not just the sadness of mourning, is commonly diagnosed in
many co-victims of homicide. Although there is some controversy
about the efficacy of antidepressant medication as opposed to "talk
therapy," the use of antidepressants with this victim population can
be quite helpful in relieving the worst symptoms and restoring
co-victims to a higher level of functioning.

I was prescribed medication on the day the murder happened, for anxiety and to help me sleep. (Mother of murder victim)

Medications, however, cannot be thought of as a panacea and should not be used to avoid dealing with the pain and grief. The prescribing of medications must be considered as only one of an array of interventions to use with co-victims of homicide.

Implications for Caregivers

The issues of mental disorders and the prescribing of drugs are of major importance in the treatment of co-victims of homicide. Many caregivers who have contact with co-victims of homicide will not be in a position, because of their disciplines and training, to evaluate or prescribe in these areas. Any caregiver who assists co-victims, however, has an obligation to determine the best ways to provide for their needs. There is opportunity for considerable abuse that can result in unnecessary pain and problems for the co-victims. Irresponsible use of medications can mean an additional second wound for co-victims, a wound over which they may have little or no control.

I've been taking Xanax and Prozac for years, others before that, I don't remember what, they didn't work. (Mother of murder victim)

The education of caregivers who are in a position to be involved in these issues and can influence the well-being of co-victims must become a priority. Physicians, especially primary care providers, are generally not well trained in the area of grief and bereavement, especially traumatic grief, and they are often not well versed in the areas of pharmacology that involve antidepressants, antianxiety drugs, and hypnotics (sleeping medication). Physicians should be given such training as a regular part of their medical school curriculum. Primary care providers may be hesitant in referring patients to specialists such as psychiatrists because they may not see it as necessary. The increasing reliance on managed care can be a serious barrier to outside referrals. The emergence of managed care, especially in the area of mental health problems, serves to emphasize the critical role of the primary care physicians and the need for them to receive better training in these issues.

While taking these medications, the patient should be strictly monitored regarding symptoms, dosage, and the length of time that the medication is taken. It is not uncommon for the client to be overmedicated and to be kept on the drug for longer than needed. On the other hand, this person may be undermedicated, making the drug ineffective. Renewals of the prescription should not be routinely written without an evaluation of the co-victim's condition and other influencing factors. A brief telephone conversation between the physician and co-victim should not be the sole basis for renewing these medications. Long-term use of many of these medications can lead to addiction.

Victim advocate: Has your doctor prescribed any medication for you since the murder?
Mother of a murdered child: Yes, Valium.
Advocate: How much?
Mother: He told me to take 5 milligrams every time that I feel upset.
Advocate: How much are you taking every day?
Mother: About 40 milligrams.
Advocate: How long have you been taking that dose of Valium?
Mother: Four months. When I run out, I just call my doctor, and he renews the prescription.

Service providers, depending on their own specialties and training, will have to be alert to the onset of problems for which they are not trained or comfortable in handling. They should be open to collaborating with other caregivers and mental health professionals as resources and for referrals. Victim advocates and other caregivers can prepare referral lists of qualified psychiatrists and other mental health professionals and make them available to co-victims. Referral lists can be built by calling hospitals, asking other co-victims and clients, asking mental health professionals, networking with colleagues, and calling the local county medical society. The lists should include specialists in grief and bereavement issues as well as in trauma. A good starting point for trauma specialists is the nearest Veterans Administration hospital or Vietnam veterans' center. It is helpful to hold a brief telephone interview with mental health professionals before placing them on a referral list to confirm that this is the type of patient seen in their practice and that they are available to take new patients. Co-victims should be given two or three names as referrals and make the decision about which doctor they wish to visit. Caregivers can only make referrals; co-victims have the right to follow up or not as they choose.

The above discussion is intended only as a guide and is not meant to supplant or replace the expertise of a physician. The matter of medication is quite complicated because it revolves not only around grief and bereavement issues but around gender questions as well. Physicians, victim advocates, and other caregivers need to be informed about these issues and be willing to educate co-victims and, if necessary, to suggest appropriate referrals. The main caveat is that judicious use of medications in the hands of a competent doctor can be helpful by assisting co-victims to find their own unique pathway through the process of reconstructing their lives.

❏ **Summary**

In the past, the array of interventions used with co-victims of homicide has been limited in scope. As caregivers become more knowledgeable about traumatic grief, there is a concurrent need to devise additional interventions to respond to the needs of co-victims. The design of these interventions must result from research that focuses specifically on the traumatic grief model. It is important to determine not only what works and what does not but also its efficacy through time. Too often, interventions for co-victims of homicide have continued to be used on the basis of anecdotal observations without concrete data.

Needed also is the development of assessment tools to determine the extent of traumatic grief of co-victims. Without such instruments, it is difficult for caregivers to determine what interventions to employ. Assessments that measure the effects of trauma and the effects of grief as isolated entities are unsatisfactory.

It is the responsibility of all caregivers who deliver services to the co-victims of homicide—victim advocates, clinicians, police, and so on—to serve as advocates for co-victims. This may mean pressing for the development of new and effectual means of serving co-victims, advocating for better quality and availability of services, and exercising case and system advocacy on behalf of individual co-victims and groups of co-victims.

7

Justice for All:
Do Co-Victims Have Legal Rights?

Interest in homicide has been historically focused on the murderer, not the victim or co-victim. The criminal justice system is defendant driven because it derives from the adversarial English common law system, which pits the state against the defendant. The system plays out a murder case in a series of steps that are controlled, prescribed, and guaranteed under the law and, furthermore, are concerned only with the defendant's apprehension, arrest, prosecution, and punishment. Prosecutors and defense attorneys tend to view the murder trial as a game, with winning as the desired outcome; everything else, including the welfare of the victim, is secondary.

The file in a murder case will read, the *State of _____ v. John or Jane Doe* (the defendant)—the victim's name does not appear on any of the legal documents. Viewed from this perspective, homicide could be a victimless crime. Photographs of the victim as a living person are usually banned from the courtroom; only pictures taken after the murder are permissible. This indifference is a hurtful shock to the many co-victims who have believed that the criminal justice system is a responsible, caring institution.

> Throughout the 10 months from murder to verdict, I felt that as a victim, I had no rights. I was at the mercy of the dictates of the court and the whim of the defendant, his lawyer, and some other ridiculous motion that had been filed. It seemed that the criminal had all the rights, I had none. The final blow was dealt when the jury returned a verdict of not guilty on all charges. I learned that the only justice in the system was for the criminal. (Girlfriend [and witness] of murder victim)

It is crucial for caregivers to review the various criticisms levied against the system regarding racial, cultural, and class biases and examine the impact of these on the co-victim. Some of this distrust of the system is warranted, and some of it may be the result of a co-victim's misperceptions. Some criticisms can be attributed to the crossover effect of a long-standing history in the justice system of racial, cultural, and class biases against defendants. If caregivers have not received cultural sensitivity training, they may not see the complexity of these issues. Caregivers should act as watchdogs for biased acts perpetrated against co-victims and actively seek to modify the system in a positive way. Co-victims expect, and deserve, to have the criminal justice system provide them with justice, a rather subjective term that might be otherwise translated as satisfaction. If their attempts to get justice are frustrated, they feel further harmed and, hence, receive a second wound.

The sociolegal model of service delivery presented here is intended as a resource for caregivers. They need to understand the nuances of the criminal justice system to provide co-victims with tools of support in this stage of their journey. All caregivers must be knowledgeable about legal issues to play their role, although victim advocates are most likely to guide co-victims in the aftermath of a murder. It is heartening to see that it is no longer an anomaly for a co-victim to be accompanied to court by a social worker.

> Three trials, two hung juries, one acquittal. It didn't work for me. I *know* the defendant was guilty, and I'm still waiting for the other shoe to drop. (Mother of murder victim)

The information in this chapter provides an overview of two areas: (a) the criminal justice system and its key players and (b) legal issues such as civil suits, victims' rights, and related legislation. Although there are differences in legal procedures and variations in victims' rights legislation from state to state, the following material focuses on the basic systems and philosophies that affect co-victims. Service providers will need to familiarize themselves with the regulations of the jurisdictions in which they work.

❏ The Criminal Justice System

Co-victims are surprised and dismayed to discover that the district attorney or prosecutor does not "represent" them or the murder victim. Many co-victims ask, "Where is my attorney?" A private attorney can be hired, but this is usually not necessary. The private attorney has no official function and cannot sit at the prosecutor's table unless invited to do so. An experienced victim service provider can provide the same service: advocacy for the victim and co-victims.

Co-victims have no legal standing unless they witnessed the murder.

Historically, co-victims have no legal standing in the case unless they were witness to the murder. They have been unwelcome participants in the criminal justice process and have been seen as irrelevant to the prosecution. The development of legal rights and services for all victims of crime has empowered co-victims with acknowledgment and a voice, albeit a small one. As a result of new policies, legislation, and advocacy by victim service providers, the criminal justice system has become more concerned about the needs and rights of co-victims and has made these issues a higher priority.

Much has been accomplished, but real change is slow to implement. Many criminal justice personnel come from a background of bureaucratic hierarchy, which is most resistant to instituting new standards of service delivery.

You feel helpless because the state takes control of the investigation even though the state never helped pay for any of his expenses, college, clothing, shelter, etc., when he was growing up. (Mother of murder victim)

The criminal justice system is a confusing maze to most co-victims. Caregivers play a critical role in guiding co-victims through the criminal justice system by performing the following tasks: (a) educating co-victims to the idiosyncrasies of the system, which includes providing information and tools to enable them to navigate the system and act as self-advocates; (b) supporting co-victims throughout the process with court accompaniment and attendance at court proceedings; and (c) acting as a liaison between co-victims and the criminal justice system to obtain factual and timely information about the status of their cases. These efforts lessen the anxiety and trauma of co-victims by reducing their feelings of loss of control and, thus, decrease the impact of the second wound.

OVERVIEW OF THE SYSTEM

Figure 7.1 provides a flow chart of the stages of the criminal justice system and services to be provided at each stage. This section discusses some of the more relevant issues that affect co-victims.

First Listings

Court accompaniment at first listings, where a co-victim is permitted to be present, is significant. A caregiver should try to be present at this critical point in the process. This hearing can be an emotional experience because it usually comes soon after the murder. It may be the first time that the co-victim will face the defendant, and it introduces the co-victim to the criminal justice system.

The purpose of the first listing is to determine whether the defendant can be held over for trial by answering the following questions: "Has a crime been committed?" and "Does the evidence show that the defendant may have committed the crime?" The type of first listing depends on the jurisdiction and the circumstances of the case.

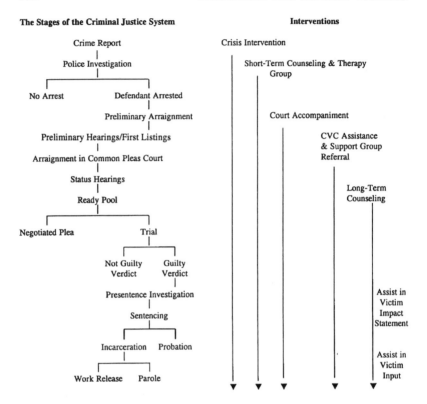

Figure 7.1. Stages of the Criminal Justice System and Interventions

It may be in the form of a preliminary hearing or may be held before a grand jury. Some grand juries may be held without any spectators permitted, whereas others allow victims or co-victims to attend.

Victim Witness Waiting Area

Many courthouses now provide a designated and secure space for victims and witnesses of crime. Co-victims should be encouraged to make use of the waiting room before and after court sessions or simply as a place for a quiet respite. Co-victims may be reluctant to use the waiting room when court is in session from fear they will miss something important. If a reliable procedure is in place to inform co-victims of the courtroom schedule, caregivers may explain it and reassure them that it is reliable. If a secure waiting area is unavailable, helping professionals should actively advocate for one.

Sequestration of Witnesses

[Sequestration] involves keeping witnesses apart from one another and outside the courtroom. It is frequently ordered by the court at the request of one of the parties in order to insure that the in-court testimony of each witness not be colored by what another witness says. (Gifis, 1984, p. 438)

This common law rule is often manipulated by defense attorneys who use it to keep the co-victims out of the courtroom and out of sight of the jury. Often, the co-victims are not true witnesses in the case but may be subpoenaed because the defense attorney states that the co-victims have some relevant information to add to the case. The co-victims must then remain outside the courtroom until their testimony is given. Sequestration can be extended when the defense attorney states that the co-victims might be called back to the stand later in the trial. Co-victims who want to be in the courtroom are usually upset about being sequestered. Caregivers will have to advocate to the prosecutor or the judge regarding sequestration. If this does not yield a positive result, then the co-victims will need extra support and an opportunity to vent their anger and frustration.

Pleas

At any time after the arraignment, the defendant can plead guilty to committing the crime. Plea bargains can occur right up to the start of the trial. If the judge accepts the guilty plea, there will be no trial. The defendant can be sentenced when the plea is given, or the court may set a later date for sentencing. A prosecutor may be interested in negotiating a plea for many reasons, including the reality that the system is overwhelmed with too many cases and the economies of not having to hold a trial. Each prosecutor's office handles plea bargains differently, especially with regard to the involvement of the co-victims in the process.

The issue of plea bargains in homicide cases is of great concern to most co-victims. A prime example of the criminal justice system's inflicting a second wound occurs when a plea is negotiated without the co-victim's prior knowledge or consultation.

> I feel more angry because she chose not to go to trial and just plead guilty before the grand jury. . . . They said she plea-bargained for life imprisonment, but I don't know if she's been sentenced. (Friend of murder victim)

Co-victims deserve to be honestly informed about this matter and to have some input, either in person or in writing. Some states already have victims' rights legislation that guarantees a co-victim's right to be heard at this stage. The pending federal constitutional amendment, discussed in the final section of this chapter, will give co-victims this right. At present, the final decision always rests with the prosecutor's office.

Continuances

A hearing or trial may be postponed for a variety of reasons—some good, some poor, and some puzzling. Cases may be repeatedly continued. This is the rule throughout the entire U.S. criminal justice system. Preparation of co-victims for this eventuality eases the resulting pain and frustration. Co-victims deserve an explanation about the reasons for the postponement. Caregivers may be able to intercede in the system when they feel that the continuances are unwarranted or too numerous.

> The preliminary hearing had been postponed six times for a myriad of reasons. Twenty members of the murder victim's family had come to each of the hearing dates, and each time they had been denied. By the sixth hearing, their emotional state was a terrible mix of pain, grief, sadness, anger, and frustration. I went over to the office of the presiding judge of the lower court. He took immediate steps to remedy the situation and wrote a letter to me which he urged that I share with the co-victims. The hearing did go on at the next date. The family was gratified by the judge's involvement, but that did not erase the wound that they received from an unresponsive and uncaring justice system. (Spungen, personal experience)

Insanity Defense

When attorneys begin to talk about competency hearings and an insanity defense, co-victims fear that justice will not be served. Some of these trepidations come from the stereotypical legacy of the insanity defense—that it will be used by a perpetrator to get away with murder. There is always a likelihood, although more remote now than in the past, that a defendant who is rich, well connected, or simply clever can fabricate mental illness as a way of avoiding the consequences of committing a violent act.

The laws governing the insanity defense vary greatly from state to state, complicating an already complex issue. As prosecutors, legislators, and juries have become less tolerant of violent crime, many states have rewritten their laws to severely limit insanity as a defense. Some states have completely abolished the use of the insanity defense, whereas a number have added new categories, such as "guilty but mentally ill." Competency is a legal mechanism to determine if defendants can understand the proceedings and assist the lawyers in their own defense. Proving defendants incompetent to stand trial has become increasingly difficult in every jurisdiction.

If competency becomes an issue in a co-victim's case, education in the applicable law should be provided by both the victim advocate and the prosecutor. If an insanity defense is employed, the co-victim should be prepared for all possible outcomes.

The Death Penalty

One of the most perplexing and controversial issues in the legal system today is the death penalty. Almost everyone has a strong opinion about the death penalty, an opinion that may be modified after a person becomes a co-victim. A commonly held misperception is that all co-victims would like to see the defendant responsible for killing their loved one executed. This is far from the truth, particularly in states in which the criminal code includes a sentence of true life without parole.

As of January 8, 1997, according to the Death Penalty Information Center in Washington, D.C., 38 states currently allow the death penalty (L. Bartle, personal communication, January 8, 1997). The case must meet certain criteria that are carefully delineated by the law. The determination to ask for the death penalty is usually arrived at by the chief prosecutor, the chief of the homicide unit, and the attorney who is prosecuting the case. Co-victims are typically not consulted because their wishes and opinions have no bearing on the matter. Many co-victims may be displeased by the death penalty decision because of their lack of understanding of the law and their obvious emotional involvement.

Another concern relating to the death penalty is attendance at the execution. If co-victims philosophically agree with the decision, they sometimes request to be present at the execution. The Death Penalty Information Center reports that co-victims are presently permitted to attend in only two states, Oklahoma and Washington. Co-victims usually are not otherwise specifically barred, but the final decision is reached by administrative hearing (L. Bartle, personal communication, January 8, 1997).

> *The effective caregiver remains neutral and nonjudgmental about the death penalty.*

> Mr. Vicker is still haunted by the assault [rape], he said, and he hopes that the execution will bring some relief.... After seeing Mr. Bonin die, he said he hopes: "It will make a big difference. He'll be dead in my eyes, in my mental videotape." ... Ms. Miller, too, said she expected a sense of closure from Mr. Bonin's death. At the moment before the injection, she said, she will be seeing her dead son Rusty in her mind and thinking, "Rusty, it's almost over. He's finally going to pay, Rusty." (Goldberg, 1996, p. A14)

It can be difficult for caregivers to deal with the co-victim's extreme emotion and pain, especially when there are conflicting feelings about the death penalty. This can unnecessarily strain the helping relationship. The most effective caregiver is one who is able to remain neutral and nonjudgmental, even when not sharing the same philosophy regarding the outcome as the co-victim. The co-victim does not have to be concerned with the opinion of the caregiver, whose primary role is to educate, inform, guide, and support the co-victim.

If neutrality is not possible, then the intervenor needs to talk to a supervisor or coworker and arrange for another service provider.

COURT ORIENTATION

Orientation is needed to acquaint co-victims with the manner in which cases progress through the system, to explain the players and their roles, and to define commonly used legal terms. Co-victims are typically anxious before court proceedings, especially before the trial. Court orientation helps predict what will occur, both legally and emotionally, and prepare co-victims for the ordeal. This is extremely helpful in reducing their anxiety.

Some of the concerns, questions, and issues that trouble co-victims may seem irrelevant to caregivers. No matter how insignificant the issues seem, they should be explored. Some questions regarding courtroom procedures should be referred to the prosecutor or the police. Many concerns of co-victims will be more practical than technical. The best advice for surviving a courtroom trial came from a co-victim who was assisting a fellow co-victim: "Bring a small pillow to sit on because the seats are hard and uncomfortable."

Formal and Informal Sessions

Service providers can educate co-victims to the criminal justice process through formal or informal means. Mental health professionals may want to consider accompanying their clients to court to learn how the system works and to better understand the emotional implications to the co-victims. Helping professionals can rely on available community resources or design innovative programs to introduce co-victims to the court system. The ideal situation is a formal court orientation program administered by a victim advocate agency or the court system. If neither exists in the jurisdiction, it may be possible to obtain funding to develop such a program. This is a prime opportunity to involve graduate interns, particularly social work students. A number of jurisdictions have orientation programs for child abuse victims that can be used as models. A formal court

TABLE 7.1 Court Orientation Guidelines

- *Purpose:* Clearly state and reiterate that the purpose of the court orientation is to provide generic information about the criminal justice system, not to provide insights into specific homicide cases. Provide co-victims with specific case information in another forum.
- *Scheduling:* Schedule sessions on a regular basis: monthly, bimonthly, or quarterly (depending on need). Offer sessions to co-victims as early in the process as possible. Sessions held later in the day are usually more convenient for co-victims to attend.
- *Handbook:* Develop a written handbook to accompany any formal court orientation. Co-victims will not remember everything they hear, and in the event that a formal session is not available, the handbook can be used as an informal overview of the system.
- *Location:* Hold court orientation sessions in an actual courtroom whenever possible. This familiarizes co-victims with the setup and atmosphere.
- *Length:* Limit sessions to 2½ hours; this is usually long enough to cover the basic information. Allow time for breaks and questions.
- *Facilitator:* Select a facilitator who is a neutral party (usually a victim advocate), rather than someone who is directly involved in the criminal justice system.
- *Content:* Organize information with a planned time frame for each topic, otherwise all information may not get covered. The following topics should always be included: (a) purpose of the orientation, (b) co-victims' rights, (c) definitions of legal terms, (d) overview and description of participants in the criminal justice system, and (e) approximate time frames for each stage of the process. Information should always be customized to the jurisdiction.
- *Invitations:* Ask appropriate co-victims who are seeking general information about the system to attend; also ask homicide detectives and prosecutors who can answer questions.
- *Evaluations:* Provide co-victims with an opportunity to evaluate the sessions. This allows caregivers to make any necessary programmatic changes and respond to any individual concerns or problems.

---

orientation program should be structured around the guidelines listed in Table 7.1.

A great deal of effort should be invested in inviting co-victims to the session and following up on their intentions to attend. This may

TABLE 7.2 Court Orientation Handbook

The following information should be included:

- Legal terms and definitions
- Overview of the criminal justice process
- Diagram of the courthouse, including locations of courtrooms, victim waiting areas, rest rooms, and elevators
- Diagram of a courtroom, including the official participants and their usual placements in the room
- Map showing location of courthouse in relation to parking lots, public transportation, and local restaurants and stores
- Crime victim compensation information and application forms
- Helpful phone numbers and addresses (i.e., district attorney's office, victim advocate agency)
- Information on handling the media
- Support group information
- Suggested reading list
- Blank paper for important information such as prosecutor's name, judge's name, and courtroom number

---

be accomplished by letter, and written material should be distributed to co-victims at the first point of contact. Co-victims' expectations and goals for attendance, as well as the expectations of the agency offering the orientation, should be discussed to ascertain if the two perspectives coincide. One co-victim complained, "I didn't like the court orientation because they told me that the killer of my son would only get 5 to 10 years for the murder." She had confused the message with the messenger and did not understand that the purpose of the session was to help her prepare for the court process and potential results of the trial.

An informal orientation can also be employed to familiarize the co-victim with the criminal justice system by use of written informa-tion, such as the handbook mentioned in Table 7.1. Table 7.2 lists the suggested content of such a handbook. When possible, co-victims can visit another murder trial in progress. Real murder trials usually do not resemble the television or movie versions, especially when co-victims have a personal involvement and stake in the proceedings. Being present in court, whether at a formal session or at an informal visit to a real courtroom, familiarizes the victim with the surroundings and depersonalizes the criminal justice process.

Child-Specific Orientations

If children are eyewitnesses to the murder of a parent, they will probably need to be prepared for court proceedings. If children are witnesses against a parent who is the defendant, the children must face issues of allegiance and guilt, as well as loss. Older children are especially affected because they understand that they can tell the story in such a way that implicates one parent more than the other (Eth & Pynoos, 1985a). In addition, as Pynoos and Eth (1985) found, child witnesses experience intense feelings of guilt connected to their imagined failures to intervene, and they often blame themselves for not having done more or for having acted cowardly.

> While preparing to testify at the trial of the murderer of her mother, father, and sister, 6-year-old Pat told her therapist, "I was a bad girl because I did not do enough to help my mommy and daddy and sister. If I had, then we would all be together now." (Spungen, personal experience)

Direct child co-victims, especially those who are required to be witnesses in court, need the assistance of a therapist who is skilled in the treatment of childhood trauma other than sexual abuse. A competent therapist can work with children not only to help make them better witnesses but also to help ensure their overall emotional well-being after participation in the process. Therapists should meet with children before the trial to prepare them on all levels. Furthermore, trauma and grief issues may reappear in the immediate pretrial period and must be dealt with in the context of the trial.

The prosecutor's office may allow child co-victims of homicide to attend a formal "court school" program intended to prepare child abuse victims. These sessions are designed to lessen children's anxiety about being in court. The inclusion of parents or caretakers can be helpful so that they know what to expect and how to deal with their children's reactions. If court school is not available, children ought to visit the courtroom to get acquainted with the physical environment. Children should be allowed to sit in the witness chair and role-play the part of those who will be serving in the courtroom, such as the judge, the court officers, the court reporter, and the prosecutor.

A collaborative effort between therapists, prosecutors, and others in the criminal justice system provides an optimum situation. Some courts will work cooperatively with prosecutors and therapists to postpone court hearings until the child is emotionally able to face the rigors of appearing as a witness. While the therapist works with the child, the prosecutor needs to establish trust and rapport with the child.

Children as young as 4 years of age have taken the stand when they were the only witnesses to a parental murder and were deemed necessary to the case. The special legal arrangements and safeguards afforded by law to children in child abuse cases are not usually extended to those children who witness murder. A caring and sensitive prosecutor, however, can provide child witnesses with the support and information needed to make them good witnesses at the trial, while at the same time safeguarding them on an emotional level.

COURT ACCOMPANIMENT

Court accompaniment should be initially offered at a first listing and should be available throughout the criminal justice process. Depending on the jurisdiction, in addition to first listings, accompaniment to court may include bail or competency hearings, status listings, trials, sentencing hearings, and posttrial hearings.

The co-victim's presence reminds the court that the victim was a real person.

The presence of the co-victim in the courtroom serves as a reminder for the judge and the jury that the murder victim was once a real living person. Not every co-victim wants to attend the court proceedings, but most do. Most co-victims report that although it proves difficult to be in the courtroom, it is even more difficult not to be present.

> It has been difficult for Alexander and Danielle to deal with both the
> loss of their father and my continued absence due to the legal proceed-
> ings. However, I will be attending all of the legal proceedings because
> it is important to me that David is represented and remembered during
> this process. (Vigoda, 1996, p. A1)

Prosecutors generally encourage the co-victim to be present in
court, but a co-victim should never be made to feel obligated or
coerced to attend or not attend. Caregivers can assist the co-victim in
arriving at a decision by providing as much pertinent information as
possible. On the other hand, many co-victims may feel pressured by
family and friends not to attend. They are told, "It's maudlin," "It's
sick," "You don't need to do that." Caregivers should support co-victims
in their decision. A co-victim should be encouraged to respond to
unsolicited advice, counsel, and comments by stating, for example,
"I hear your concern, but I have made up my mind to attend. I'd
appreciate it if you would support me in my decision."

> We attended the trial to know what was happening and to let the jurors
> know that Lewis had family and was loved and very much missed. . . .
> If I hadn't gone and someone told me that 12 people found him
> innocent, I wouldn't have believed it. (Mother of murder victim)

Knowing that a service provider will be in the courtroom throughout the proceedings relieves much of the co-victim's anxiety. The
primary role of the caregiver who provides court accompaniment is
to offer support and guidance through the criminal justice process.
Under certain circumstances, the caregiver may also be called on to
act as an advocate on behalf of the co-victim. Additional support can
be provided by the presence of family members and friends.

During court proceedings, the caregiver should be alert to safety
and security issues. This might include shielding co-victims from
unwanted intrusions of the media or protecting them from possible
harassment from the defendant's family and friends. The caregiver's
responsibility is to assess a potentially threatening or dangerous
situation and, if necessary, ask for assistance from police, court
officers, or sheriff's deputies.

In addition, advocates need to prepare co-victims for upcoming
testimony and evidence so that they can decide whether to stay in

the courtroom. For example, without proper preparation, co-victims may find the medical examiner's presentation too trying. Co-victims should always be allowed to make their own choices. Having a choice is empowering and often provides the emotional strength to endure the courtroom testimony.

There are rules governing behavior and decorum in a courtroom. The co-victim's demeanor will be carefully scrutinized by the court officers, the judge, the defense attorney, and the jury. A co-victim should be apprised of this beforehand and encouraged to act accordingly. Refusing to adhere by the rules may jeopardize the prosecutor's case or result in permanent removal from the courtroom. Some behaviors that may be offensive are crying openly, verbal outbursts, and gestures. Helping professionals should be alert to signs of potential problems and accompany co-victims out of the courtroom if necessary.

If a limited number of service providers are available for court accompaniment, victim service agencies may be forced to make difficult decisions. Caregivers may feel the stress of being pulled in a number of directions at once. For example, when some members of the family are in the courtroom and some are outside, it is difficult for intervenors to know where and when their services are most essential. Cases may be prioritized depending on the particular needs of co-victims. Criteria for making these decisions include whether a co-victim is alone or has a supportive cadre of family and friends, the emotional state of the co-victim, and special circumstances of the murder or the trial. If there are not enough caregivers to cover all the cases on a given day, service providers can visit every courtroom where a co-victim is attending a trial at the beginning of the morning and afternoon court sessions. By checking in on a regular basis, the caregivers have an opportunity to reassess the needs and the emotional state of the co-victims and provide some level of assistance. This may not present the ideal court accompaniment situation, but the co-victims will still feel supported. The caregivers can also inform co-victims where they can be reached in an emergency.

AFTER THE TRIAL

In the days following a trial, co-victims report a wide variety of surprising and even frightening emotions. During this critical stage, some may feel a letdown or even an overwhelming depression. Co-victims may also experience a brief period of elation immediately after the verdict, which may soon turn to feelings of anger, sadness, grief, and pain, causing this posttrial phase to be one of their most critical emotional phases.

Co-victims should be prepared to expect strong emotions to sur-face after the trial and to realize that these are quite normal. Many co-victims have unrealistic expectations about the consequences of the completion of the trial and the giving of a verdict. They may be shocked to discover that it does not really change things to any great degree—the victim is still dead. In addition, the grief process for some co-victims may have only just begun, while support systems may withdraw, leaving them feeling quite alone and bereft. Service providers should be alert to this and continue to offer support, referrals to counseling, encouragement to return to counseling, or information about attending a homicide support group.

INTERACTING WITH MEMBERS OF THE SYSTEM

During their journey through the criminal justice system, co-victims will have numerous contacts with police, judiciary, prosecutors, and defense attorneys. All these members of the criminal justice system have the potential to inflict a second wound. Some will do so because they are insensitive and uncaring; others, because of lack of training and understanding. Dealing with co-victims is a relatively new ex-perience for most of these participants, many of whom have been part of the system for a long time.

> They've basically been supportive, and I try to remember that this is just their job and that they have to be distant because if they got too close to people it would be hard for them. But it's really difficult sometimes when they don't deal with you as a person; to them we're just number 100 for 1994. (Daughter of murder victim)

Victim advocates should strive to establish lines of communication and working relationships with individuals in the various divisions of the criminal justice system, such as homicide detectives or super-visors, the prosecutor's office, individual prosecutors, and judges and their support staff. When a positive connection with the system exists, the co-victim feels more involved and, as a further benefit, may be more forthcoming in providing pertinent information about the case and more likely to attend court proceedings.

During the last decade, remarkable changes have been accomplished by victim advocates and other caregivers as well as by co-victims who go on to informally advocate within the system. Participation in formalized trainings, sensitivity sessions, and impact of crime panels are examples of advancements.

Many police officers, members of the judiciary, and prosecutors always treat co-victims with the dignity, fairness, and respect that they deserve. Others simply do not care and are not interested in changing their behavior. Of greatest concern are the supervisory entities who have not addressed victims' issues by institutionalizing new protocols for personnel to follow. The following discussion highlights concerns for caregivers to be aware of when working with members of several of the criminal justice divisions.

Police

After a homicide, co-victims usually have their first criminal justice contact with the police, and the relationship may continue for years. Many police officers treat co-victims with kindness and sensitivity, but this is usually not as a result of any special direction from the police department.

Victim sensitivity issues are usually not a priority in police academy curricula or in-service programs, although this situation seems to be slowly changing. Police seem to be more openly antagonistic than are other criminal justice personnel to anything that is called "training" or that has a caring or an emotional component it. Commonly, police are resistant to being associated with any form of assistance that resembles "social work." Attention and acquiescence to the importance of victim issues from the top supervisory level can create a more supportive environment for victims.

Police departments, as well as individual police officers, often display biases in their work that can be harmful to co-victims. Many of these attitudes have to do with cultural, racial, and class issues. Instances of intolerance often do not receive priority attention from the police department unless a high-profile incident occurs. Until police departments openly sanction debriefing, focus groups, and specialized sensitivity training, second wounds will continue to be inflicted—intentional and unintentional.

One police department practice that is becoming more widely accepted and that shows great promise in addressing these problems is the incorporation of police-based victim advocates. This has the advantage of providing direction for change from within, making police more amenable to examining and possibly modifying some of their actions. In recent years, the issue of dealing with co-victims, and all victims of crime, has garnered increasing interest and attention from police departments. It is a step in the right direction, but much more remains to be done before co-victims will be assured that they will receive respectful and unbiased treatment from the police.

Judiciary

By definition, the function of judges is to determine controversies between parties; they are not advisers or investigators (Gifis, 1984). A judge is to remain impartial, fair, and neutral to both parties. Anyone who is familiar with judges, however, realizes that they all have idiosyncrasies that affect what occurs in their courtrooms. Although some judges remain impartial and even exhibit some level of empathy for all courtroom participants, others may gain a reputation as "defendant oriented" or "prosecutor oriented."

The judge sets the tone for everyone who works in the courtroom.

A judge is in complete control of the courtroom, and courtroom procedures are usually sacrosanct. Except for the most egregious of actions, participants in a criminal justice proceeding have almost no recourse to a judge's behavior. Every state has a judicial conduct board or committee to look into complaints made by witnesses, victims, and defendants. Those serving on these boards are usually from the judicial sector, which may make it difficult to get an objective hearing or a redress of grievances. Going public with a complaint by bringing it to the attention of the media may cause unwanted publicity and motivate the judge to be more willing to take a different position. Victim advocates have reported the following as examples for which there is no redress: judges who eject co-victims when they look like they are crying, will not allow a victim advocate to sit next to the co-victim during the proceedings, and will not permit the co-victim to have a drink of water while in the courtroom.

Judges usually receive in-service training during judicial conferences, but because of the concern that any training involving victim issues may affect their impartiality, workshops or panels of this nature are not widely implemented. Some programs that describe the impact of crime on victims and update current victims' rights legislation have been considered acceptable. How much of this material is actually integrated into a judge's courtroom philosophy remains to be seen. Some judges will permit a co-victim to wear a campaign pin bearing the photograph of the murder victim or hold a picture or other memento of the victim or will order a short recess when the testimony has gotten too overwhelming for the victim to tolerate.

Court personnel, such as court officers, sheriffs, and court clerks, may also inflict a second wound. The judge has varying degrees of responsibility and authority over these individuals, but training and supervision may come from other departments in the system. The judge sets the tone for everyone who works in the courtroom. Personnel may be abrupt, surly, and insensitive when dealing with co-victims. One victim advocate reported that a court officer said, "Why is there a victim advocate here? The victim is dead." Unacceptable behaviors and comments should first be reported to the prosecutor; if the prosecutor cannot, or will not, deal with the situation, they should be brought to the attention of the judge.

Prosecutors

As mentioned earlier, the role of the prosecutor, or district attorney, is to try the case and prove the defendant guilty. During court proceedings, the prosecutor must concentrate all efforts on the case and has limited time to explain proceedings or answer questions. In addition, some prosecutors are not comfortable with providing emotional support and shy away from extended personal interaction. This is less a reflection of institutionalized biases than a lack of understanding of what a co-victim expects in the relationship. The chief prosecutor dictates the conduct of prosecutors and will have a significant influence on an individual prosecutor's treatment of co-victims. There are individual differences among prosecutors, and many develop warm and personal relationships with co-victims.

> They needed to make us more a part of the case. . . . Lewis was our son. We always were an important part of his life and in death we weren't. (Mother of murder victim)

Many district attorneys' offices now include training for new personnel in working with crime victims. This may not benefit co-victims, however, because homicide cases tend to use only the most senior prosecutors, whose orientation may have been conducted quite some time ago. Small jurisdictions may also have part-time prosecutors brought in from private practice who may know the law but are not educated in working with co-victims. On the other hand, many prosecutors have been in the forefront of the movement to have victim advocates work with them because they do not or cannot provide the necessary support and services that co-victims deserve.

In the past, private, nonprofit victim agencies provided services for co-victims, and a small number of prosecutors invited these agencies to house an advocate within their office or the courthouse. A positive development in the last 3 to 5 years has been the trend of district attorneys' offices to integrate victim advocates into their staff to provide services to co-victims.

Defense Attorneys

It would be remiss not to mention the position that defense attorneys play and the influence they have on co-victims. During many murder trials, the bulk of the co-victim's anger has been observed to shift from the defendant to the defense attorney (this observation has not been validated by research). Caregivers need to be cognizant of the issues raised in this context to respond to co-victims. It is common to hear a co-victim say, "I do not understand how that attorney can represent that murderer."

Under the Constitution of the United States, every criminal defendant is guaranteed a defense, and the co-victim should be educated about this. The question of the equality of this defense is not a matter to be raised here. Nevertheless, the defense attorney is hired to do a job, and whether or not the co-victim likes or appreciates the methods employed, the defense attorney's right to be present must be accepted as an incontrovertible fact. The defense attorney may be hired privately by the defendant, work for the public defender's office, or be hired by the court through a private law firm. For a defendant to qualify for a free defense, the defendant must prove indigence by taking a "pauper's oath" and swear to having no assets such as money, property, or other financial resources for a private attorney.

> I attended the trial to try to understand why John was murdered. Sometimes I still don't understand why all the lies were told. Justice was not done. (Mother of murder victim)

It is extremely painful and frustrating for co-victims to sit in the courtroom and hear the defense attorney heap blame on the victim, their loved one. Co-victims have little recourse, legal or otherwise, to pursue. Homicide victims cannot defend themselves, and co-victims are not permitted to rebut information presented by the defense attorneys, even when they go beyond the facts and resort to attacks on the victim's character through insinuations and innuendos. Knowing that prosecutors will attempt to offset this defense can help the co-victims prepare for the humiliation and pain they will experience on hearing the testimony in court.

Defense attorneys may also attempt to irritate and upset the co-victims by exhibiting certain behaviors. It is unlikely that caregivers will be able to influence the defense attorneys' conduct, but some opportunities may arise. A victim advocate who was providing court accompaniment to co-victims during a trial was witness to the following scenario:

> During breaks in the court proceedings, the defense attorney would parade in front of them with a smirk on his face. The judge was hearing the case. It was not a jury trial, and members of the media were seated in the jury box. The attorney's interactions with the press usually

consisted of asides about the case and a series of bad jokes, all within earshot of the co-victims. The advocate was able to put an end to the offensive behavior by directly addressing the attorney.

Co-victims have difficulty understanding when the defense attorney and prosecutor engage in small talk, jokes, and banter when court is in session and during breaks. The relationship between prosecutor and defense attorney may be quite amicable outside the courtroom proceedings. A game is played out in the courtroom between the attorneys; the primary goal of the competition is the winning of the case. Once the trial is over, win or lose, I have witnessed a number of defense attorneys approach the victim's family and graciously offer their condolences. One defense attorney, after losing the case, walked over to the co-victims, hand extended, and said, "I hope that you feel justice has been served." Most co-victims seem moved by these gestures and are accepting of the olive branch.

❏ Additional Legal Issues

Co-victims have the right, and often the need, to seek redress for pain and suffering. In addition to the court of criminal justice, civil suits and crime victim compensation (CVC) are the other major avenues of recourse for co-victims. Caregivers should familiarize themselves with all current applicable legislation and statutes to advise, inform, educate, guide, and support co-victims regarding these legal issues. The following overview of civil suits and victims' rights legislation will give service providers an appreciation and increased awareness of the range of issues.

CIVIL SUITS

There is a growing trend in the United States toward filing civil suits on behalf of crime victims. These suits have emotional and economic significance for victims and co-victims who believe they are an effective way to get compensation from those they surmise are culpable for their pain. In *What the Lawsuit Against Simpson Is Really*

About, Nelson (1996) writes, "To the victims' families this case is about justice. It's about accountability. It's about closure" (p. 2). The decision of whether to file a civil liability suit involves important considerations, including the viability of the case. A successful outcome will provide psychological and monetary benefits for a co-victim, but this is not accomplished without emotional hardship. One of the principal obstacles may be that the co-victim will have to testify and confront the perpetrator in civil court. A co-victim who has already faced the perpetrator in a criminal court proceeding may not be ready or willing to be retraumatized. Because civil court dockets are filled to capacity, the case may not go to trial for a number of years, which can work both for and against a co-victim's emotional state. Table 7.3 lists key concepts for caregivers to be aware of regarding homicide civil law issues.

Intervenors need not be experts on every relevant legal issue, but they should have sufficient knowledge to make co-victims aware of the difference between civil and criminal law and first- and third-party lawsuits. A good resource for helping professionals is a basic legal dictionary such as *Law Dictionary* by Gifis (1984). An excellent training manual available from the National Victim Center (NVC) is *Legal Remedies for Crime Victims Against Perpetrators: Basic Principles* (Carrington, 1994).

Just as victim service agencies maintain referral lists of mental health professionals, it is also prudent for them to compile a list of qualified attorneys who can provide in-depth information and assessment of a civil case. Referrals should be made to attorneys who have experience in dealing with wrongful death, malpractice, and personal injury cases. Former prosecutors who are in private practice also make good candidates because they may have more experience than other attorneys in dealing with victims of crime. The local bar association or other attorneys, including prosecutors, may be able to suggest attorneys who are experienced in this type of civil litigation. Several national victims' organizations, such as the NVC Civil Litigation Project and National Organization for Victim Assistance (NOVA) can provide additional advice and counsel on legal suits (see Resources). Caregivers may become involved in this issue in one of two ways: They may be approached by co-victims with questions or concerns regarding a civil suit, or they may provide outreach by

202 HOMICIDE: THE HIDDEN VICTIMS

TABLE 7.3 Civil Law

- A private or civil wrong is called a *tort.*
- The criminal prosecution or conviction of the defendant is not necessary before a victim can bring a civil suit.
- The burden of proof in a civil case is much lower than in a criminal case. In a criminal action, the prosecutor seeks proof *beyond a reasonable doubt* that the defendant is guilty of a degree of murder; the only issue in the wrongful death suit is whether it has been shown by a *preponderance of the evidence* that the defendant has caused the victim's death and is legally responsible to pay the damages.
- The statute of limitations sets the time within which the plaintiff must take action. Each state will vary with respect to time limits.
- "Wrongful death statutes in most jurisdictions create a separate cause of action for the surviving relatives or heirs of the victim for injuries they suffer as a result of the death of the victim" (Stark & Goldstein, 1985, p. 208). This creates a separate case from the one conducted by the state against the defendant.
- Wrongful death suits fall into two sometimes overlapping categories: (a) first-party actions in which the co-victim brings a suit against the individual who caused the death or assisted the perpetrator in causing the death and (b) third-party lawsuits that hold others legally responsible whose negligence may have aided or facilitated the murder of the victim.
- *Damages* are the monetary compensation that co-victims or plaintiffs seek to redress harm done to them. *Actual* or *compensatory* damages are sought for those losses that can be directly attributed to the murderous act, such as out-of-pocket losses, funeral costs, pain and suffering, and so on. *Exemplary* or *punitive* damages, in addition to compensatory damages, are assessed as a form of punishment for the perpetrator. *Pecuniary* damages are the loss of money such as financial support or potential income that would have been provided by the deceased.

---

informing co-victims that they might have grounds for a suit and should seek legal counsel for a definitive opinion.

A wrongful death action is customarily handled by an attorney on a contingency basis, which means that the attorney takes no fee unless there is a successful outcome in the case, and any court costs are borne by the co-victim. The fee, commonly set at one third or one half of the award, should be thoroughly discussed and accepted by both parties before signing any legal agreement. Attorneys are generally not interested in taking a contingency case without a strong possibility that the case can be won and that there will be a reasonably large settlement attached to it. Attorneys feel there is a disincentive, considering the time and effort involved, in pursuing a civil case against an indigent defendant. Most attorneys will not take on a wrongful death case just because the co-victim wants a symbolic victory. The co-victim needs to be prepared for this possibility.

Wrongful death cases are complicated and difficult to litigate. Many of the suits fail in the civil system because they are thrown out of court for being without merit or frivolous. In addition, few actions result in the recovery of any money because most defendants in murder cases have no assets and are considered judgment proof. Nevertheless, many co-victims still want to pursue this course of action.

Third-party suits. The defendants in third-party suits are usually schools, colleges and universities, hotels and other public establishments, employers, and landlords. Although money may not be the prime motivation for a co-victim to institute a civil suit, third-party suits often yield large settlements. The third-party defendant is often referred to as having "deep pockets" because of its ability to pay the specified damages. If the suit is successful, the judgment may be paid directly by the third-party defendant or, more likely, by the insurance carrier. Third-party suits have a higher probability of being settled out of court than do other wrongful death suits because the insurance carrier, by negotiating a settlement with the co-victim, will save the cost of putting on a defense at a lengthy trial and avoid the risk of the court's ordering an even larger amount. These suits have the potential to prevent a certain amount of victimization by making third parties take steps to prevent future crimes to protect themselves from lawsuits.

Tort of outrage. Under certain specific circumstances, a co-victim might also have grounds to sue for intentional infliction of emotional distress, sometimes referred to as the *tort of outrage.* As a general rule, courts have permitted co-victims to recover damages for emotional distress *only* if they were present at the scene of the crime and the defendant inflicted the emotional distress intentionally or recklessly (e.g., a child who witnessed a parent's murder). Learning of the murder of a loved one by telephone, from a police officer, from the media, or by discovering the victim will, in most cases, have the same impact as presence at the actual act. Therefore, it is incomprehensible to many co-victims that they cannot sue for intentional infliction of emotional distress. John W. McNamara (1986), an attorney whose younger brother, Darren, was murdered, writes,

> It is harsh irony that perhaps the most outrageous of all conduct— murder—is rarely actionable under the tort of outrage. The main obstacle to such a suit continues to be the requirement that the plaintiff be present at the murder. . . . In light of the degree of wrongfulness associated with murder, common sense notions of justice dictate that a murderer should not be shielded from liability for distress suffered by family members. There is no basis in either reason or policy to deny recovery to the immediate members of a murder victim's family merely because they were not present at the scene of the murder. Although there may be a practical necessity to limit liability by draw- ing a line somewhere . . . (p. 587)

As more co-victims initiate lawsuits against defendants in the civil court system and as the law regarding the rights of crime victims in civil matters continues to evolve, new precedents regarding torts will be established. A good source of current information on the issues in this field is the NVC's *Crime Victims' Litigation Quarterly* and *Crime Liability Monthly*, which highlight current settlements and verdicts in the civil liability arena (see Resources).

VICTIMS' RIGHTS LEGISLATION

In 1985, Stark and Goldstein stated, "What are commonly called victims' rights are really a broad range of rights, privileges, policies, and practices" (p. 5). In the last decade, the codification of many of these rights as statutes by the individual states has been achieved. Victim agencies, networks, coalitions, and individual crime victims have provided much of the impetus in effecting critical changes to broaden the scope of victims' rights legislation. All agencies that serve crime victims should ensure that staff members are fully cognizant of current legislation, both in their jurisdiction and on a national level, to educate, guide, and support co-victims; monitor compliance of the criminal justice system to ensure that the victims have their rights protected; and introduce and familiarize criminal justice personnel with state statutes, case law regarding rights of co-victims, and the philosophy inherent in the material.

Victims' rights legislation includes an enumeration of specific rights pertaining to crime victims as well as a list of the responsibilities of law enforcement agencies, the criminal justice system, and state departments of corrections and parole. In state statutes, commonly referred to as the Victims' Bill of Rights, and the proposed federal amendment, the following rights are granted: (a) notification of, and the right to attend, court proceedings, including bail hearings and parole hearings; (b) eligibility for compensation and restitution; (c) freedom from intimidation and harassment by the defendant; (d) fair and dignified treatment; (e) victim input at various stages of the criminal justice process; (f) information about the release or escape of defendants; (g) prompt return of victims' property; and (h) notice of all the rights in legislation.

When the first states enacted and implemented victims' rights legislation, victim advocates and crime victims began to realize that although this was a significant step in guaranteeing rights to victims, enforcement mechanisms were not incorporated in most of the statutes. There continue to be many incidents of noncompliance with the statutes by members of the criminal justice system without any remedies or imposition of penalties available to victims or their advocates. As of 1996, 29 states had passed constitutional amendments to rectify this oversight by incorporating statutes with procedures that offer an opportunity to seek redress. In some states, the process to enact a constitutional amendment is so burdensome that it may be almost impossible to accomplish. The passage of such amendments should not be viewed as a panacea for the problems of the faulty original statutes.

There has been a recent national movement to overcome the weaknesses of state statutes by amending the U.S. Constitution to protect

the rights of crime victims and to create a level playing field nationwide. Supporters of the amendment aspire to balance the rights of
perpetrators that are guaranteed in the Constitution by also providing constitutional rights for crime victims. Although many persons
object to tinkering with the Constitution and are concerned about the
pragmatic effect of the amendment on prosecutions, the proponents
of the amendment have not been deterred from taking action. A
Crime Victims' Rights Constitutional Amendment was introduced as
a joint resolution both in the House of Representatives and Senate in
the spring of 1996 and reintroduced in 1997 (H.R. J. Res. 71; S. J. Res. 6),
bringing national attention to victim issues.

Several existing statutes relevant to co-victims are presented here
in general terms because they differ greatly in each state. The major
principles and goals contained in each are similar—to establish and
protect the rights of crime victims. The focus here is on areas particularly
relevant to co-victims and in which caregivers can interact with co-victims
and the criminal justice system. These are (a) victim impact statements
(VIS), (b) victim input before parole, (c) notoriety for profit or "Son
of Sam" statutes, and (d) crime victim compensation.

Victim Impact Statements

Once a verdict has been reached in a criminal trial, a sentencing
hearing is scheduled. Defendants have the right to allocution, to
speak on their own behalf, as part of the sentencing procedure.
Victims also deserve to have their day in court, to have their beliefs
heard. The President's Task Force on Victims of Violent Crime
(Herrington, 1982) recommended the following: "Judges should allow for, and give appropriate weight to, input at sentencing from
victims of violent crime" (p. 72). The Supreme Court noted in *Payne v.
Tennessee* (1991) that

> it is an affront to the civilized members of the human race to say that
> at a sentencing . . . a parade of witnesses may praise the background,
> character, and good deeds of Defendant . . . without limitation as to
> relevancy, but nothing may be said that bears upon the character of,
> or the harm imposed, upon the victims. (quoted in NVC, 1996, p. 231)

The concept that the victim has the right to participate at sentencing has met with opposition by those who feel that the VIS may exert undue influence on the judiciary. Proponents of VIS continue to assert that "the goal of victim participation is not to pressure justice, but to aid in its attainment" (Herrington, 1982, p. 78). The NVC reports that by 1995, every state had granted the right of the co-victim to be heard at sentencing through the VIS (S. Howley, personal communication, December 12, 1996).

Current crime victims' rights bills generally include a section outlining the right of a crime victim to submit a VIS, along with specific instructions governing its use. Most states allow the co-victim to submit a written statement, included in the presentence report that the judge orders at the time of an adjudication of guilt, and a verbal statement to be presented at the sentencing hearing. Most states allow both and require that the judge consider the VIS at the sentencing hearing. In some jurisdictions, the decision to allow a co-victim to testify at sentencing may reside with the trial judge. If a co-victim is too distressed to read the statement in court, this right may be delegated to a family member, friend, advocate, or other spokesperson. The co-victim should view the VIS as an opportunity to inform the court about the effects of the trauma and physical, spiritual, psychological, social, and financial stresses experienced as a result of the homicide.

In most larger jurisdictions, a presentence investigation division of the court system generally has the primary responsibility to handle the preparation of the VIS and to include it in the presentence report. The presentence unit is usually available to answer questions about the VIS and to assist the co-victim in the actual writing of the VIS. Although the victims' service agency may not play an official role in the preparation of the VIS, it still has a obligation to get involved in the process. The VIS is one of the few legal rights that co-victims have, and it is imperative for them to be informed about and encouraged to exercise this right. Caregivers should recognize that the final decision to prepare the VIS is the co-victim's. Most co-victims who are familiar with the process are eager to participate. An excellent

The victim impact statement is one of the few legal rights of co-victims.

source for service providers is *A Victim's Right to Speak, A Nation's Responsibility to Listen*, available from the NVC (see Resources).

> For 15 months, the family of Eddie Polec, the 16-year-old Fox Chase boy fatally beaten on the steps of St. Cecilia's Church, watched as the wheels of justice ground on. Yesterday, it was their turn to speak. The victim's father . . . said "Your actions that night allowed my son to die. . . . I can never forgive you for that." Kristie Polec, 20, the sister of the victim . . . said her brother's death had "affected our lives beyond anything I could have imagined." . . . She worries "that I'll get a phone call that somebody else in the family has been taken away." (Loyd, 1996, pp. A1, A13)

Service providers may want to recommend that a co-victim keep a journal or notebook to record significant feelings, thoughts, and events related to the aftermath of the murder. This task may prove helpful, even therapeutic, and also serves as a technique for planning and preparing the VIS. No special skills are needed because the journal in its original form is not meant for others to read. If this is too burdensome for some co-victims, the same information can be put on a tape recorder.

If the defendant is acquitted of the murder, if there is a guilty verdict that carries with it a mandatory sentence imposed immediately after a guilty verdict, or possibly if the death penalty is imposed, a co-victim may not have the opportunity to present a VIS. In the latter situation, if permitted, the co-victim should still prepare a VIS and submit it to the state department of corrections or prisons to be held in the defendant's file for future reference. The issues of commutation or pardon may arise later, and the VIS might be considered at that time.

In the penalty phase of a capital case, the defendant is permitted to present evidence of any mitigating circumstances that may influence the jury's decision on the appropriate penalty. At this juncture, the right of a co-victim to testify should be considered. In the last decade, there have been a number of constitutional questions regarding the VIS in capital cases, which resulted in two U.S. Supreme Court cases: *Booth v. Maryland* (1987), which denied the right of a co-victim to present a statement in a capital case, and *Payne v. Tennessee* (1991), which overturned the earlier decision. The right of the co-victim to submit a VIS during the penalty phase of a capital case is an area marked by change due to state constitutional issues. In some state statutes, there is no differentiation between a VIS and a VIS presented during the penalty phase of a capital case. These statutes are problematic, and many are currently being tested in state courts to determine their constitutionality. In all likelihood, if these nonrestrictive statutes are overturned, new statutes will be introduced to address the problem.

Victim Input Before Parole

The right of a victim to provide input before the state parole board has received a great deal of attention from victim advocates and co-victims in the last decade. The impact of parole, or early release of the defendant, on the co-victim needs to be considered by the parole board before a decision is rendered. Victim advocates have been firm in the belief that statutes should give the co-victim the same right of allocution that is given to the defendant at a parole hearing. As a result, many states have revised current statutes or enacted new ones to expand the rights of co-victims in this matter. Forty-three states currently allow co-victims to offer written or oral input to the parole board at the parole hearing. In most cases, this testimony is submitted in confidence to the parole board, but the constitutional issue of nondisclosure still remains to be resolved in the courts. A new victim notification program has been created in many states that provides a mechanism, including the appointment of a victim advocate, for notification of a co-victim within a specific time frame (commonly 30 to 90 days) before the impending parole hearing of the defendant. The co-victim has the responsibility to enroll in the program and make notification of any change in address. Service providers need to emphasize to co-victims the role they have in maintaining contact with the program and ensure that co-victims have the necessary paperwork.

The co-victim can make written comment to the board, personally appear before the board, or both. In recent years, the right of the co-victim to be present and to offer input has been greatly extended in many states. There is a growing trend to also include in this legislation the right to be notified of the parole board's decision prior to the release of the defendant. Before the enactment of these new statutes, many co-victims first learned of the defendant's release when they saw the defendant walking down the street or in front of their home. This is quite traumatic and another example of the second wound inflicted by the criminal justice system.

A movement is under way in the United States to abolish parole and to use determinate sentences: 20 years means 20 years. This idea is gaining support from some who work in corrections and who are interested in the concept of restorative justice. There is a potential that the parole system, as we know it, may be abolished in some states. If this occurs, it will generate major changes in the criminal justice and corrections systems.

Notoriety for Profit or "Son of Sam" Statutes

These laws apply to all victims of crime but bear specific attention in the context of legal issues that affect co-victims.

> In 1977, the New York state legislature passed a statute that became known as the "Son of Sam" law. It was enacted to prohibit a notorious convicted murderer, David Berkowitz, also known as "Son of Sam," and other criminals like him, from profiting from their crimes by selling accounts of his various crimes. (NVC, 1993, p. 1)

This is a complex legal issue, but caregivers should be cognizant of the basic premise to be able to counsel and support co-victims regarding this matter.

> The concept behind Son of Sam laws is that it is contrary to public policy and a sense of public decency to allow violent criminals to profit from the retelling of their crimes while their victims continue to suffer financially and endure the added emotional pain from the publicizing of such accounts. This is not an entirely new idea. The public policy of Son of Sam laws is based on a precedent over one hundred years old. (NVC, 1993, p. 2)

Since 1977, more than 40 states and the federal government have enacted Son of Sam statutes. These have been contained in the

Victims' Bill of Rights and may also be duplicated in other legislation. These laws have always been controversial, and in 1991, the New York State statute was struck down by the U.S. Supreme Court, placing in doubt other comparable state statutes. Since that time, some states have amended their Son of Sam laws to take into account the constitutional issues raised in the New York decision. A wide divergence of statutory language is found in different jurisdictions. On the most basic level, these statutes require that anyone entering into a contract with an accused or convicted criminal must notify the state and supply copies of all pertinent documents. The state then escrows the money into a special account for a time. If the defendant is subsequently convicted of the crime and the co-victim sues for civil damages, any judgment that is ordered will be paid from the escrowed funds.

It is becoming more common for defendants involved in high-profile crimes to be offered large sums of money as fees and royalties for their stories. The Son of Sam statutes may not aid a large number of co-victims in recovering damages, but they do serve as a symbol that convicted criminals will not profit from their crimes.

Crime Victim Compensation (CVC)

CVC, a legislatively created benefit program, is a prime example of an area in which the state becomes involved in victims' legal rights. This is accomplished by the administration of a fund to compensate victims for the harm done to them by criminals. CVC is administered by an official state-run CVC board, agency, or other entity. It serves as the ultimate authority over all CVC matters. It needs to be strongly emphasized to co-victims that the service provider who assists with the completion of the CVC application does not represent the CVC board in any capacity.

> All states, the District of Columbia, and the Federal government have enacted crime victim compensation laws. These laws generally provide that crime victims, their survivors and persons who are responsible for the maintenance and support of victims, or those who have suffered economic loss due to the victims' injuries or death, are eligible for compensation if certain conditions are met. (Carrington, 1994, p. 321)

CVC is funded by monies collected from fines imposed on convicted criminals in the state, not by tax dollars. CVC statutes vary widely regarding issues such as dollar amounts, eligibility, and contribution. Because this is considered a civil matter, CVC boards never pay claims for pain and suffering. Co-victims may apply to CVC for reimbursement for funeral expenses and related expenses associated with the funeral (i.e., flowers, grave marker, and clothing for the deceased). Other items that may be covered are hospital bills for the deceased if associated with the crime and, under certain conditions, counseling expenses for the co-victims. If the deceased was working at a legitimate job and was the sole support of the family, and there is documented evidence such as payroll vouchers and IRS tax returns, a claim for loss of support may be filed. From the service provider's perspective, CVC is by far the most significant area of involvement with co-victims regarding victims' rights and legal issues. Completing the CVC process becomes an important part of the grief work for co-victims. The assistance of a service provider with this practical task can be incredibly beneficial, even therapeutic, for co-victims at a time when they may be feeling cheated and hurt. Because of the sheer volume of CVC applications processed, victim service agencies tend to develop an expertise in CVC matters. Agencies that receive federal Victims of Crime Act (1984) funding have a legally mandated responsibility to provide this assistance to co-victims. The official state agency commonly provides a CVC handbook or brochure for distribution to co-victims, but service provider agencies should prepare additional materials to clarify the process.

> *Crime victim compensation is funded by monies collected from fines imposed on convicted criminals.*

Co-victims may wish to complete the CVC forms on their own, but victim service providers should still offer assistance. Table 7.4 highlights a number of key issues for caregivers to be concerned with in dealing with CVC.

Caregivers should be aware of the factual issues of the case that could influence the claim. It is helpful for the agency to determine, before assisting with a CVC claim, whether there was any contribution

TABLE 7.4 Crime Victim Compensation

- Official notification of the right to apply for CVC is commonly the responsibility of the police department. Caregivers should offer CVC information in the event that the co-victims may not have been previously notified for any reason.

- Caregivers need to be aware of regulations referring to specific time limitations for filing CVC. In the majority of jurisdictions the time frame is one year. Exceptions may be made under special circumstances.

- It is preferable to assist a co-victim with CVC forms in person and not over the phone. If appropriate, the agency should co-sign the CVC form and keep a copy of it and all associated documents. In this way, the agency will be able to monitor the application in case of problems and keep track of the award amount for record-keeping purposes.

- Prior to the CVC appointment, a co-victim should receive a CVC checklist of necessary documentation. This will greatly facilitate the process and often avoid the need for a second visit.

- An hour and a half is a reasonable time to allow for a co-victim to complete the CVC application. Additional office time for follow-up paperwork is usually required.

- A co-victim may become quite emotional while filling out the application, providing the caregiver with an excellent opportunity to offer support, short-term counseling, and referrals to other services.

- Co-victims need to be informed of the procedures to follow to challenge a denied or reduced claim.

- Special circumstances may affect the amount of the CVC claim. Most states have regulations regarding life insurance and civil suits. As a rule, any monies collected by a co-victim from the victim's life insurance policy are applied against the expenses. If a judgment is awarded to a co-victim as a result of a civil suit and it is the same as or greater than the amount of CVC funds received, that amount will have to be repaid.

- "Contribution on the part of the deceased may reduce or negate any CVC award. This issue is often a very sensitive one for the advocate to broach with the co-victim, because they may be unwilling or unable to face the reality of their loved one's alleged involvement. All state compensation statutes intend that awards should either be denied or reduced when victims through their own misconduct have contributed to their injuries or death. Yet, these statutes generally fail to define clearly 'misconduct' or 'contribution.' This has permitted wide discretion on the part of compensation boards in their decision making." (Smith & Eddy, 1989, pp. 13-14)

---

to the death by the victim (i.e., drugs or illegal activity) by talking to the medical examiner, prosecutor, or police. If this information shows evidence of a high probability of contribution, there are still some good reasons for filing a CVC claim: (a) If the case goes to trial, a different version of the incident may be presented that will clear the victim of contribution, and (b) the CVC board may, at some future time, change its regulations regarding certain contributory circumstances, which may provide an opportunity to have the claim reviewed. The co-victim must be made aware of the circumstances, the regulations in the CVC statute, and the possibility that the claim may be either denied or reduced.

Co-victims need to be informed about the realistic time frame for receiving CVC reimbursement. In many states, it may take months for the CVC board to process the claim. In the event that an award is ordered, it may be as long as a year before they receive the payment. Unfortunately, in many states, the CVC boards cannot keep up with the volume of claims, and an entire bureaucracy has been developed to handle CVC.

Restitution. The right to restitution is included in most crime victims' bills but is not typically a viable option in homicide because of the difficulty of collecting money from defendants who are serving lengthy prison terms or life sentences. There is currently a growing effort from the victims' rights community and co-victims for the court to consider imposing restitution on defendants who are found guilty of murder. Judges are reluctant to do this because restitution orders are generally based on the defendant's ability to pay. Many prisoners earn small amounts of money in prison, and there may be some ability, however limited, for the defendant to pay restitution to the co-victim. If restitution is ordered at the time of sentencing, a convicted murderer who is released from prison after serving the sentence may then have to pay restitution as a condition of parole.

To make certain Mr. Blenden did not forget the child whose life he took, the judge also ordered him to pay a $520 fine, in weekly increments mailed to the family of the victim. . . . "It's not like I don't remember that she is gone until I see that check, . . . but at least I know that he has to be reminded of her once a week. He will have to think about her and what he did." (Bragg, 1996, pp. A1, A16)

Co-victims have difficulty understanding why the judge does not exercise the court's coercive power and order the defendant to pay restitution. Restitution payments may not make a major monetary difference to a co-victim, but the act of a defendant's being ordered to make restitution can hold great symbolic meaning for co-victims.

❑ **Summary**

Service providers have significant roles to play regarding the legal rights of crime victims in their search for justice. One of the intervenor's major duties is to provide direct service to co-victims—the backbone of the victim assistance system—by accompanying, guiding, supporting, and educating co-victims throughout their contacts with the criminal justice system. Equally important is the advocacy performed, on both a micro- and macrolevel, by caregivers to secure additional legal rights, seek better services, and ensure access to these services.

Can co-victims find justice within the system as it exists today? Great strides have been made in expanding the legal rights of crime victims in the last 20 years. Many professionals and crime victims alike can be proud of the accomplishments that just a few years ago seemed so unattainable; now they look to the future. They echo the words of Martin Luther King Jr. in his speech in Washington, D.C., August 28, 1963: "No, no, we are not satisfied, and we will not be satisfied until justice rolls down like waters" (cited in *Columbia Dictionary of Quotations*, 1993).

8

Facing the Media

The media play an important role for a co-victim in the aftermath of a homicide. Whether the media covers the event will have serious consequences for the co-victim, given that the actions of the media have the power to turn private grief into a public spectacle. The quality and the quantity of media coverage can be helpful or hurtful to the co-victim, often both simultaneously.

Historically, the media's view of murder is defendant driven. This perspective, similar to that of the criminal justice system, is reflected in the pictorial representation of victims as anonymous body bags or splotches of blood on the street, rather than as real people. Some might say that the press is simply responding to the public's voracious interest in violence and murder. For example, murder is almost always the lead story on the nightly TV news and on the front pages of the newspaper. Nevertheless, when members of the media cover murder trials, writing about the most minute details of the crime, they usually focus on the defendant while overlooking the victim and the co-victims' experience.

Murder is also big business for the media: A "good" murder and subsequent trial can sell a lot of newspapers, gain viewers for the nightly news, and provide material for docudramas and miniseries. In other words, the media are in a position to capitalize on some of society's worst fears and anxieties and decide what is "newsworthy."

> *The quality and quantity of media coverage can help or hurt the co-victim.*

The above issues are critical to co-victims and have long-term ramifications. Caregivers may not have a principal role in handling media issues for co-victims, but they can advise, support, stand in, and advocate in matters relating to the media. Service providers may also exercise their right as individual citizens to sensitize the media to victim issues.

Although this chapter is not an appropriate forum for an in-depth discussion of the role of the press in U.S. society, it highlights issues that affect both the media and the co-victim, influence their interactions with each other, and affect the public's perceptions of both. Topics covered include media perspectives, such as legal issues; the "second wound"; positive effects of media coverage; and strategies for caregivers working with the media.

❏ Media Perspectives

To understand the impact of the media, alternatively called the press, on the co-victim, there must be some understanding of what is needed for the media to function effectively. It is easy for intervenors and co-victims to make judgments without considering the perspective of the media. Thus, there are a number of areas to consider, such as the media's (a) goals and strategies, (b) legal rights and remedies, (c) moral and ethical dilemmas, and (d) stress factors.

MEDIA GOALS AND STRATEGIES

The media may try to be responsive to victims' needs, but their goals are different from those of victim advocates or co-victims.

Members of the media may say they are merely responding to what their viewers, listeners, and readers want on the basis of ratings and readership. In other words, the consumer ultimately decides what the media do. As a result, the media find themselves in the middle of a dilemma.

The media need certain elements to put together a newsworthy story. First, it must be determined whether a story is going to be printed, where it will appear in the newspaper, or how much time it will be given on television or radio. Some of the hooks that the media look for in a story include new or unique stories, appeal to the general public or impact on the community, controversial content, and time-liness or relation to some other current event. In addition, television needs a story that is highly visual and action oriented, and newspapers want good photographic opportunities. Larry Platt, during his appearance on *ABC News Nightline,* said it well: "If it bleeds, it leads" (Bettag, 1996).

Electronic Versus Print Media

Television is more likely to seek the quick story, whereas print has the time and space to generate a more in-depth approach to the news. On radio, it is not enough to "hear" a co-victim talk about pain and grief; it does not speak for itself as it does on television. Because the audience cannot see the speaker, radio requires a verbally articulate participant and stories that paint a visual image.

Greenfield (1986) explains what makes the medium of television different:

> 1) Television is at its best delivering personal, dramatic, emotional data. . . . Thus, the experience delivered by TV is simply more intense than that of any other medium; 2) television also brings you, as a viewer, closer to the process of gathering the story; and 3) TV news is consumed differently than is print news. (p. 19)

Stories on television can speak for themselves, but this quality also makes the medium inherently more intrusive as a result of the lights, cameras, news crews, and news vans. If more than one television station arrives at a murder scene, hospital, co-victims' house, or courthouse, the resulting media circus can be overwhelming and frightening to the co-victims.

Furthermore, television is constantly challenged to compress a story into 20-second sound bites, often referred to as "shake and bake" news. Co-victims may willingly have given a lengthy interview, but so much footage gets edited out that they feel shortchanged. Television reporters generally do not inform co-victims about the television news process, so their expectations are rarely met.

The initial television footage—glimpses of the victim's body bag, bloodstains on the street or sidewalk, chalk marks outlining the body—may be replayed for years as the murder case progresses through the criminal justice system or as other events put the story back in the news. Retraumatization of the co-victim will occur each time these pictures are witnessed. The mere presence of the media can trigger traumatic memories even if the co-victim feels that the reporters have done a good job. Caregivers need to take this into account, particularly in cases that receive extensive coverage.

The last 5 years have seen the emergence of the "tabloid news" show. Programs such as *Hard Copy* and *Inside Edition* represent more examples of violence as entertainment. This type of show will often pay large sums for interviews, which are not typically offered by regular news or magazine-style shows. Tabloid news shows are usually not amenable to requests to consider the privacy, pain, and grief of the co-victim when making production decisions. The reporters from these shows can be persistent and intimidating. If the co-victim is unwilling or unable to participate, the show may still feature the murder case without the acquiescence of the co-victim.

Caregivers will need to educate co-victims about how these shows operate so that they can make an informed choice about whether to appear. Service providers will also need to understand the co-victims' possible embarrassment or loss of control and privacy because of their decision.

Being interviewed on the radio is usually less stressful for co-victims because it is far less intrusive than other media and the time constraints are not as limiting. If co-victims are planning to go on a call-in show, however, it is best to prepare for having to answer difficult, personal, and sometimes inappropriate questions. A good strategy is for advocates to accompany co-victims to the show and stay with them while on the air.

Print journalists may be more subtle, but pens, pencils, tape recorders, and cameras can be equally intimidating.

> "I thought you would want to know: We're running a whole feature on your daughter. If you don't talk to me, it's going to be an unflattering portrait. I'm sure you'll find it upsetting. If you'd only give me a few minutes I'll say whatever you want me to say." . . . What easy marks we were that day. What a smoothie he was. He was, in effect, saying, "Give me an interview or your daughter gets screwed in print." (Spungen, 1983, pp. 379-380)

Often, what is ultimately printed in a newspaper is a much shorter, edited version of the interview. Co-victims may be disappointed that the news article did not say what they expected and feel pain over the sensationalized headlines. Reporters often do not explain what it means to talk "off the record," and co-victims may feel misled about what is to appear in print.

Crime stories have been an integral part of newspapers for 150 years. Print journalists, more than electronic journalists, are likely to regard what they do as sacred and can be defensive about criticisms. Collectively, the print medium is most reluctant to open its internal process to any level of outside scrutiny or influence. Compared with print, television is still in its infancy, and news directors and reporters tend to be more amenable to changing the way they treat crime victims. A good example of this is a nationwide trend to reduce the number of body bags and murder victims' bloodstains shown on television. Victim advocates and co-victims have clearly made a difference by communicating with members of the electronic media and should continue to address the issues with individual reporters, editors, and news directors. It is also helpful to the entire community to acknowledge reporters who write news articles that treat co-victims in a sensitive and dignified manner. For instance, a newspaper should receive kudos for printing information in a separate box or sidebar that highlights issues regarding personal safety or services available to victims of crime.

LEGAL RIGHTS OF THE MEDIA

> Congress shall make no law respecting an establishment of religion, or prohibiting the free exercise thereof; *or abridging the freedom of speech, or of the press* [italics added]; or the right of the people peaceably to assemble, and to petition the Government for a redress of grievances. (U.S. Constitution, Amendment 1)

The First Amendment to the U.S. Constitution is the basis on which the power of the press in this country resides. The First Amendment, however, belongs to *all* citizens. Greenfield (1986) states, "I sometimes believe that we journalists use the first amendment the way a diplomat uses his passport when he's stopped for drunken driving—a way to claim immunity from the consequences of what we do" (p. 21).

> *Co-victims have the right not to disclose information or give interviews to the press.*

Members of the press have the right to try their best to obtain an interview from the family of a murder victim, or barring that, write a story using any sources they can find. And co-victims also have rights: (a) the freedom *not* to disclose information; (b) the freedom *not* to cooperate by giving interviews; and (c) the freedom *not* to allow the press access to their home, office, or property. The press may feel that the First Amendment is notice enough, but prior to a murder, most co-victims are unaware of their rights. There is no legal requirement for the press to read a list of rights such as the police are required to read to the accused. In the immediate aftermath of a homicide, co-victims are usually in a vulnerable state and may later regret what they say to an eager reporter. The consensus of victim advocates is that both the press and co-victims are best served if co-victims are informed of their right to refuse an interview.

MORAL AND ETHICAL DILEMMAS OF THE MEDIA

The place of the victim of violence in crime stories continues to be a hotly debated subject for members of the media profession.

> The police answered only questions we asked and promised to return and tell us the rest of the story. Before that could happen, a TV news report devastated our family with the account, including pictures, of where she was taken and set afire. (Mother of murder victim)

One key area of concern is the publication of the victim's or co-victim's address or the showing of the residence on television. Another problem is the humiliation and shame co-victims may experience by having their grief made so public or having others know certain details and circumstances of the murder. In cases in which there is no arrest, co-victims may fear that information in the media could be used to threaten or harm them. Still others may worry that this information could expose them to anonymous calls from mentally ill strangers or to criminals who might burglarize or vandalize their property.

> The *Post-Dispatch* reported a September, 1987, robbery of a St. Louis supermarket in which seven store employees were shot, five fatally. Not only did the paper run grisly photographs of the crime scene but three times printed the exact addresses of all seven victims. (NOVA, 1991, p. 1)

> Within the last decade both crime victims and journalists have begun to ask whether crime reporting is victimizing the victims again. The issue is not what newspapers and the electronic media have a right to do legally. It's what we ought to do ethically. (Thomason, 1986, p. 2)

It is not a simple decision whether to publish or televise information; every choice that an editor, news director, or reporter makes is fraught with ethical considerations.

How do we, as a country, resolve the complex issues that strike at the heart of one of America's basic freedoms? The mere idea of a code of ethics is an anathema to many members of the press. There is increasing pressure, from both inside and outside the profession, however, that the media must begin to police themselves. Although this is a controversial topic, more news organizations are setting guidelines for the coverage of violence and the victims of crime. For example, when television station KVUE-24 in Austin, Texas, issued crime coverage guidelines in response to viewers' and community input, the news director stated, "This project is *not* about 'family sensitive' news, censorship, or going 'soft' in our news coverage. We will still report on crime, but we're raising the standard on why we report crime and how we present it" (C. C. McFeaters, personal communication, February 8, 1996).

Whether news organizations will sincerely implement and enforce policies for codes of ethics remains to be seen. All attempts to incorporate sensitivity to victims' issues, however, are seen as positive steps.

Right to know versus right to privacy. In recent years, many victims, victim advocates, members of the press, and individual citizens have begun to question "the tension between the press as a commercial enterprise and as a human institution, between earning a profit and behaving with decency" (Gissler, 1989, p. 5). Again, the blame for insensitivity and intrusiveness cannot all be placed at the media's feet. George Will labeled the public's fascination with crime as "the pornography of grief" (Greenfield, 1986, p. 22). But which, ultimately, will be more compelling—the right to know or the right to privacy?

> The reporters were back. . . . They crammed our front porch and spilled out onto the lawn, jabbering with each other, jockeying for position close to the front door. There were photographers and television cameramen. There were microphones and tape recorders and lights. One of the reporters rang the doorbell. He kept his thumb down on it so it rang over and over and over again, demanding my attention and cooperation. . . . The freak show was on again. (Spungen, 1983, p. 1)

STRESS OF REPORTING VIOLENCE

The topic of how stress affects journalists is given little attention, and members of the press may deny its very existence. Editors, news directors, and other supervisory personnel do not encourage or give permission to their staff to discuss this troubling area. As a result, many reporters, much like police personnel, develop a way of denying their feelings to the detriment of their careers, their emotional lives, and the needs of victims and co-victims.

Journalists need permission to talk about anxieties and concerns that are provoked by the pressures of their jobs with peers and supervisors. In especially stressful or traumatic circumstances, journalists should be provided with debriefing sessions conducted by professionals. Informal sessions on a weekly basis, much like those employed by mental health professionals, could provide a venue to discuss such matters in a timely fashion. A variety of focus groups, including either individually or collectively current staff, viewers, and victims of crime and their advocates, could also offer a setting to open up some dialogue on media stress. It seems more expedient if attendance by the staff were compulsory. It has been my experience that when the press does implement any of these programs without that requirement, attendance is usually by staff who need it the least. The stress of reporting violence continues to receive little acknowledgment both from within and outside the profession. This can be further evidenced by the paucity of specialized curricula, training programs, and research that clearly identifies the needs of the press and addresses and evaluates its means of responding.

❏ **Impact of the Media on Co-Victims:
The Second Wound**

The circumstances of a murder case may transform co-victims from ordinary citizens into household names. Their reputations, as well as the reputation of the murder victim, can be seriously maligned in the process. If what they do or say is broadcast inaccurately, co-victims are faced with a possible lose-lose dilemma: (a) Speak to the press in an often futile attempt to set the record straight and possibly intensify the media coverage, or (b) remain silent in the hope that this inaccessibility will make the press lose interest.

The media are responsible for perpetrating a second wound on the co-victim almost as often as is the criminal justice system. This harm is caused by a general insensitivity to and lack of understanding of the co-victim's situation. One newspaper editor lamented, "Reporters are often accused of exploiting horror, harassing traumatized families, invading the privacy of mourners. Alas, it can happen" (Gissler, 1989, p. 11).

MEDIA EXPLOITATION

The creation of celebrity co-victims is usually engineered by the press who see the stories and the actors involved in certain murder cases as infinitely more compelling than others. Often, the case revolves around what may be considered an innocent and vulnerable murder victim, such as a child, or an association with some other intriguing or high-profile case. The co-victims must possess some attributes that will magnify their attractiveness to the media, such as being available, articulate, physically appealing, or able to show emotion but with a level of control. Examples are Marc Klaas, the father of 12-year-old murder victim Polly Klaas, who was kidnapped from her own home by a paroled sexual offender and later found murdered, and Fred Goldman, whose son, Ron, was found murdered with Nicole Brown Simpson, ex-wife of former football star O. J. Simpson, in 1994.

The role of celebrity may allow the co-victim an opportunity to speak out about murder and its effects on the family and to address larger issues such as violence in our society, victims' rights, and the criminal justice system. On the other hand, is the price the co-victim pays too high? The lure of the media and the possibility of 15 minutes of fame may be too seductive for a co-victim to decline. It is difficult for a co-victim, even with the advice and support of a victim advocate or other caregiver, to judge the long-term effects of this media exposure. Although they do not relish this newfound fame, some co-victims cooperate simply because they feel they ought to use their new role as an opportunity to accomplish something positive.

Television talk shows are among those that often exploit co-victims and their experience. Not all shows of this genre sensationalize the murder events or take advantage of the emotions of co-victims, but appearances on these shows can nevertheless be quite damaging to co-victims. Victim advocates' agencies are often besieged by talk show personnel who request, "Get me a victim." The television producer often specifies bizarre criteria such as someone who has had all her family members murdered at one time or someone who was killed by a female teen. Service providers often face a quandary when approached by a talk show on which the co-victim would stand little chance to benefit. Many advocates are reluctant to expose a co-victim to the dangers of such shows. Some co-victims, however, may want an opportunity to speak out regardless of the emotional risk.

COURTHOUSE COVERAGE

The issue of television cameras in the courtroom is quite controversial and complex. Some states do allow cameras in the courtroom but always at the judge's discretion. The coverage of the O. J. Simpson trial in 1995 and the Court TV cable station have catapulted the issue into the forefront.

> Some news media lawyers and outside experts say they expect the Simpson trial to lead to more challenges of televised coverage of trials. And already, the trial has renewed the debate over whether cameras damage or enhance the criminal justice system. (Associated Press, 1995, p. 35)

> Many believe that courtroom cameras were responsible for turning the first trial into an extended circus by intimidating Judge Lance Ito and inspiring the lawyers to grandstand at every opportunity. Because of that, some judges are more reluctant than ever to allow cameras in their courtrooms. (Seplow, 1996, p. A2)

Of concern here is the impact of this coverage on co-victims. The camera's watchful eye is always available to examine every move and expose their grief and pain. This sideshow is often accompanied by on-air, play-by-play analysis from reporters and legal specialists. There is almost never a victim advocate or professional to provide insight into the victim experience that is unfolding in the courtroom. This level of societal scrutiny is an excruciating experience for the co-victim.

In addition, the media can be quite aggressive at preliminary hearings of high-profile cases. Much of this confusion and jockeying for position is caused by the competitiveness of the various stations and news media to obtain the best possible coverage. Cases at a homicide preliminary, grand jury, or other first hearing stage are still fresh stories. A year or more down the road, when the trial is held, the case may no longer hold the same allure. Television coverage at these hearings tends to border on the sensational—shots of grieving co-victims, fights between the families of a homicide victim and the defendant, and pictures of the defendant being led away in handcuffs and leg chains. When the still photographers from the newspapers, accompanied by their reporters, and the microphones and reporters from the radio stations are added, the net result is a welcoming committee that resembles a swarm of killer bees. This is the scene that generally awaits co-victims as they approach the courthouse or courtroom.

When co-victims get within sight of the camera crews, a collective shout goes up from the press, "There they are!" and the entire media group runs forward like a pack of wolves going in for the kill. The camera lights bob and weave as the camera crews race toward their prey. Anyone in their path is unceremoniously bumped, shoved, jostled, or knocked out of the way. Co-victims are left shaking, frightened, and often in tears at this display of the freedom of the press at its worst. Even if co-victims' relationships with the media are well established and amicable, co-victims are usually so intimidated by this exhibition that any thoughts of speaking to the media are quickly forgotten as they lower their heads in a defensive posture.

Not much can be done to influence the media to behave in a different way in such a highly competitive setting. Nevertheless, a service provider who is knowledgeable about the media and their impact can help prepare co-victims to deal with the experience. Victim advocates should arrange to accompany the co-victims to court and may request additional escorts such as police, court officers, and sheriff's deputies to minimize the trauma and facilitate safe passage through the crush of the media. Sometimes, an alternate route can be found that avoids the press, but complete evasion of the media may not be possible.

The criminal justice system in a number of localities is responding to the situation that the media, particularly the electronic media, have created. Experiments to control the media presence in the courthouse and its environs are not an attempt to diminish First Amendment rights but are out of concern for the safety of witnesses and victims. Individual state rules of criminal procedure may provide the authority to curtail broadcast or photography. When the city of Philadelphia opened its criminal justice center in September 1995, it enacted a policy of excluding the media camera people at the new courthouse. An official Philadelphia Local Rule of Court, based on policies practiced in the Philadelphia Federal Courthouse, still welcomes the press, but no microphones, tape recorders, or cameras of any type are permitted inside the courthouse. Reporters can approach victims for interviews; the cameras and photographers, however, must wait outside. This has greatly reduced the media circus that used to exist in the hallways and has restored a level of decorum and respect to court proceedings. The media are able to get coverage, albeit not to the same extent as before, and co-victims and victim advocates are pleased to have the possibility of additional trauma greatly reduced.

QUALITY AND DEPTH OF MEDIA COVERAGE

> In the town where it happened, they had the victim's and the murderer's names switched; they portrayed us as animals ready to pounce on him. (Family of murder victim)

The quality of reporting about the victim and the media's attempt to involve the co-victim unnecessarily in that process become major issues to add to the co-victim's trauma and the infliction of a second wound. For example, in covering a murder case, the media tend to look at the victim as one extreme or the other—a *good* victim or a *bad* victim. The proclivity of the press to automatically assign labels and euphemisms, however accurate or inaccurate, to a murder victim greatly increases the co-victim's second wound. Labels and euphemisms in the headline of a story are generally the responsibility of a copy editor, not the reporter. Reporters often receive the blame for headlines, although they have had nothing to do with their construction and may not approve of them. Copy editors, however, are not

> *The media tend to look at the victim as one extreme or the other.*

readily accessible, and there are few appropriate arenas in which they can be educated about the issue. The challenge is that once the label or euphemism has appeared, it is difficult to overcome even if additional facts later reveal that this appellation is wrong.

The second wound can be exacerbated by the depth of either coverage or noncoverage of certain cases. High-profile cases usually involve a well-known person, an intriguing location, or unusual circumstances such as the age of the murder victim. Some homicide cases are relegated to the back pages of a newspaper or a squib (a small news article written without a reporter's byline) or are completely ignored by the press. For many co-victims, that can be equally traumatic. Lack of coverage can make them feel as if a loved one did not count as a human being, that the co-victim's loss was so negligible that it was not worth mentioning.

> His murder was not in the news; that made me feel like my son was not nobody and that really hurt. (Mother of murder victim)

CULTURAL AND RACIAL BIAS

Members of the press often feel they are unjustly accused of racial bias. It is possible that what appear as racial prejudices are media reactions in response to short time frames and deadlines. Cultural and racial bias is often influenced by whether the media coverage is local or national. Local press may exhibit biases based on the cultural and racial makeup of the community. Local television news coverage, especially in urban cities, often portrays blacks as perpetrators and whites as victims. Several recent studies have indicated that there "is a pattern of news portrayal that implies that the atypical is typical: the unlikely likely" (Jamieson & Romer, 1995, p. E5). In 1994, a study of Philadelphia television coverage intimated that blacks were usually the perpetrators of crime and whites were the victims of violent crime. Yet "statistics showed that in 1993 only 6 percent of the reported homicides in Philadelphia involved a black perpetrator and a white victim" (1995, p. E5).

Many black co-victims feel that their loved one's homicide has been given little or no coverage in the media as a reflection of race.

This seems to be a fairly common grievance when the victim is a black male between the ages of 18 and 30 and the perpetrator is also black. The lack of attention paid to black-on-black homicide may be because news stories highlight the unusual, and intraracial crime among blacks is more common. In an urban setting, another murder of a young black male is no longer regarded by many in the media as news.

Another criticism levied against the media involves the labeling of black murders as drug involved before the case is fully investigated or brought to trial. This type of coverage reinforces the stereotype of young male blacks as violent and involved in the drug trade. In the event that this implication turns out to be incorrect, it is difficult to retract. Most of the time, any new information goes unmentioned or unnoticed, and the co-victim is further traumatized.

❏ Positive Effects of Media Coverage

> We fully cooperated with the media. First, we wanted our daughter found; second, we wanted those responsible for her murder held accountable; third, we wanted to thank others for their kindnesses; fourth, we wanted the world to know the real Stephanie. (Mother of murder victim)

The many instances in which the media have made positive contributions should also be noted. The benefits that may accrue from a media story are too often overlooked. If there were more opportunities for dialogue among the co-victims, the victim advocates, and the members of the press, it might be possible to increase the potential of the media to do good and not increase harm. Focus groups or seminars in which all the interested parties can get together provide such a forum. It is also important for co-victims and service providers to better understand what the press needs to accomplish its goals and objectives.

> Seeing the story of his murder on TV, I was amazed; it seemed surreal. I wish I had used the media to my advantage. (Mother of murder victim)

The media can use their power in many ways to make a positive contribution in the aftermath of a murder. Reporters and decision makers can (a) highlight some harm or peril that can come to a person so that others will be more vigilant; (b) give special meaning to an ordinary person's life and death; (c) aid in the grieving process by providing co-victims a platform to talk about a loved one and their pain and grief over the murder; (d) provide the public with information about the murder and suspects in no-arrest cases to help solve the crime and make an arrest; (e) facilitate the grieving process of the community by focusing on the manner in which the media deal with murders; and (f) educate the public by presenting information about grief, victims' rights, victim services, and the criminal justice system.

USING THE MEDIA TO SOLVE CASES

The following newspaper article illustrates the power of the media in helping to solve murder cases.

> The inspector in charge of the Homicide Division said the pictures may have been the key to the case. "The information that came available today was probably brought about by the attention that the media had given the picture." . . . Police had made the pictures available last Thursday, and they were printed in *The Inquirer* and other newspapers and broadcast on television. The result, police said, was the tip identifying Harrison [the suspect]. (Gibbons & Gelles, 1996, p. A1)

If the interest of the media is piqued, reporters may be willing to do a feature on an unsolved case. It is difficult to determine what unsolved cases might prove to be of interest to them. In recent years, there has been a rise in national television shows featuring unsolved crimes, such as John Walsh's *America's Most Wanted* and *Unsolved Mysteries*. Some years ago, John Walsh's own son was abducted and murdered, and to date there has not been an arrest in the case. Mr. Walsh showcases no-arrest cases because he truly understands the pain and frustration of the co-victim.

It is difficult for an individual co-victim to get a case highlighted because the shows are not restricted to unsolved murders. In addition, the producers have stringent criteria and parameters regarding what cases they are willing to showcase. Generally, homicide cases more than 10 years old are considered difficult to solve and are therefore not chosen. Co-victims often have high expectations about getting the case on the show and can be left feeling even more frustrated when they are unsuccessful in doing so. And if the case is on the show but the murder remains unsolved, co-victims are often inconsolable.

Many local television stations have a "Crime-Fighters" or "Crime-Stoppers" show as part of the regular news. These programs concentrate on local unsolved violent crimes, especially homicide. Local shows often get referrals of cases directly from law enforcement personnel, rather than from victim advocates or co-victims. Although many cases are solved from this venue, it is fraught with the same problems that face co-victims on national shows in access and unfulfilled expectations.

❏ Strategies for Working With the Media

Educating co-victims as soon as possible after a homicide about their *rights* in dealing with the media is helpful. Average citizens are not usually interested in or knowledgeable about such information until they become victims. The NVC (1990) pamphlet "Victims' Rights and the Media" is the best resource available and can serve as a guide for caregivers to use and to offer to co-victims.

An important first step in working with co-victims is to make an assessment. If the media have not yet picked up on a story, a caregiver can be proactive in discussing the influence of the media. Some questions that may help caregivers gain insight into the co-victims' feelings and misconceptions about the media are these:

Do you feel media coverage would be useful? How?

Has anyone from the media contacted you?

What is one thing you would most like the public to know?

Do you want to be on TV? Radio? Have your picture in newspapers?

How do you feel about the media coverage so far (if applicable)? Was it fair and accurate? Will it help? (Stein, 1995, p. 2:20)

It is the caregiver's responsibility to provide co-victims with an accurate representation of their rights. Victims have the right to

1) not talk to, pose for a picture, or provide photographs to the media; 2) choose a spokesperson or "family liaison" to represent their point of view; 3) release a written statement to reporters in lieu of speaking; 4) choose the time and place for an interview; 5) conduct a television interview using a silhouette or give a newspaper interview without having a photograph taken; 6) request specific reporters or decline speaking to specific reporters; 7) ask to review a story before it appears, if there is time; 8) be treated at all times with dignity and respect by the media. (Stein, 1995, p. 2:20)

LEGAL REMEDIES

The following information is included as a guide for caregivers to be able to educate, guide, and support co-victims who feel so aggrieved by the behaviors of the media that they want to pursue legal action. For more information, they should go to the original sources or contact a lawyer who specializes in First Amendment cases.

The case of a co-victim versus the media is one situation in which there is a low expectation for any success in the courts. The power of the press and the right to free speech will severely limit the co-victim's ability to redress grievances or perceived grievances in the legal arena. This may intensify feelings of frustration, anger, and helplessness and, in some cases, lead to further traumatization.

In today's litigious society, the tendency is to want to sue to right some wrong. There are three main barriers to instituting a civil suit against the media: (a) Precedence or prior legal rulings almost preclude any chance of success, (b) any case involving First Amendment issues needs to be handled by an attorney who specializes in that area of the law, and (c) the cost of mounting such a case can be prohibitive for most co-victims because First Amendment Civil lawsuits are usually not headed on a contigency basis.

If a case is viable, the co-victim may seek legal redress from the media at two stages. The first is prior to the publication of a news story, airing of a television program, or communication of information. This action is considered prior restraint and provides almost no opportunity for the co-victim to restrict the media. "Under the First

Amendment guarantees of free speech and press, prior restraints are subject to strict scrutiny and bear a heavy presumption against constitutional validity" (Gifis, 1984, p. 363). The possibility that a co-victim may be upset by information to be released in the future is insufficient legal grounds to halt its release. This issue may be difficult and painful for co-victims to comprehend. Co-victims have the right to appeal directly to the media not to release the offensive information. This approach may or may not meet with success, but it is worth trying.

The other stage at which a co-victim might seek vindication is after information is released. At this point, there are two causes of action under which a co-victim can seek damages: invasion of privacy and intentional infliction of emotional distress.

The *invasion of privacy* argument is available to anyone who is concerned by media disclosures of private facts. "Tort law protects one's private affairs with which the public has no concern against unwarranted exploitation or publicity that causes mental suffering or humiliation to the average person" (Gifis, 1984, p. 244). The rights of the public may be superior to the rights of the individual, however. In a privacy claim, the plaintiff must establish several factors for the case to be actionable. The information disclosed has to be an embarrassing private fact. In high-profile cases, much of the information becomes part of the public domain and is, therefore, no longer private. Next, "the disclosure must be highly offensive to a person of reasonable sensibilities. It is not enough that the victim is genuinely offended" (Anderson, 1986, p. 8). Finally, if the disclosure of an embarrassing public fact is considered to be in the public interest, then it is not actionable. A further complication for the co-victim in a privacy case is that there is no cause for action regarding another's privacy. The law gives no redress to the co-victims in reference to the invasion of the murder victim's privacy either in the name of the victim's estate or for the co-victims themselves. Although privacy issues are well established as a cause of action, a plaintiff will likely not prevail in the courts.

Intentional infliction of emotional distress is another cause of action, sometimes taken by an attorney in an attempt to avoid the hazards of the privacy case, that has its own set of weaknesses. This tort has limited application; therefore, it has been of little help to co-victims.

To reiterate, co-victims do have First Amendment rights, but they are not likely to be vindicated in the courts. Often, co-victims' only recourse is to become better informed in dealing with the media and to educate and persuade the press to deal with co-victims in a fair and sensitive way.

INTERPERSONAL STRATEGIES

Co-victims, with the help of caregivers, may identify a particular strategy that makes them feel comfortable in dealing with the media. Some find that saying a few well-chosen words when the media appear or holding a controlled press conference and answering a minimum of questions with brevity serves them best. For others, any attention is more than they can bear, and they need to strategize ways to avoid facing the media.

Caregivers, especially therapists, need to understand the emotional toll that interactions with the media can take on co-victims and offer opportunities for them to vent their emotions and concerns to the appropriate persons. A brainstorming session among a caregiver, advocate, and co-victim to formulate some sort of strategy can empower the co-victim and allow him or her to take some action even if that cannot change what happened.

It is worthwhile for caregivers to invest in forging a working relationship with the media. When trying to initiate change in how the media deal with victim issues, the best route to take is a one-on-one approach. I know this works because as a victim advocate, I have been talking to individual members of the media in the courthouse halls for many years. I know most of the television reporters and camera people, and we have established a respectful, but wary, relationship. As I chat informally with them during breaks in court, I attempt to give them small doses of insight into the co-victim experience without preaching or telling them how to do their job.

Last year, I was escorting the mother of a murder victim from the courtroom to the rest room. This was a high-profile case, so the halls were filled with members of the press milling about, waiting for a break in the courtroom action so they could catch the co-victims, defendants, prosecutors, or defense attorneys as they went in and out of the courtroom. The television news crews were standing behind

yellow police barriers in the hallway. As we started out the door and
began the long walk down the hallway, the camera crews immediately recognized the mother. They all put their lights on, and at least
five or six camera crews started to run alongside us. The mother was
in a fragile state and near physical collapse due to her pain and grief
over the recent, brutal murder of her son. The commotion and the
heat of the camera lights seemed to make her melt into my arms, and
I was almost carrying her. I turned to the camera crews and put my
hand up as a signal for them to go away, this was not a good time.
Much to my amazement and relief, they turned off the lights, put
down the cameras, and went back to their vigil at the courtroom door.
When we returned from the rest room, I expected a replay of the
earlier scene. I cradled the co-victim close to me in a protective hug
as we approached the camera crews one more time. This time, they
did not turn on the lights or the cameras. I saw several camera people
looking at us with an empathy that I had never noticed before. I silently
mouthed a "thank you" to them, and many of them nodded back.

In dealing with television news, there is little opportunity for
recourse when inaccuracies do occur. One approach might be for
co-victims to contact the station's news director, preferably in writing, to voice their complaints. Some television news organizations
have established a vehicle for reporting concerns, but its presence is
not usually well publicized.

Many newspapers have an ombudsman to contact about the publication of incorrect facts. A copy of a letter to the ombudsman should
be sent to the reporter and the editor of the newspaper. The act of
committing grievances in writing can help reduce anger and anxiety
for a co-victim even if there is no guarantee that anything concrete
will be done to rectify the situation. At best, the newspaper may have
a "Corrections Column" that may print a brief notice. Newspapers
will rarely print a full retraction of a news article. At the least, the
ombudsman or the reporter may respond with an empathetic letter
or an apology for causing the co-victim additional pain. If none of
these techniques gets a response, victim advocates and co-victims
can also write a letter to the editor or an op-ed piece for the editorial
page.

An excellent technique to employ regarding the use of offensive
pictures taken at the crime scene or an unsuitable picture of the

murder victim is to offer more appropriate copies of the victim's picture. Often, the press are appreciative of this type of assistance. This is an example of a win-win circumstance in working cooperatively with the media.

> An 18-year-old high school student had been beaten to death by a gang of teenagers in a case of mistaken identity. This was a very high-profile case due to the circumstances surrounding the murder and the fact that the father of the victim was a police officer. The media repeatedly showed views of the crime scene which focused on pools of the victim's blood or a picture of the victim as a much younger child. The parents had received copies of his high school yearbook picture just days after his murder. They had copies made of the photograph and brought them to the preliminary hearing and distributed them to the members of the media. The reporters were very touched by the family's efforts and replaced the old pictures with the new photograph from that point on through the case. (A victim advocate)

❏ Summary

Yes, the public does have a right to know, especially if the reasons are compelling and if the reporting of the event can be helpful to the public's safety and well-being. A co-victim's not wanting to see the story in print or on television is not sufficient cause for the media to desist and go away. News organizations need to be aware of co-victim issues; what to report and how to cover the story, however, will continue to be a controversial issue. Many in the media believe that no matter how careful the reporting might be, some news stories will still be met with a feeling of pain and even outrage by the co-victim. Gissler (1989) reminds us that "it remains a balancing act for the media to cover the news about death and tragedy with balance, to provide compelling reports but with reasonable sensitivity" (p. 7).

9

Reconstructing a New Life: Endings and Beginnings

"The process of reconstructing a new life . . . has a similarity to the physical healing of the body after a deep wound" (Young, 1994, p. 5:21). One of the major goals of *Homicide: The Hidden Victims* is to provide intervenors with a framework for understanding the co-victim's experience. Service providers can employ this material as a guide to assisting co-victims in reconstructing new lives within the context of their own experience. This process can be "adjusted to incorporate new information in a way that enables the individual to experience pleasure and satisfaction in his or her life" (McCann & Pearlman, 1990a, p. 8).

> I'm sadder, but more forgiving. Less judging, more willing to try to separate the important from the frivolous. More anxious to have fun, let stuff slide. Just take things as they come, realizing how little control I have. What a tough lesson! (Mother of murder victim)

❏ Healing

Highlighted here are primary elements that I believe must be incorporated into the healing process. Although some of these may have been touched on earlier in the book, this in-depth look is needed to underscore their importance. These items include (a) the dual myths of getting over it and closure; (b) spirituality, including forgiveness; (c) social activism; (d) tears; and (e) laughter and humor.

THE DUAL MYTHS OF
GETTING OVER IT AND CLOSURE

Co-victims and caregivers often mistakenly believe that the goal for co-victims is "to get over it." Pressure is put on co-victims by their personal universe—families, friends, coworkers, neighbors, and others they regularly come in contact with—to go back to living normal lives; the key word here is *back*. A question commonly asked of co-victims, "Aren't you over that yet?" reinforces the impression that their trauma and grief are simply a transitory phase.

Closure conveys the same implications as "getting over it." It is often used to suggest that the co-victim should, and will, achieve a final resolution and state of completeness to the trauma, grief, and pain that have resulted from the murder. A level of resolution may be accomplished for co-victims at various stages, such as after the defendant is arrested or the trial is over. Suggesting that total closure is possible, however, is to offer an illusory hope. Instead of pressure for closure or to get over it, co-victims need assistance and encouragement in reconstructing a new life, a realistic and achievable objective.

Klass (1983) articulates the impossibility of the finality to grief: "But we cannot 'get over it,' because to get over it would mean we were not changed by the experience. It would mean we did not grow by the experience. It would mean that our loved one's death made no difference in our lives" (p. 1).

THE SPIRITUAL DIMENSION

Spirituality, as defined by Young (1994), "refers to the essential core values and the animating force within human beings. . . . For some, religious principles guide their understanding of spirituality. For most, their sense of spirituality helps to define their value systems" (p. 8:1). One's spirituality after the violent death of a loved one can be either a steadying or challenging force. "Whether a member of an organized religion or not, one's beliefs, including faith in God (or a higher power) often change as a result of the death. . . . One may increase, decrease or change particular practices as a result of his processing" (Gyulay, 1989, p. 17). Co-victims may find spirituality to be a troublesome issue, adding to the trauma and pain, as they search for acceptable responses to their theological doubts and questions and attempt to reach an understanding of their spirituality and its significance.

Co-victims should be given permission and the opportunity to explore these issues with a service provider who is available to listen in a nonjudgmental manner and whose training included an over-view of different religious faiths and practices. "People forget that often it is just such an exceptionally difficult external situation which gives man the opportunity to grow spiritually beyond himself" (Frankl, 1985, p. 93).

When planning for a loved one's funeral, cremation, or memorial service, co-victims may also ask their clergy or spiritual leader for guidance. Many clergy have not received special training as grief or pastoral counselors and, although well-meaning, may respond to the co-victim with inappropriate responses or euphemisms such as "Forgive the murderer," or "Your loved one is better off in heaven." In *Victims: A Manual for Clergy and Congregations,* Delaplane and Delaplane (1993) call such statements and advice "misguided compassion" and say that "such advice is not only infuriating but painful to hear" (p. 172). In the early stages after the murder, clergy may need to focus on their capacity to be with the co-victims in their pain and not to engage in discussions about religious philosophies.

"I spoke to a priest last night because I still couldn't understand why this happened to us, and to Ryan," says Sandy, a legal secretary. "I just needed an answer. Father Kelly said you have to just ask God to guide you." I ask if that helped and she waits on her own answer. Her lips part, managing a faint *yes* [italics added]. But the rest of her says no. (Lopez, 1997, p. A9)

Forgiveness or Restorative Justice

The issue of forgiveness is complex because it holds different meanings for different people within their belief systems. There are often both outside and internal pressures on co-victims to forgive the defendant. Organized religion, as well as a personal fear of God, plays a major role in influencing co-victims' feelings and actions regarding the subject of forgiveness.

In addition to more conventional spiritual and religious resources to address these issues, a number of formal programs have been developed in the last decade to assist co-victims in achieving a feeling of peace as well as some level of closure through the context of restorative justice. In the United States and Canada, the Quakers and Mennonites are credited with greatly contributing to the development of new paradigms of restorative justice programs to replace the old idea of retributive justice. Programmatic examples in the emerging field of restorative justice theory are victim-offender reconciliation programs and victim-offender mediation programs. The number of such programs throughout North America, Canada, and Europe is increasing rapidly. These programs are based on the principle that the crime was committed not only against the state but against the individuals and the wider community as well.

> Instead of placing the victim in a passive role and reinforcing an adversarial dynamic that often results in little emotional closure for the victim and little, if any, direct accountability by the offender to the victim, the mediation process actively facilitates personal conflict resolution. (Umbreit, 1993, p. 70)

This new justice model is not without its critics and is a controversial issue in some quarters. Many service providers and criminal justice experts are concerned that the victim may be further harmed through participation in these programs. They believe that the focal point of any restorative justice program has to be the co-victim first, with the offender and the community interests being addressed last. This may not always be the situation because the sponsoring group may not have a clear notion of its own agenda or may not fully consider the impact of the process on the co-victim. To protect the interests of the co-victim, service providers should participate in all phases of the process, including the development of restorative justice programs, the evaluation process, debriefing of co-victims, and monitoring of outcomes.

Before making any decision to become involved in a restorative justice program, co-victims need to be aware of the underlying philosophy of the program and its availability in their jurisdiction. They also need an understanding of their own motives and the possible personal consequences if they choose to be involved. There must be a strong interest by all parties; key to the success of this theory is that neither co-victim nor offender should be coerced in any manner to participate. The co-victim's acceptance of the notion of forgiveness for the defendant should not be made a prerequisite for participation. It may happen at a later time, or it may never happen. The decision to forgive or not forgive the defendant must always remain the co-victim's choice. Involvement in the program can still be valuable for the possible insights and self-knowledge that may result. Achieving a sense of self-forgiveness, often an important issue for co-victims, may be a surprising and beneficial outcome for the co-victim. The concept of restorative justice should be presented to co-victims as only one of a variety of options available to assist them in the reconstruction of their lives.

Involvement in restorative justice programs should be voluntary.

WHY SOCIAL ACTIVISM?

> I would never wish this experience on anyone, but I know that it will keep happening. I only hope that I can help someone who is going through what I went through. I'd like to touch and influence someone's life the way everyone who helped me over the past 21 months has influenced me. (Girlfriend of murder victim)

A substantial number of co-victims seek a resolution to their experience by becoming involved in social action. Some co-victims take on new personas in their pursuit of public action. Eventually, their lives become defined not by the homicide but by social activism.

Following this course offers co-victims a way to transcend their trauma and grief

> by making it a gift to others. The trauma is redeemed only when it becomes the source of a survivor mission. Social action offers the survivor a source of power that draws upon her own initiative, energy, and resourcefulness but that magnifies these qualities far beyond her own capacities. (Herman, 1992, p. 207)

Co-victims can direct their energies to a variety of social actions. The co-victims who feel especially aggrieved by the criminal justice system, its treatment of others, or both tend to work within this area, whereas others may take on larger social issues such as violence prevention. Caregivers should encourage, educate, and support co-victims in their desire to become involved. Co-victims should first be cautioned, however, about not undertaking any action prematurely before they have had time to deal with their own grief and pain. Too often, they set out to take public action without a clear understanding of the pertinent issues and their own agenda. They may become frustrated because they have unrealistic expectations of what can be accomplished. For some, the act of participation is not enough. Co-victims who are ill prepared to take on this arduous and visible role may have to discontinue their activities; this can leave them feeling angrier and even more out of control.

> In a strong case, with overwhelming evidence, everything went wrong! Our exclusion from the trial, like non-persons, the indignities, exploitation, and the lenient sentence re-victimized us. Our family's experience was the catalyst for the victims' movement in Maryland and changes in the criminal justice system. (Mother of murder victim)

Co-victims who turn anguish into action are surprised that they often face criticism and negative responses from others, especially family members and friends. They may find that many, especially legislators, do not take them seriously. Co-victims may often be confronted with statements such as, "Why don't you let it rest?" and "You can't move on with your life if you constantly do things that remind you of what happened." They may also be addressed in meetings and public forums as "Mary-Jo's mother" or "the victim's father," rather than by their own names.

It is true that some co-victims get involved as social activists to postpone dealing with their own pain and grief. The majority of co-victims who take social action, however, have a clear picture of what they need to do and why they do it. "Although giving to others is the survivor mission, those who practice it recognize that they do it for their own healing. In taking care of others, survivors feel loved and cared for themselves" (Herman, 1992, p. 209).

There is limited empirical research regarding the co-victims who choose this path; any inferences must be drawn from observations and qualitative research. Parents of murdered children are more likely than other co-victims to employ social activism as a means of externalizing and modifying their anger, frustration, and pain.

> But for the family of a victim to reach out to the family of an offender is rare. . . . It is amazing that these two men can understand what they have in common and share a goal of making something good come out of something very, very terrible. . . . Instead of curling up inside of himself, he [the father of the victim] got to a point where he could look beyond his personal pain. (Cannon, 1996, p. A25)

In addition, some surprising gender differences have been noted. For example, the mother of a murdered child is more apt than the father to take on the activist role. This behavior, which may be out of character for her, can be attributed to the desire to communicate her pain and anger and her willingness to do so in a more public forum. On December 7, 1993, Carolyn McCarthy's husband was shot and killed and their adult son was severely wounded in what became known as the Long Island Railroad massacre.

> This turned McCarthy, 52, a nurse by vocation, a housewife and mother into a spokeswoman for the families of victims. Later, she became a student of the nation's gun laws and a strident activist against the national gun lobby. And now she finds herself running for Congress in an effort to change the laws. [Although Carolyn McCarthy was not given much chance of winning, she was elected to Congress on November 5, 1996.] "The journey kept taking on a life of its own. . . . There was nothing I could do about what happened on the train.

But crusading against guns was manageable. This was something over which I have some control." (Samuel, 1996, p. A3)

In the last 20 years, co-victims who have pursued the course of social activism have accomplished many significant goals that stand to benefit others, some who have not yet experienced the consequences of the violent death of a loved one. In *Man's Search for Meaning*, Frankl (1985) states,

> We must never forget that we may also find meaning in life when confronted with a hopeless situation, when facing a fate that cannot be changed. For what matters is to bear witness to the uniquely human potential at its best, which is to transform a personal tragedy into a triumph, to turn one's predicament into a human achievement. When we are no longer able to change a situation . . . we are challenged to change ourselves. (p. 135)

HOW TEARS HELP

Tears shed during anger and grief are an important part of the healing process, both emotionally and physiologically; they help rid the body of a buildup of certain chemicals. In American society, tears are not a commonly sanctioned method of dealing with emotional stress. There are so many cultural prohibitions against crying for both men and women that some co-victims do not give way to crying from fear of being labeled weak. As a result, many co-victims are not afforded the opportunity for this release. They may resort to crying in private or attempt to hold back their tears. Service providers should acknowledge the need for co-victims to shed their tears and offer them a safe and accepting environment in which they will feel comfortable in doing so.

> Crying produces salt water. It purges, protects and expands the spirit. Crying is a release, a cleansing, an expression. However, we must learn to cry with an agenda. Are you crying to release, purify, to cleanse? Are you angry, frightened, worried or elated? We may cry because of a particular situation, but there is underlying emotion we really need to express. (Vanzant, 1993, p. 81)

THE ROLE OF HUMOR AND LAUGHTER

Humor and laughter serve as an emotional outlet, in much the same way as crying does. Laughter can provide a release for individuals who are experiencing the worst of what life has to offer. In the initial period after the murder, co-victims may view laughter and humor, whether emanating from themselves or others, as constituting a lack of respect for the victim and, consequently, as distasteful. On the other hand, service providers need to be alert to co-victims who exhibit humor and laughter in the extreme. Inappropriate use of these may be a substitute for other emotions that have been denied or suppressed.

Just as co-victims need permission to cry or express anger, they also need the approval of caregivers and others to laugh again. "The return of humor is a real sign of healing. . . . Caring, sensitive, and shared laughter is indeed one of the best medicines for recovery" (Gyulay, 1989, p. 28).

❑ Summary

Not too long ago, I was on a sort of suicide watch. I couldn't bear the pain so I wanted to die. After some time passed, I began to feel like maybe I could survive, maybe I could go on. . . . Life went on. I liked that it went on, and I no longer want to take that away from me. Enough has been taken from me. (Daughter of murder victim)

The journey that a co-victim faces is challenging and takes a lifetime. Life is truly changed forever; there is no going back. Spirituality, tears, and laughter all contribute to co-victims in the transformation of their lives. In many instances,

> *The journey that a co-victim faces is challenging and takes a lifetime.*

there are happy endings, lives returned to "normal" again, although it is a different "normal" than before the murder. Once more, co-victims may find the courage and optimism to greet the morning with a smile as they say, "Hello, day!"

You may well be isolated in your anguish. You can't believe that this could happen to you. Others want to believe that the aftermath is not as bad as you claim. If it should happen to them, they could handle it better, be stronger, recover sooner. . . . They say that by now you should be back to normal. . . . Now in addition, and by yourself, you must try to repair all that his crime has destroyed: and what you cannot repair, you must endure. (Herrington, 1982, pp. 12-13)

The final report of the President's Task Force on Victims of Crime (Herrington, 1982) was published 15 years ago. Today, co-victims are no longer forgotten; they no longer have to go through their experience alone. Service providers play an indispensable role in helping co-victims find their individual pathways. By recognizing the underserved and forgotten, the co-victims of homicide, caregivers have altered society's perception of violence, leading to an increased recognition of its impact on individuals and the community. Intervenors have often given so much of themselves to those they serve that in an amazing metamorphosis, many co-victims have turned into caregivers.

The most significant gift you can give your griever is your presence. I wish you peace and gentleness in your own journey. (Gyulay, 1989, p. 30)

Resources

❏ Organizations

Anti-Violence Partnership (AVP) of Philadelphia, Families of Murder Victims (FMV) Program, 1421 Arch Street, Philadelphia, PA 19102, (215) 686-8033.

Association of Traumatic Stress Specialists (ATSS), 7338 Broad Rive Road, Irmo, SC 29063, (803) 781-1096.

Association for Death Education and Counseling (ADEC), 638 Prospect Avenue, Hartford, CT 06105, (860) 586-7503.

International Critical Incident Stress Foundation, 4785 Dorsey Hall Drive, Suite 102, Ellicott City, MD 21042, (420) 730-4311.

International Society for Traumatic Stress Studies (ISTSS), 60 Revere Drive, Suite 500, Northbrook, IL 60062, (708) 480-9028.

Mothers Against Drunk Driving (MADD), 511 East John Carpenter Freeway, Suite 700, Irving, TX 75062, (800) GET-MADD.

National Association of Crime Victim Compensation Boards, P.O. Box 16003, Alexandria, VA 22303, (703) 370-2996 (contact for listing of individual state CVC programs).

National Criminal Justice Referral Service (NCJRS), P.O. Box 6000, Rockville, MD 20850, (800) 851-3420.

National Organization for Victim Assistance (NOVA), 1757 Park Road NW, Washington, DC 20010, (202) 232-6682.

National Victim Center (NVC), 2111 Wilson Boulevard, Suite 300, Arlington, VA 22201, (703) 276-2880.
Parents of Murdered Children (POMC), 100 East 8th Street, Suite B-41, Cincinnati, OH 45202, (513) 721-5683.
Vidocq Society, P.O. Box 51256, Philadelphia, PA 19115, (215) 389-0299.

❏ Books and Journals

Alexander, D. W. "A Creative Healing Book" series. Available from the Bureau for At-Risk Youth, 135 Dupont Street, P.O. Box 760, Plainview, NY 11803-0760, (800) 999-6884.
Alexander, E. K., & Lord, J. H. (1994). *A victim's right to speak, a nation's responsibility to listen.* Available from National Victim Center (NVC), 2111 Wilson Boulevard, Suite 300, Arlington, VA 22201, (703) 276-2880.
Brener, A. (1993). *Mouring and Mitzvah: A guided journal for walking the mourner's path through grief to healing.* Woodstock, VT: Jewish Lights Publishing.
Caplan, S., & Lang, G. (1995). *Grief's courageous journey: A workbook.* Oakland, CA: New Harbinger.
Crime Liability Monthly. Journal of the National Victim Center, Arlington, VA.
Crime Victims' Litigation Quarterly. Journal of the National Victim Center, Arlington, VA.
Cushner, K., & Brislin, R. W. (1996). *Intercultural interactions: A practical guide* (2nd ed.). Thousand Oaks, CA: Sage.

❏ Audiovisual Material

Crime victim compensation: A good place to start [Videotape]. (Doc. No. NCJ 1623591H). Available from Office for Victims of Crime Resource Center, (800) 627-6872.

❏ Clinical Instruments

Grief and Mourning Status Interview and Inventory (GAMSII). From Rando, T. A. (1993). *Treatment of complicated mourning.* Champaign, IL: Research Press.
Posttraumatic Stress Diagnostic Scale (PDS). *PDS Manual* (1995). Minneapolis, MN: National Computer Systems (NCS). Available from NCS, P.O. Box 1416, Minneapolis, MN 55440.
Traumatic Intake Assessment (2nd revision, 1994). Available from MaryDale Salston, 2039 North Meridian Road, Number 220, Tallahassee, FL 32303.
Traumatic Stress Institute (TSI) Belief Scale (Revision L). Available from Traumatic Stress Institute, 22 Morgan Farms Drive, South Windsor, CT 06074, (860) 644-2541.

References

American Psychiatric Association. (1994). *Diagnostic and statistical manual of mental disorders* (4th ed.). Washington, DC: Author.

Anderson, D. A. (1986). Crime victims: Do they have privacy rights? In T. Thomason & A. Babili (Eds.), *Crime victims and the news media* (pp. 7-10). Fort Worth: Texas Christian University Department of Journalism.

Applebaum, D. R., & Burns, G. L. (1991). Unexpected childhood death: Posttraumatic stress disorder in surviving siblings and parents. *Journal of Clinical Child Psychology, 20*(2), 114-120.

Associated Press. (1995, September 17). Simpson case backlash keeps cameras out of other courtrooms. *New York Times*, p. 35.

Baker, R. (1993, September 10). A slight plague of murder. *New York Times*, p. 21.

Barnard, A., & Henson, R. (1996, June 26). Father slays son, 2½, then kills himself. *Philadelphia Inquirer*, pp. B1, B4.

Bastian, L. D. (1995). Criminal victimization 1993. *Bureau of Statistics Bulletin* (NCJ-151658). Washington, DC: U.S. Bureau of Justice Statistics.

Beckmann, R. (1990). *Children who grieve: A manual for conducting support groups*. Holmes Beach, FL: Learning Publications.

Bell, C. C., & Jenkins, E. J. (1990). Preventing black homicide. In J. Dewart (Ed.), *The state of black America 1990*. Washington, DC: National Urban League.

Bell, C. C., & Jenkins, E. J. (1991, November). *Community violence and children on Chicago's southside*. Paper presented at the NIMH conference on Community

Violence and Children's Development: Research and Clinical Implications, Bethesda, MD.

Bettag, T. (Executive Producer). (1996, September 24). *ABC News Nightline*. New York: American Broadcasting Company.

Blumenthal, R. (1990, November 6.). With detective hard pressed, family joins hunt for killer. *New York Times*, pp. B1, B5.

Booth v. Maryland, 482 U.S. 496, 107 S. Ct. 2529 (1987).

Bowlby, J. (1980). *Attachment and loss: Vol. 3. Loss: Sadness and depression*. New York: Basic Books.

Bragg, R. (1996, December 26). Prisoner's pittance is meant as a reminder of a great loss. *New York Times*, pp. A1, A16.

Brom, D., & Kleber, R. J. (1989). Prevention of post-traumatic stress disorders. *Journal of Traumatic Stress, 2*, 335-351.

Burgess, A. W. (1975). Family reaction to homicide. *American Journal of Orthopsychiatry, 45*, 391-397.

Cannon, A. (1996, December 25). Father of slain man joins kin of teen killer to fight violence. *Philadelphia Inquirer*, p. A25.

Carrington, F. (1994). *Legal remedies for crime victims against perpetrators: Basic principles* (Rev. ed.). Arlington, VA: National Victim Center.

Centers for Disease Control. (1990). Homicide among young black males: United States, 1978-1987. *Morbidity and Mortality Weekly Report, 39*, 869-873.

Centers for Disease Control. (1994). *Suicide fact sheet*. Atlanta, GA: National Center for Injury Prevention and Control, Division of Violence Prevention.

Chesnais, J. (1992). The history of violence: Homicide and suicide through the ages. *International Social Science Journal, 44*, 217-234.

Cipriano, R. (1996, June 13). Business scrubs away death. *Philadelphia Inquirer*, p. A3.

Clines, F. X. (1993, March 9). Police killers offer insights into victims' fatal mistakes. *New York Times*, pp. A1, A16.

Colimore, E., Raphael, M., & Sanginiti, T. (1994, November 3). Wife of a Cherry Hill rabbi found beaten to death at home. *Philadelphia Inquirer*, pp. A7, A17.

Columbia dictionary of quotations. (1993). New York: Columbia University Press. (Caedmon recordings reproduced by arrangement with HarperCollins)

Cook, J. A. (1988). Dad's double binds: Rethinking fathers' bereavement from a men's studies perspective. *Journal of Contemporary Ethnography, 17*, 285-308.

Crime Victims' Rights Constitutional Amendment, H.R. J. Res. 71, S. J. Res. 6, 105th Cong., 1st Sess. (1997).

Daughen, J. R., Costantinou, M., & Sheehan, K. (1994, January 12). Woman slain on highway. *Philadelphia Daily News*, pp. 5, 22.

Davis, M., Eshelman, E. R., & McKay, M. (1988). *The relaxation and stress reduction workbook* (3rd ed.). Oakland, CA: New Harbinger.

Delaplane, D., & Delaplane, A. (1993). *Victims: A manual for clergy and congregations*. Washington, DC: U.S. Department of Justice, Office for Victims of Crime.

Doka, K. (Ed.). (1988). *Disenfranchised grief: Recognizing hidden sorrow*. Lexington, MA: Lexington Books.

Elias, R. (1993). *Victims still: The political manipulation of crime victims*. Newbury Park, CA: Sage.

English, G. (1995, October 8). Abuse victims say case spoke volumes on domestic violence. *Philadelphia Inquirer*, p. A20.

Eron, L. D. (Chairman). (1993). *Violence & youth: Psychology's Response Volume I.* (Summary report of the American Psychological Association Commission on Violence & Youth). Washington, DC: American Psychological Association.

Eth, S., & Pynoos, R. S. (1985a). Developmental perspective on psychic trauma in childhood. In C. R. Figley (Ed.), *Trauma and its wake* (pp. 36-51). New York: Brunner/Mazel.

Eth, S., & Pynoos, R. S. (1985b). Interaction of trauma and grief in childhood. In S. Eth & R. S. Pynoos (Eds.), *Post-traumatic stress disorder in children* (pp. 168-186). Washington, DC: American Psychiatric Press.

Eth, S., Baron, D. A., & Pynoos, R. S. (1987). Death notification. *Bulletin of the American Academy of Psychiatry and the Law, 15,* 275-281.

Figley, C. R. (1992, November). Posttraumatic stress disorder: Part IV. Generic treatment approaches. *Violence Update, 3*(3), 1, 4-8.

Figley, C. R. (Ed.). (1995). *Compassion fatigue: Secondary traumatic stress disorder in those who treat the traumatized.* New York: Brunner/Mazel.

Figley, C. R. (1996, February 17). *The active ingredients in efficient treatments of PTSD.* Paper presented at IATC Conference, San Francisco.

Flitcraft, A. H., Hadley, S. M., Hendricks-Matthews, M. K., McLeer, S. V., & Warshaw, C. (1992, September). American Medical Association diagnostic and treatment guidelines on domestic violence. *Archives of Family Medicine, 1,* 39-47.

Florida State University. (1994). *Eliminating posttraumatic stress disorder: The active ingredient symposium series* [Brochure]. Tallahassee, FL: Author.

Fowlkes, M. R. (1990). The social regulation of grief. *Sociological Forum, 5,* 635-652.

Frankl, V. E. (1985). *Man's search for meaning* (Rev. ed.). New York: Pocket.

Freud, S. (1953). Mourning and melancholia. In J. Strachey (Ed. and Trans.), *The standard edition of the complete psychological works of Sigmund Freud* (Vol. 14). London: Hogarth. (Original work published 1917)

Fried, J. (1990, December 14). Confession forces a family to relive decade-old killing. *New York Times,* pp. B1, B4.

Frogge, S., & Cantrell, C. (1991). *We hurt too: A guide for adult siblings* [Brochure]. Irving, TX: Mothers Against Drunk Driving.

Gammage, J. (1993, June 18). Shooting took a life, shattered a second, and shook many more. *Philadelphia Inquirer,* p. A1.

Gerbode, F. A. (1993). *Traumatic incident reduction: A simple trauma resolution technique.* Menlo Park, CA: Institute for Research in Metapsychology.

Getzel, G. S., & Masters, R. (1984). Serving families who survive homicide victims. *Social Casework: The Journal of Contemporary Social Work, 65*(3), 138-144.

Gibbons, T. J., & Gelles, J. (1996, November 21). Arrest in killing of Penn chemist. *Philadelphia Inquirer,* p. A1.

Gifis, S. H. (1984). *Law dictionary* (2nd ed.). Woodbury, NY: Baron's Educational Series.

The girls who had everything. (1986, October 22). *New York Times,* p. A30.

Gissler, S. (1989, February 16). *Death and the media: An editor's dilemmas.* Paper presented at the Interdisciplinary Education Conference on Bereavement and Grief, Yeshiva University, New York.

Goffman, E. (1963). *Stigma: Notes on the management of spoiled identity.* New York: Simon & Schuster.

Goldberg, C. (1996, February 22). Boys' families hope for release as freeway killer's execution nears. *New York Times,* p. A14.

Goodman, H. (1995, December 3). 2d jury convicts ex-guard in '84 Drexel slaying. *Philadelphia Inquirer*, pp. A1, A13.

Greenfield, J. (1986). TV: The medium determines impact of crime stories. In T. Thomason & A. Babili (Eds.), *Crime victims and the news media* (pp. 19-23). Fort Worth: Texas Christian University Department of Journalism.

Gross, J. (1990, August 12). Bystander deaths reshape city lives. *New York Times*, p. 18.

Gutierrez, A. (1993, Fall). Strategies for reaching Hispanics. *The MADDvocate, 6*(2), 18-19.

Gyulay, J. E. (1989). Grief responses. *Issues in Comprehensive Pediatric Nursing, 12,* 1-31.

Halporn, R. (1993, Fall). Asian-Americans in loss and grief. *The MADDvocate, 6*(2), 16-17.

Haran, J. (1988). Use of group work to help children cope with the violent death of a classmate. In G. S. Getzel (Ed.), *Violence: Prevention and treatment in groups* (pp. 79-92). New York: Hawthorn.

Henry-Jenkins, W. (1993, Fall). African-American grief. *The MADDvocate, 6*(2), 14-15.

Herman, J. L. (1992). *Trauma and recovery.* New York: Basic Books.

Herrington, L. H. (Chairman). (1982, December). *President's task force on victims of crime: Final report.* Washington, DC: Government Printing Office.

Horowitz, M. J. (1986). Stress-response syndromes: A review of posttraumatic and adjustment disorders. *Hospital and Community Psychiatry, 37,* 241-249.

James, G. (1992, December 24). The endless quest for a daughter's killer. *New York Times*, pp. B1, B5.

Jamieson, K. H., & Romer, D. (1995, August 27). If it's (black and white) crime, television will give it time. *Philadelphia Inquirer*, p. E5.

Janoff-Bulman, R. (1985). The aftermath of victimization: Rebuilding shattered assumptions. In C. R. Figley (Ed.), *Trauma and its wake* (pp. 15-35). New York: Brunner/Mazel.

Janoff-Bulman, R. (1992). *Shattered assumptions: Towards a new psychology of trauma.* New York: Free Press.

Jones, C. (1995, October 13). Nicole Simpson, in death, lifting domestic violence to the forefront as a national issue. *New York Times*, p. A28.

Kahn, A. S. (Ed.). (1984). *Victims of crime and violence* (Final report of the American Psychological Association task force on the victims of crime and violence). Washington, DC: American Psychological Asssociation.

Karen, R. (1992, February). Shame. *Atlantic Monthly, 269,* 40-70.

Kauffman, J. (1988). Intrapsychic dimensions of disenfranchised grief. In K. J. Doka (Ed.), *Disenfranchised grief: Recognizing hidden sorrow* (pp. 25-29). Lexington, MA: Lexington Books.

Kilpatrick, D. G., Amick, A., & Resnick, H. S. (1990). *The impact of homicide on surviving family members.* Charleston: Medical University of South Carolina, Crime Victims Research and Treatment Center.

Klass, D. (1983). Reflections on time and change. *Healing, grieving, growing.* Oak Brook, IL: Compassionate Friends.

Klass, D. (1993). Solace and immortality: Bereaved parents' continuing bond with their children. *Death Studies, 17,* 343-368.

Kolbert, E. (1994, December 14). Television gets closer look as a factor in real violence. *New York Times*, pp. A1, D20.

Koop, C. E., & Lundberg, G. D. (1992). Violence in America: A public health emergency. *Journal of the American Medical Association, 267*(22), 3075-3076.

Laker, B., & O'Dowd, J. (1993, December 22). Medical student killed: Newlyweds' plans end in tragedy. *Philadelphia Daily News*, pp. 4, 5.

Leary, W. E. (1994, October 23). Gun violence leading to better care for injuries. *New York Times*, p. 32.

Lerner, M. J. (1980). *The belief in a just world: A fundamental delusion*. New York: Plenum.

Lerner, M. J., & Miller, D. T. (1978). Just world research and the attribution process: Looking back and ahead. *Psychological Bulletin, 85*, 1030-1051.

Levy, R. (1996, January). The Vidocq Society. *Greater Philadelphia Bulletin, 14*(1), 1, 10.

Lewis, C. (1995, November 29). Our fear of crime is exaggerated, and lurid news stories are to blame. *Philadelphia Inquirer*, p. A19.

Lindemann, E. (1994). Symptomatology and management of acute grief. *American Journal of Psychiatry, 151*(6), 155-160. (Original work published 1944)

Lohmann, R. A. (1977). Dying and the social responsibility of institutions. *Social Casework, 58*(9), 538-545.

Lopez, S. (1997, January 1). Enduring the loss of a child to violence. *Philadelphia Inquirer*, pp. A1, A9.

Lord, J. H. (1993). *Death notification seminar* (Rev. ed.). Irving, TX: Mothers Against Drunk Driving.

Lore, R. K., & Schultz, L. A. (1993). Control of human aggression: A comparative perspective. *American Psychologist, 48*, 16-25.

Loyd, L. (1994, December 7). Man sentenced to die for shooting teen during deli dispute. *Philadelphia Inquirer*, p. B5.

Loyd, L. (1995, November 1). Life sentence for man who killed officer. *Philadelphia Inquirer*, p. B1.

Loyd, L. (1996, February 28). Polecs get chance to tell killer their pain. *Philadelphia Inquirer*, pp. A1, A13.

MacKellar, F. L., & Yanagishita, M. (1995, February). *Homicide in the United States: Who's at risk?* (Population Trends and Public Policy, Vol. 21). Washington, DC: Population Reference Bureau.

Man tells of learning about wife's slaying. (1995, January 25). *New York Times*, p. B4.

Marzuk, P. M., Tardiff, K., & Hirsch, C. S. (1992). The epidemiology of murder-suicide. *Journal of the American Medical Association, 267*(23), 98-102.

Matza, M. (1991, July 28). The innocent bystander as victim. *Philadelphia Inquirer*, pp. A1, A10.

McCann, I. L., & Pearlman, L. A. (1990a). *Psychological trauma and the adult survivor: Theory, therapy, and transformation*. New York: Brunner/Mazel.

McCann, I. L., & Pearlman, L. A. (1990b). Vicarious traumatization: A framework for understanding the psychological effects of working with victims. *Journal of Traumatic Stress, 3*(1), 131-149.

McGoldrick, M., & Gerson, R. (1989). Genograms and the family life cycle. In B. Carter & M. McGoldrick (Eds.), *The changing family life cycle* (2nd ed., pp. 164-186). Needham Heights, MA: Allyn & Bacon.

McKay, M., Davis, M., & Fanning, P. (1983). *Messages: The communication book*. Oakland, CA: New Harbinger.

McKay, M., Rogers, P. D., & McKay, J. (1989). *When anger hurts: Quieting the storm within*. Oakland, CA: New Harbinger.

McNamara, J. W. (1986). Murder and the tort of intentional infliction of emotional distress. *Duke Law Journal, 1986,* 572-587.

Mitchell, M. A. (1992). An overview of children as witnesses to violence. In D. F. Schwartz (Ed.), *Children and violence report of the 23rd Ross roundtable on critical approaches to common pediatric problems* (pp. 77-86). Columbus, OH: Ross Laboratories.

National Clearinghouse for the Defense of Battered Women. (1995). Battered women charged with crimes: Results of criminal cases. *Statistics packet* (3rd ed.). Philadelphia: Author.

National Organization for Victim Assistance. (1985, October). Survivors of homicide victims. *Network Information Bulletin, 2*(3), 1-10.

National Organization for Victim Assistance. (1991). Crime news policies at the Post-Dispatch. *National Organization for Victim Assistance Newsletter, 15,* 1-5.

National Victim Center. (1990). *Victims' rights and the media* [Pamphlet]. Arlington, VA: Author.

National Victim Center. (1993). *Notoriety-for-profit/Son of Sam statutes.* Arlington, VA: Author.

National Victim Center. (1996). *1996 victims' rights sourcebook: A compilation and comparison of victims' rights legislation.* Arlington, VA: Author.

Nelson, D. T. (1996, November). Trial of the century, Part II: What the lawsuit against Simpson is really about. *Crime Victims' Litigation Quarterly, 3*(4), 1-2.

Newberger, E. H., & Newberger, C. M. (1992). Treating children who witness violence. In D. F. Schwarz (Ed.), *Children and violence report of the 23rd Ross roundtable on critical approaches to common pediatric problems* (pp. 87-97). Columbus, OH: Ross Laboratories.

Osterweis, M., Solomon, F., & Green, M. (Eds.). (1984). *Bereavement: Reactions, consequences, and care.* Washington, DC: National Academy Press.

Oxford English dictionary (2nd ed.). (1989). Oxford, UK: Clarendon.

Paik, A. (1995, March 11). Kin's anger erupts in a murder trial. *Philadelphia Inquirer,* p. B7.

Payne v. Tennessee, 501 U.S. 808 (1991).

Phillips, N. (1991, July 21). Memorial for a child slain at five. *Philadelphia Inquirer,* p. B2.

Prothrow-Stith, D. (1991). *Deadly consequences.* New York: HarperCollins.

Pynoos, R. S., & Eth, S. (1985). Children traumatized by witnessing acts of personal violence: Homicide, rape, or suicide behavior. In S. Eth & R. S. Pynoos (Eds.), *Post-traumatic stress disorder in children* (pp. 17-43). Washington, DC: American Psychiatric Press.

Pynoos, R. S., & Nader, K. (1990). Children's exposure to violence and traumatic death. *Psychiatric Annals, 20,* 334-344.

Quinney, R. (1972, November). Who is the victim? *Criminology, 10,* 314-323.

Rando, T. A. (1988). *How to go on living when someone you love dies.* Lexington, MA: Lexington Books.

Rando, T. A. (1993). *Treatment of complicated mourning.* Champaign, IL: Research Press.

Redmond, L. M. (1989). *Surviving: When someone you love was murdered: A professional's guide to group grief therapy for families & friends of murder victims* (1st ed.). Clearwater, FL: Psychological Consultation and Education Services.

Richardson, L. (1993, July 1). For a grieving mother, freshened tears. *New York Times,* p. B6.

Rinear, E. E. (1985, April 22). *Signs and symptoms of post-traumatic stress disorder among surviving parents of child homicide victims.* Paper presented at the 62nd annual meeting of the American Orthopsychiatric Association, New York.

Rynearson, E. K., & McCreery, J. M. (1993). Bereavement after homicide: A synergism of trauma and loss. *American Journal of Psychiatry, 150*(2), 258-261.

Sabatini, R. V. (1996, June 26). Murder-suicide ruled in Bristol fire deaths. *Philadelphia Inquirer,* p. R3.

Samuel, T. (1996, July 16). Victims' kin running for office to change nation's gun laws. *Philadelphia Inquirer,* p. A3.

Schur, E. M. (1984). *Labeling women deviant: Gender, stigma, and social control.* New York: Random House.

Sehnert, K. W. (1981). *Stress/unstress: How you can control stress at home and on the job.* Minneapolis, MN: Augsburg.

Seplow, S. (1996, November 27). Without camera, trial isn't as riveting. *Philadelphia Inquirer,* p. A2.

Sherman, L. W., Steele, L., Laufersweiler, D., Hoffer, N., & Julian, S. A. (1989). Stray bullets and "mushrooms": Random shootings of bystanders in four cities, 1977-1988. *Journal of Quantitative Criminology, 5,* 297-316.

Sherman, R. (1994, April 18). Crime's toll on the U.S.: Fear, despair and guns. *National Law Journal, 1,* 19-20.

Skorneck, C. (1990, December 22). Shootings no longer faze D.C. children. *Philadelphia Inquirer,* p. A3.

Smith, M., & Eddy, D. (1989, July/August). *The prostitute, the blind pig, and the gambler: Contributory conduct and illegal activity* [Technical assistance supplement]. Alexandria, VA: National Association of Crime Victim Compensation Boards.

Spungen, D. (1983). *And I don't want to live this life.* New York: Random House.

Spungen, D. (1993). *Victim services for homicide co-victims.* Philadelphia: Anti-Violence Partnership of Philadelphia.

Stark, J. H., & Goldstein, H. K. (1985). *The rights of crime victims.* New York: Bantam/American Civil Liberties Union.

Stein, A. J., & Winokuer, H. R. (1989). Monday mourning: Managing employee grief. In K. Doka (Ed.), *Disenfranchised grief: Recognizing hidden sorrow* (pp. 91-101). Lexington, MA: Lexington Books.

Stein, J. (1995). *Guide for victim advocates on working with the media: Part II.* Washington, DC: U.S. Department of Justice, Office for Victims of Crime, in cooperation with the National Organization for Victim Assistance.

Symonds, M. (1980). The "second injury" to victims. *Evaluation and Change* (Special issue), 36-38.

Tarasoff v. Regents, 17 Cal.3d 425, 131 Cal.Rptr. 14, 551 P.2d 334 (1976).

Terry, R. J., Colimore, E., & Gibbons, T. J., Jr. (1996, July 11). Wait for answers in Dellapenna case grows one day longer. *Philadelphia Inquirer,* p. R3.

Thomason, T. (1986). The issue is ethics. In T. Thomason & A. Babili (Eds.), *Crime victims and the news media* (p. 2). Fort Worth: Texas Christian University Department of Journalism.

Umbreit, M. S. (1993). Crime victims and offenders in mediation: An emerging area of social work practice. *Social Work, 38*(1), 69-73.

Uniform crime reports for the United States. (1993). Washington, DC: U.S. Department of Justice, Federal Bureau of Investigation.

Valbrun, M. (1996, January 12). A Philadelphia officer is mourned as colleague, mother, friend. *Philadelphia Inquirer,* pp. A1, B7.

Van der Kolk, B. A. (1987). The role of the group in the origin and resolution of the trauma response. In B. A. Van der Kolk (Ed.), *Psychological trauma* (pp. 153-172). Washington, DC: American Psychiatric Press.

Vanzant, I. (1993). *Acts of faith: Daily meditations for people of color.* New York: Fireside.

Victims of Crime Act of 1984 (as amended), 42 U.S.C. § 10601 *et seq.*

Vigoda, R. (1996, December 10). Judge rules du Pont ready to stand trial. *Philadelphia Inquirer,* pp. A1, A14.

Vines, S. W. (1988). The therapeutics of guided imagery. *Holistic Nursing Practices,* 2(93), 55-65.

Violence Against Women Act of 1994, 42 U.S.C. § 13701 *et seq.*

Weiner, J. (1995, June 8). A shooting victim now crusades against violence aimed at gays. *Philadelphia Inquirer,* p. G4.

Weinfeld, I. J. (1993, Fall). Help for the bereaved: The Jewish traditions. *The MADDvocate,* 6,(2), 20-21.

Wolfelt, A. D. (1992). Men in grief: A naturally complicated experience. In *Helping men in grief* [Special issue]. *Bereavement: A Magazine of Hope and Healing.*

Woodall, M. (1995, August 20). When mom's boyfriend gets violent, children die. *Philadelphia Inquirer,* pp. A1, A16, A17.

Worden, J. W. (1991). *Grief counseling and grief therapy: A handbook for the mental health practitioner* (2nd ed.). New York: Springer.

Young, M. A. (1994). *Responding to communities in crisis: The training manual of the crisis response team.* Washington, DC: National Organization for Victim Assistance.

Zawitz, M. W., Klaus, P., Bachman, R., Langan, P., Graziadei, H., & Harlow, C. W. (1994). Domestic violence: Violence between intimates [Selected findings]. *Bureau of Justice Statistics Bulletin* (NCJ-149259). Washington, DC: U.S. Bureau of Justice Statistics.

Index

Abuse:
   battered woman syndrome, 89-90
   domestic violence, 86-87
   link to murder, 87-91, 114
   of children, 85
Advocacy, 145-146
   distinction from counseling, 142-143
   See also Victim advocates
African Americans:
   lack of coverage of crime against,
      229-230
   media portrayals of, 14, 229-230
   mourning among, 53
Alcohol, 172
   See also Drunk driving murders
Alternative therapies, 165-166, 167
Amendments, victims' rights, 205-206
American Indians, 51-52
American Psychological Association
   Task Force on the Victims of
   Crime and Violence, 155
American Red Cross, 165

And I Don't Want to Live This Life
   (Spungen), 13
Anger, 44
   at victim, 46-47
   functions of, 44-45
   in domestic violence cases, 89
   normalization of, 46-47
   of spouses, 70
   revenge fantasies, 45-46, 76
   targets of, 47, 198
Antidepressants. *See* Medication
Anti-Violence Partnership, 40
Anxiety, 57, 58-59
Asian Americans, 52
Association of Traumatic Stress
   Specialists (ATSS), 141
ATSS. *See* Association of Traumatic
   Stress Specialists
Attorneys:
   for civil cases, 201, 202-203
   See also Defense attorneys;
   Prosecutors

Autopsies, of Jewish victims, 54

Battered woman syndrome, 89-90
Behavior modification, 157
Bereavement:
    response phases, 26
    See also Grief; Mourning
Berkowitz, David, 210
Bills of information, 111-112
Blacks. *See* African Americans
Blame:
    placed on mothers, 33
    placed on victims, 11-13, 15, 29, 89
    self-. *See* Guilt
Booth v. Maryland, 208
Bowlby, J., 26-27
Brothers. *See* Siblings
Bystander killings. *See* Random killings

Capital cases, 185-187, 208-209
Caregivers, 139
    confidentiality, 152
    coping strategies, 153-154
    duty to warn, 152-153
    knowledge of legal issues, 201
    legal issues, 152-153
    practical assistance, 151
    relationships with media, 235-236
    relationships with members of
        criminal justice system, 194-195
    second wounds inflicted by, 10-11
    services, 144-147, 179, 181
    skills needed, 145, 147-152, 155
    training, 145, 155
    vicarious traumatization, 153-154
    See also Mental health professionals;
        Victim advocates
Cartoons, 5
Case advocacy, 145
Centers for Disease Control and
    Prevention (CDC), 3, 5
Children:
    abuse of, 85
    aggression linked to violence in
        lives, 3-4
    deaths of, 65-67, 85-86
    exposure to violence in media, 4

    increasing violence of, 5-6
    pedicide, 85-86, 115
    random killings of, 108-109
    violence witnessed by, 3-4, 35-36
Children, as co-victims, 70
    adult, 73-74
    court orientation, 190-191
    direct co-victims, 72-73
    discussing death with, 37-39, 71-72
    emotional responses, 71, 72, 190
    family relationships, 168
    funeral attendance, 71
    grief reactions, 36-37, 38, 39
    indirect co-victims, 71-72
    interventions with, 166-171
    of police officers, 94, 98
    post-traumatic stress symptoms, 72
    siblings of victim, 74-75
    support groups, 169-170
    witnesses of homicide, 72-73, 190-191
Civil law terminology, 202
Civil suits, 200-204
    against media organizations, 233-235
    awards and crime victim
        compensation, 213
    damages, 202
    third-party, 203
    tort of outrage, 203-204
Clergy, 240
Closure, 239
Commemorations, of victims, 39-40, 71
    at crime scenes, 132
Communication skills, 147-148
Community disasters, 110-112, 164-165
Complicated mourning, 23, 31
Concerns of Police Survivors (COPS), 98
Confidentiality issues, 152
Constitutions:
    state, 205
    See also U.S. Constitution
Continuances, 184
Controlled dreaming, 158
COPS. *See* Concerns of Police Survivors
Counseling, 143-144
    distinction from advocacy, 142-143
    family therapy, 158-159
    for children, 168-169
    group therapy, 159-161
    in cases of intrafamily homicide, 84

individual, 158
in no-arrest cases, 106, 107
in police departments, 98
post-trauma, 41, 156-158
supportive, 146
Court accompaniment, 146-147, 179,
191-193
at first listings, 181
dealing with media, 227
Courts:
orientation to, 187-191
personnel, 197
victim witness waiting areas, 182-183
See also Judges; Trials
Co-victims:
active roles in investigations, 104-105
activities required of, 24-25
common responses, 63-64
definition, 8-10
diaries, 157, 208
inner representations of victims, 43
input at sentencing, 206-209
input before parole, 209-210
input to plea negotiations, 184
lack of legal standing, 180-181
life philosophy changes, 59
loss devalued by others, 13-15, 29
media exploitation of, 225-226
nervous system changes, 23
no-arrest cases, 101-107
numbers of, 10
physical health, 60-61
privacy issues, 222, 223, 234
reluctance to seek assistance, 139
rights in dealing with media, 221, 233
trauma experienced by, 18-22, 41, 43
views of criminal justice system, 179
See also Children, as co-victims;
Grief; Parents; Reconstruction of
life; Second wounds
Coworkers, as co-victims, 78, 81-82
Crime. See Homicide; Violence
Crime scenes:
cleaning, 130-131
visiting, 132
Crime victim compensation (CVC),
211-214
assistance with claims, 147, 212-214
contribution of deceased, 213, 214

expenses covered, 144, 212
Crime Victims' Rights Constitutional
Amendment, 205-206
Criminal justice system:
activists and, 243
biases in, 179, 195-196
controversies over victim programs,
140
dealing with, 68
distrust of, 179
focus on defendants, 178
guidance by caregivers, 181
handling of drunk driving murders,
100
lack of legal standing for co-victims,
180-181
providing information on, 146, 181,
187-191
restraining orders in domestic
violence cases, 88-89, 116
second wounds inflicted by, 68, 179,
194-200
stages, 181, 182
treatment of murder victims,
111-112, 178-179
See also Trials
Crisis intervention programs, 145
for police officers, 97-98
Crisis intervention stress debriefings.
See Critical incident stress
debriefings
Critical incident stress debriefings, 112,
164-165, 170-171
Cross-cultural awareness, 148-151
Crying, 245
Cultural differences:
attitudes of police, 195-196
awareness of, 148-151
biases in criminal justice system, 179,
195-196
biases in media, 229-230
in grieving process, 51-54
languages, 150
spatial relationships, 150-151
CVC. See Crime victim compensation

Death notification:
by police, 122-123, 135-136

by telephone, 128-129
common reactions, 134-135
compassion in, 123
consequences of poorly delivered,
    133-134
debriefing following, 122, 136-137
determining next of kin, 124
effects of performing, 135-136
following up, 132-133
from other sources, 129
goals of, 123
impact, 119-120, 133-134
improvements needed, 137
information provided, 123-124
in hospitals, 127-128
in workplace, 128
persons performing, 122-123
preparation for, 123-124
protocol, 124-127
role of caregivers, 120-121
training in, 121-122, 135-136, 137
Death penalty, 185-187, 208-209
Deceased. *See* Victims
Defendants:
    executions, 186
    focus on, 178, 216
    insanity defense, 185
    parole, 209-210
    pleas, 183-184
    related to or acquainted with
        victim, 6
    sentencing, 111-112, 206-209
    Son of Sam statutes, 210-211
    traits shared with victims, 4
Defense attorneys:
    co-victims' anger at, 47, 198
    potential to inflict second wounds,
        198-200
    relationship with prosecutors, 200
    See also Trials
Depression, 57-59, 173
Detectives, homicide, 103-105, 194-195
    See also Police officers
*Diagnostic and Statistical Manual of
    Mental Disorders*, 18
Diaries, 157, 208
Disasters. *See* Community disasters
Disenfranchised grief, 28-29, 79, 94-95
District attorneys. *See* Prosecutors

Doctors:
    need for training in traumatic grief,
        174-175
    presence at death notification, 127
    See also Medication
Doka, K., 28-29
Domestic violence. *See* Abuse
Dreaming, controlled, 158
Drugs. *See* Medication
Drunk driving murders, 99-101
    co-victims as witnesses, 100
    support groups, 100-101
Duty to warn, 152-153

Executions, 186
Extended families, 78-79
Extramarital affairs, 80-81
Eye movement desensitization and
    reprocessing, 167

Families:
    changes to system, 64, 76-78, 83-84,
        158-159
    coping mechanisms, 65
    extended, 78-79
    grandparents, 67-68, 86
    impact of murder, 64-65
    notification. *See* Death notification
    role of protector in, 64
    siblings, 74-78
    support for children, 168
    See also Children; Intrafamily
        homicide; Parents
Families of Murder Victims (FMV),
    xviii-xix, 9, 40, 106, 116
Family therapy, 158-159
Fathers:
    grieving process, 31-33, 55
    protector role, 64
    See also Parents
Fear, 47-48, 66
Figley, Charles, 165
First Amendment, 221, 233-235
First listings, 181-182
FMV. *See* Families of Murder Victims
Forgiveness, 84, 89, 241
Fowlkes, M. R., 13

Frankl, V. E., 245
Freedom of press, 221, 233-235
Freud, Sigmund, 25-26
Friends, as co-victims, 78-79
Funerals, 40
    attendance by children, 71
    roles of significant others, 79

Gay partners, 80-81
Gender differences:
    in grieving, 31-33, 54-56
    in use of medication by co-victims, 56
Genograms, 159
Gerbner, George, 6
Goffman, E., 14
Goldman, Fred, 225
Goldman, Ronald, 85, 225
Grand juries, 182
Grandparents, 67-68, 86
Grief:
    acute, 31
    anger and, 44-47
    circular model, 27
    cultural influences, 51-54
    disenfranchised, 28-29, 79, 94-95
    distinction from mourning, 24, 27
    fear and, 47-48
    gender differences, 31-33, 54-56
    interruptions in process, 28, 30-31
    linear structure, 26-27
    mental health implications, 56-60
    of children, 36-37, 38, 39
    pathological, 31
    physical symptoms, 60-61
    process, 23-24, 30
    rituals and commemorations, 39-40,
        53, 71, 132, 171
    shame and, 50-51
    subsequent temporary upsurge of
        (STUG), 42-43
    traumatic, 40-42, 43, 56-60
    See also Mourning
Grief work, 24-25
    Freud on, 25
    tasks, 26, 27-28
Group crisis intervention. See Critical
        incident stress debriefings
Group therapy, 159-161

Guided imagery, 167
Guilt, 49-50
    anger and, 47
    confusion with shame, 48-49
    of children, 190
    of parents, 66
    survivor, 49-50

Healing, 239
    humor and, 246
    tears and, 245
    use of term, 19
Hearings:
    continuances, 184
    media coverage, 226-227
    parole, 209-210
    preliminary, 182
Hispanics, 53
Homicide:
    causes, 2-5
    clearance rates, 97, 101
    crime scenes, 130-131, 132
    definition, xvii
    link to domestic violence, 87-91
    multiple, 110-112
    no-arrest cases, 101-107, 231-232
    notification. See Death notification
    rape and, 15-16
    rates, 5-6
    serial, 110-112
    suicide and, 112-117
    victim precipitation, 15
    See also Victims
Homicide detectives, 103-105, 194-195
    See also Police officers
Hospitals, death notification in, 127-128
Humor, in healing process, 246

Individual therapy, 158
Infanticide, 85
Inner representations, of victims, 43
Innovative therapies, 165-166, 167
Insanity defense, 185
Insurance:
    life, 213
    mental health coverage, 144, 158,
        174-175

International Critical Incident Stress
    Foundation, 165
Intervenors. *See* Caregivers
Interventions:
    addressing existing trauma, 155-156
    advocacy, 145-146
    alternative therapies, 165-166, 167
    assistance with crime victim
        compensation (CVC) claims, 147,
        212-214
    child-specific, 166-171
    court accompaniment, 146-147, 179,
        181, 191-193, 227
    crisis intervention, 97-98, 145
    critical incident stress debriefings,
        112, 164-165, 170-171
    information on criminal justice
        system, 146, 181, 187-191
    police deaths, 97-98
    referrals to specialists, 147, 175-176
    See also Counseling; Support groups
Intrafamily homicide, 83-85
    infanticide, 85
    murder-suicide cases, 114-115
    pedicide, 85-86, 115
    rates, 6

Janoff-Bulman, R., 19-21
Jewish Americans, 54
Journalists. *See* Media
Journals, 157, 208
Judges:
    potential to inflict second wounds,
        194-195, 196-197
    training for, 197
    See also Trials
Justice:
    restorative, 241-242
    See also Criminal justice system;
        Victims' rights
Just world hypothesis, 11-12

Kauffman, J., 50
King, Martin Luther, Jr., 215
Klaas, Marc, 225

Latinos, 53
Laughter, in healing process, 246
Lawsuits. *See* Civil suits
Lawyers. *See* Attorneys; Defense
    attorneys; Prosecutors
Legal terminology, 202
Lerner, M. J., 11
Lesbian partners, 80-81
Liability issues, 152-153
Life insurance, 213
Lightner, Candy, 99
Lindemann, E., 26, 31

MADD (Mothers Against Drunk Driv-
    ing), 99, 100, 121, 130
Managed care, limits on mental health
    coverage, 144, 158, 174-175
McCann, I. L., 153
McCarthy, Carolyn, 244-245
McNamara, John W., 204
Media:
    caregivers' relations with, 235-236
    cases solved with help of, 231-232
    competitiveness, 226-227
    courthouse coverage, 226-227,
        235-236
    coverage of multiple murders,
        110-111
    coverage of murder-suicide cases, 114
    co-victims' rights in dealing with,
        221, 233
    cultural and racial biases, 229-230
    dealing with, 220, 232-233, 235
    exploitation, 225-226
    focus on defendants, 216
    freedom of press, 221, 233-235
    goals and strategies, 217-220
    invasion of privacy, 222, 223, 234
    legal action against, 233-235
    moral and ethical dilemmas, 221-223
    photographs used by, 236-237
    portrayals of homicide victims, 14,
        221-223, 228
    portrayals of random killings,
        108-109
    portrayals of violence, 4-5, 6-7
    positive effects, 230-232

preparing co-victims to deal with, 232-233, 235
print, 220, 228-229
quality and depth of coverage, 228-229
radio, 218, 219-220
reporting of police deaths, 94-95
responding to inaccuracies in, 236
second wounds inflicted by, 224-225, 228-229
stress of reporting violence, 223-224
See also Television
Medical examiners, 129-130
Medication, 171-176
antianxiety, 58-59
gender differences in prescription rates, 56
monitoring, 175
pros and cons, 172-174
self-prescribed, 172
Memorial services, 40, 71, 171
Men:
grieving process, 31-33, 54-56
in support groups, 56
killed by abuse victims, 89-90
suicide rates, 114-115
victim advocates, 142
See also Fathers; Spouses
Mennonites, 241
Mental health professionals, 142-143
helping co-victims deal with media, 235
paying for services, 144, 158
recommendations for skill building, 155
referrals to, 147, 175-176
services, 143-144, 158-161
trauma specialists, 175, 190
Miller, D. T., 11
Minority victims, 14
mothers of, 33
See also African Americans
Mothers:
blame placed on, 33
children killed by boyfriends, 85-86
dealing with criminal justice system, 68
grieving process, 31-32, 33
minority, 33

social activism of, 244
See also Parents
Mothers Against Drunk Driving. *See* MADD
Mourning:
complicated, 23, 31
distinction from grief, 24, 27
Freud on, 25-26
normal, 23
six R processes, 30
See also Grief
Movies, violence in, 4-5
Multiple homicide, 110-112
Murder. *See* Homicide
Murderers. *See* Defendants
Murder-suicide cases, 112-113
frequency, 113-114
media coverage, 114
number of co-victims, 113-114
pedicide, 115
reactions of co-victims, 117
revenge cases, 115-116
services for co-victims, 116-117
spousal, 114-115

National Law Journal (NLJ), 7
National Organization for Victim Assistance. *See* NOVA
National Victim Center (NVC), 201, 204, 207, 208, 232
National Victims' Rights Week, 40
Native Americans, 51-52
Neurolinguistic programming, 167
Newspapers:
coverage of crime, 220
headlines, 228-229
ombudsmen, 236
New York (state), Son of Sam statutes, 210-211
Next of kin, 124
See also Death notification
No-arrest cases, 101-107
desire for resolution, 102-103
longing for justice, 103-105
reactions to arrest, 107
reward money, 105
support for co-victims in, 105-106
television shows on, 231-232

Vidocq Society and, 105
Notoriety for profit, 210-211
NOVA (National Organization for
    Victim Assistance), 121, 156, 165,
    201
NVC. *See* National Victim Center

Obsessive-compulsive thoughts, 59-60

Parents:
    as co-victims, 65-67, 68-69
    children murdered by, 85-86, 115
    dealing with criminal justice system,
        68
    emotional responses, 66
    grieving process, 31-33, 35, 55
    marital problems, 32, 34-35
    of married children, 67
    protector roles, 64
    reactions of adult children to deaths
        of, 73-74
    single, 32
    social activism of, 244
    step-, 67
    See also Children
Parents of Murdered Children (POMC),
    xvii-xviii
Parole:
    input of co-victims before, 209-210
    movement to abolish, 210
Payne v. Tennessee, 206, 208
Pearlman, L. A., 153
Pedicide, 85-86, 115
Peer support groups. *See* Support
    groups
Philadelphia (Pennsylvania):
    district attorney's office, xviii
    policies on media in criminal justice
        center, 228
Photographs, of victims, 131-132,
    236-237
Platt, Larry, 218
Pleas, 183-184
Poetry, 39
Police departments:
    crisis intervention programs, 97-98
    support system for families, 95-96

unsolved cases units, 104
victim advocates in, 196
Police officers:
    biases of, 195-196
    children of, 94, 98
    clearance rate of murders, 97
    communicating with co-victims,
        103-105, 194-196
    co-victims of murdered, 93-99
    death notification by, 122-123,
        135-136
    fellow officers as co-victims, 95-96
    female, 98
    spouses, 96, 98
POMC. *See* Parents of Murdered
    Children
Post-incident analysis:
    in domestic abuse cases, 90-91
    in murder-suicide cases, 116-117
Post-trauma counseling, 41, 156-158
Posttraumatic stress disorder (PTSD),
    18
    diagnostic criteria, 20-21
    early interventions, 156
    experienced by children, 72
    experienced by co-victims, 21, 22, 41,
        43
Preliminary hearings, 182
President's Task Force on Victims of
    Violent Crime, 206
Press. *See* Media
Privacy:
    invasion of, 222, 234
    right to, 223, 234
Prosecutors:
    plea negotiations, 183-184
    potential to inflict second wounds,
        194-195, 197-198
    relationship with defense attorneys,
        200
    victim advocates in offices of, xviii,
        198
    working with child witnesses, 191
    See also Trials
Prothrow-Stith, D., 4
Proxemics, 150-151
Psychiatrists, 171
    See also Medication; Mental health
        professionals

Psychological autopsies. *See*
     Post-incident analysis
Psychologists. *See* Caregivers; Mental
     health professionals
Psychopharmacologists, 171
PTSD. *See* Post-traumatic stress disorder

Quakers, 241

Radio:
     call-in shows, 219-220
     news, 218, 219
Rage. *See* Anger
Random killings, 107
     children as victims, 108-109
     emotional responses to, 109
     impact on community, 109-110
     media portrayal, 108-109
     trends, 107-108
Rando, T. A., 29-30, 31
Rape-murder cases, 15-16
Reconstruction of life by co-victims, 19,
     238, 239, 246-247
     change in assumptions, 19-22, 59
     closure, 239
     forgiveness, 241
     healing, 239
     humor and, 246
     restorative justice, 241-242
     social activism, 242-245
     spiritual aspects, 239-240, 241
     tears and, 245
Recovery, use of term, 19
Redmond, L. M., 41, 160
Religious beliefs, 239-240, 241
Rendell, Edward, xvii
Reporters. *See* Media
Restitution, right to, 214-215
Restorative justice, 241-242
Restraining orders, 88-89, 116
Revenge:
     as motive for murder-suicide, 115-116
     fantasies, 45-46, 76
Rituals:
     children's participation, 71, 171
     mourning, 39-40, 53

Schools:
     critical incident stress debriefings,
          170-171
     random killings in, 109-110
     violence prevention programs, 171
Secondary victimization, 10
Second wounds, 10-11
     from members of criminal justice
          system, 68, 179, 194-200
     inflicted by media, 224-225, 228-229
     plea negotiations, 184
     release of convicted defendant, 210
Sentencing:
     input of co-victims, 206-209
     treatment of victims, 111-112
Sequestration, of witnesses, 183
Serial murders, 110-112
Service providers. *See* Caregivers
Services. *See* Interventions
Shame, 29, 50-51
     anger and, 47
     confusion with guilt, 48-49
Sheriffs, 197
Siblings, as co-victims:
     adult, 75-78
     children, 74-75
     guilt feelings, 74-75
     revenge fantasies, 76
Significant others, 78-81
     children killed by mother's
          boyfriend, 85-86
     murders by, 87-88
     socially forbidden relationships,
          80-81
     See also Spouses
Simpson, Nicole Brown, 85, 86, 225
Simpson, O. J., 85, 89, 225, 226
Sisters. *See* Siblings
Smith, Susan, 85
Social activism, 242-245
Social workers. *See* Caregivers; Mental
     health professionals
Somatic disturbances, 60-61
Son of Sam statutes, 210-211
Spatial relationships, 150-151
Spirituality, 239-240, 241
Spouses:
     as co-victims, 69-70
     murders by, 87-88

murder-suicide cases, 114-115
of police officers, 96, 98
    See also Significant others
Spungen, Nancy, xvii, 13
States:
    constitutional amendments on
        victims' rights, 205
    co-victim input allowed at
        sentencing, 207
    Son of Sam statutes, 210-211
Stepparents, 67
Stigmatization, of homicide victims, 11,
        12-16, 29, 50-51
    See also Shame
Stress:
    anger as defense, 44-45
    experienced by journalists, 223-224
    in performance of death notification,
        135-136
    reaction to trauma, 18, 22
    See also Post-traumatic stress disorder
STUG. See Subsequent temporary
        upsurge of grief
Subsequent temporary upsurge of grief
        (STUG), 42-43
Suicidal ideation, of co-victims, 57-58
Suicide:
    attempts, 58
    rates, 114-115
    See also Murder-suicide cases
Support groups, 55-56, 161-164
    children in, 169-170
    facilitators, 162
    following up, 164
    format, 163
    guidelines, 162-163
    in cases of intrafamily homicide, 84
    in drunk driving murder cases,
        100-101
    in no-arrest cases, 106, 107
    in police death cases, 98
Supportive counseling, 146
Supreme Court. See U.S. Supreme Court
Survivor guilt, 49-50
Survivors. See Co-victims
System advocacy, 145

Tarasoff v. Regents, 152

Tears, 245
Teenagers, as co-victims, 72
    counseling for, 168-169
    support groups, 169-170
    See also Children, as co-victims
Television:
    cartoons, 5
    Court TV, 226
    talk shows, 225-226
    unsolved cases programs, 231-232
    violence portrayed on, 4-5
Television news:
    courthouse coverage, 226-227,
        235-236
    coverage of crime, 6-7, 218-219,
        222-223
    dealing with, 220
    local, 232
    responding to inaccuracies, 236
    tabloid shows, 219
Therapists. See Mental health
        professionals
Therapy:
    alternative, 165-166, 167
    family, 158-159
    for children, 168-169
    group, 159-161
    individual, 158
    See also Counseling
Thought field therapy, 167
Thought stopping, 157
Tort of outrage, 203-204
Torts, 202
Trauma:
    counseling for, 41, 156-158
    experienced by co-victims, 18-22
    grief and, 40-42, 43
    long-term symptoms, 22
    physical and emotional responses,
        18-19
    vicarious, 153-154
    working through, 22-23
    See also Posttraumatic stress disorder
Traumatic incident reduction, 167
Treatments. See Interventions
Trials:
    behavior of co-victims, 193
    capital cases, 185-187, 208-209
    continuances, 184

court accompaniment, 146-147, 179,
191-193, 227
defense attorneys, 198-200
emotional reactions, 193-194
intrafamily homicide cases, 84-85
media coverage, 226-227, 235-236
treatment of victims, 111-112, 178-179
victim witness waiting areas, 182-183

U.S. Constitution:
freedom of press, 221, 233-235
proposed victims' rights
amendment, 205-206
U.S. Supreme Court:
Booth v. Maryland, 208
Payne v. Tennessee, 206, 208
ruling on "Son of Sam" statute, 211

Vicarious traumatization, 153-154
Victim advocates:
confidentiality issues, 152
facilitators of support groups, 162
genders of, 141-142
history, 140-141
in district attorneys' offices, xviii, 198
in police departments, 196
professional organizations, 141
relationships with members of
criminal justice system, 194-195
roles, 140-142
services, 142
training, 141
See also Caregivers
Victim impact statements, 206-209
Victim-offender mediation programs,
241
Victim-offender reconciliation
programs, 241
Victim precipitation, 15
Victims:
ages, 73
blame placed on, 11-13, 15, 29, 89
characteristics, 4, 8
common reactions, 10
definitions, 7-8
from minority groups, 14
identifying, 129-130

inner representations, 43
media portrayals, 14, 221-223, 228
multiple, 110-112
photographs of, 131-132, 236-237
related to or acquainted with
murderers, 6
spoiled identities, 13-15
stigmatization of, 11, 12-16, 29, 50-51
traits shared with murderers, 4
treatment by criminal justice system,
111-112, 178-179
women, 14-15
See also Co-victims
Victims of Crime Act, 212
Victims' rights:
input at sentencing, 206-209
input before parole, 209-210
movement, xviii, 8, 40
restitution, 214-215
Son of Sam statutes, 210-211
victim impact statements, 206-209
See also Crime victim compensation
(CVC)
Victims' rights legislation, 204-205
proposed federal constitutional
amendment, 205-206
state constitutional amendments, 205
Victims of Crime Act, 212
Victim witness waiting areas, 182-183
Vidocq Society, 105
Violence:
attitudes toward, 2, 6-7
in American culture, 2, 3, 4-5
media portrayals of, 4-5, 6-7, 108-109
prevention programs, 171, 243
witnessed by children, 3-4, 35-36
young perpetrators, 3-4, 5
Violence Against Women Act, 86, 88-89

Walsh, John, 231
Widows and widowers. See Spouses
Will, George, 223
Witnesses:
children, 3-4, 35-36, 72-73, 190-191
of drunk driving murders, 100
programs for, 140
sequestration of, 183
waiting areas in courts, 182-183

Women:
    battered woman syndrome, 89-90
    domestic violence and, 86-91
    grieving process, 31-32, 33, 55-56
    homicide victims, 14-15
    police officers, 98
    victim advocates, 141-142
    See also Mothers; Spouses

Worden, J. W., 27-28
Workplaces:
    coworkers as co-victims, 78, 81-82
    death notification in, 128
    random killings in, 109-110
    revenge killings in, 116
Wrongful death actions. *See* Civil
    suits

About the Author

Deborah Spungen founded Families of Murder Victims (FMV) and served as Executive Director from 1985 to 1993. In 1991, she helped develop and introduce the Student Anti-Violence Education Program (SAVE) under the auspices of FMV. An umbrella organization, the Anti-Violence Partnership of Philadelphia (AVP), was formed in 1993 to encompass FMV and SAVE to better represent the entire cycle of violence. She served as Executive Director of AVP from its inception until 1994 and now is Special Projects Director for AVP and an active member of its Board of Directors.

She received her Master of Social Service (M.S.S.) and Master of Law and Social Policy (M.L.S.P.) from Bryn Mawr College Graduate School of Social Work and Social Research. In addition, she is a Certified Trauma Specialist (CTS). She has taught as an adjunct professor at Chestnut Hill College and as a visiting instructor at Bryn Mawr College Graduate School. She has appeared on more than 400 television and radio shows throughout the United States; given numerous print interviews; and presented at conferences, lectures, and workshops. She authored *And I Don't Want to Live This Life*, the story of the murder of her daughter Nancy and her family's survival in the aftermath of Nancy's death. In 1995, she was the recipient of the Presidential Crime Victims Service Award as well as an honoree at the Philadelphia Womens Way "Woman Triumphant" Awards.